PAVEL FLORENSKY:
A METAPHYSICS OF LOVE

T0374710

ROBERT SLESINSKI

PAVEL FLORENSKY: A METAPHYSICS OF LOVE

ST. VLADIMIR'S SEMINARY PRESS
CRESTWOOD, NEW YORK 10707

Library of Congress Cataloging-in-Publication Data
Slesinski, Robert, 1950-
Pavel Florensky: a metaphysics of love.

Includes bibliographical references and index.
1. Florenskii, P.A. (Pavel Alexsandrovich), 1882-
1943. 2. Theology, Doctrinal—History—20th century.
3. Metaphysics. 4. Orthodox eastern church—Doctrines—
History— 20th century. 5. Russikaia pravoslavnaia tserkov'—
Doctrines -History – 20th century. I Title.
BX597.F6S55 1984 230'.193 83-27130
ISBN-13: 978-0-88141-032-7
ISBN-10: 0-88141-032-2

Pavel Florensky:
A Metaphysics of Love

Copyright © 1984 by
ST VLADIMIR'S SEMINARY PRESS
575 Scarsdale Road, Crestwood, NY 10707
www. svspress. com • 1-800-204-2665

ISBN 978-0-88141-032-7

PRINTED IN THE UNITED STATES OF AMERICA

To
BISHOP MICHAEL OF PASSAIC
without whose support and
confidence in the author
this study
would never have been written

Table of Contents

Foreword

Appearing in the year marking the fortieth anniversary of Fr. Pavel Florensky's death, here is the first monograph in English on one of the most extraordinary figures of contemporary Orthodoxy. Florensky could perhaps be recognized today as one of the major speculative theologians of the twentieth century.

Actually some such recognition might still be forthcoming. Florensky's manuscripts, preserved by relatives and friends, are gradually being published, both in his native Russia and abroad. Significantly, they appear in the Soviet Union even in some state publications which recognize not only Florensky's philosophical talents but also his achievements in purely scientific research and in building up Soviet technology in the twenties. But the greater and most important texts are being published in the periodicals of the Moscow Patriarchate.

This authority and recognition of Pavel Florensky both by the secular and by the ecclesiastical circles of his country —where the two are generally so deliberately and systematically segregated—is an extremely interesting and important phenomenon which may prove quite significant in the slowly moving but very apparent religious revival within the Russian intelligentsia.

Priest, theologian, philosopher, and scientist, Florensky has sometimes been compared with Teilhard de Chardin, or even Leonardo da Vinci. But beyond and above such comparisons stands his personal witness to Christ and the Gospel. A professor of the Theological Academy of Moscow, he always refused to participate in politics or to emigrate. Remaining in his country, he rather attempted the impossible: to serve as a priest, wearing beard, pectoral cross, and cassock, while assuming high responsibilities in major research institu-

11

tions of the new atheistic state. Faithful to the end, he eventually died in distant exile (1943), a confessor of the faith, far from church, friends, family, and books. As a philosopher and a theologian, Florensky is not above controversy. In pre-Revolutionary Russia he was one of the leaders of the "sophiological" school, associated with Vladimir Soloviev, and a close friend of Sergius Bulgakov. However, systematic criticism of "sophiology" by Nicholas Berdyaev and particularly by Georges Florovsky, and, eventually, Metropolitan Sergius of Moscow, came later. In 1912-14, the major "sophiological" book of Florensky—his dissertation entitled *The Pillar and Foundation of Truth*—won the highest academic recognition at the Moscow Theological Academy. In his later publications, however, Florensky on his own initiative modified many of his original conceptions and moved somewhat away from sophiology. In any case, his academic career and achievements witness to the openness, the breadth, and the creative potential of that brief period of spiritual freedom in Russia which preceded the Revolution.

It is highly desirable that the thought of Pavel Florensky become better known. His seminal work, *The Pillar and Foundation of Truth,* recently appeared in a French translation (Editions l'Age d'Homme, Lausanne: 1975). The unusual and very personal style of that book, and some of its philosophical method, may make an initiation to Florensky's thought rather difficult. The appearance in print of some of his more recent works could be more helpful.

In this respect the present publication is a welcome event. Written by a young American theologian belonging to the Greek Catholic tradition, it introduces the reader to the fascinating world of Pavel Florensky in a clear, gentle, and open-ended way. It is to be hoped that Fr. Slesinski's book, as well as the recent accessibility of a large body of writings by Florensky himself, will contribute to a new dialogue between Orthodoxy, the West, and the contemporary world of science, which was the goal of Florensky's life, so tragically interrupted by the darkness of a Siberian concentration camp.

—John Meyendorff

Preface

Much, even though not all, Russian religious thought in the twentieth century can be classified according to two notable tendencies. A first current is highly speculative in nature and concerns the attempts to give philosophical articulation to the experience of the world's organic wholeness. In this current, we can place the sophiological school of Fathers Pavel Florensky and Sergius Bulgakov, the pan-unity school of Lev Karsavin and Simeon Frank, and even the thought of Nicholas Lossky, who, although he is a stern foe of all sophiological and pan-unity theorizations, shares their speculative concern to offer a philosophic accounting of cosmic experience.

A second, and decidedly less systemic tendency, is also to be found among Russian Orthodox thinkers. These, headed by Father Georges Florovsky and Vladimir Lossky, have sought a return to the patristic and liturgical sources of Orthodoxy in order to rediscover the true roots of Orthodox thought and, on this basis, to revive past visions and to create aspirations for future developments and innovations in Orthodoxy. Even though the sophiologists themselves frequently appeal to patrology, their application of it would be criticized by the likes of a Florovsky. In our own day, the concern for patristic-liturgical authenticity carries the predominant weight in Orthodox circles. Thinkers such as Fathers Alexander Schmemann and John Meyendorff immediately come to mind. In their writings considerable fruit is still being borne for Orthodox thought today.

The sophiological school, on the other hand, has borne virtually no noteworthy fruit since the death of Bulgakov in 1944. This fact should not, however, be taken as a sign of the futility of the sophiological enterprise and, even less so, of its intellectual sterility. Indeed, one of the immediate aims of this study is to rehabilitate the name of sophiology; it seeks also to revive interest in this kind of speculation. This study, however, restricts itself to a detailed, critical-interpretative analysis of only one of the sophiologists, Father Pavel Florensky. Less well-known in the West than Vladimir Soloviev and Bulgakov, the two figures generally associated with this train of thought, Florensky in his own time was one of the capital figures of the Russian intelligentsia. He was variously the personal friend, colleague, collaborator—even spiritual father—of many, if not most, of the leading person-ages on the Russian intellectual scene of his day.

In the course of this investigation it will become clear that many of the original ideas and novel insights accredited to such diverse, seminal thinkers as Heidegger, Whitehead, Marcel, and Buber, all known for their overriding concern for a radical revitalization of western philosophical thought, had been earlier expressed by Florensky from an eastern perspec-tive in a specifically Russian and Orthodox idiom. In this way, it is equally hoped that the possibilities of philosophy for ecumenism will become manifest. Philosophy in an ecumen-ical key, indeed, can show that in the spiritual depths of man, in the deepest recesses of the human soul, where St. Augustine said God was more inward than his inmost self (see *Con-fessions,* III, 6), men truly are *one.* Not only has Orthodox philosophical thought much to contribute to the West, but western thought also can enrich it. Specifically, it will be suggested that the doctrine of analogy, especially as regards to the analogy of intrinsic attribution as elaborated by Catholic Thomists, can provide an important key for unlocking the secrets of sophiology and for freeing it from bondage to pantheism.

The title of this study, however, indicates that the topic under discussion is love. It is maintained that with the theme of love one can tie Florensky's manifold insights together. This may not be apparent at the start, but after our investiga-tion begins to take shape, the necessary methodological and epistemological preliminaries having been dealt with, the centrality of love for Florensky's thought should become evident. The twofold core of his metaphysics, the principle of dynamic identity and consubstantiality, will come to the fore at the same time.

The limits of the present investigation do not permit an exhaustive examination of Florensky's thought. Certain aspects, chiefly historical, like the influence of German idealism, especially as it is found in Kant and Schelling, on Florensky as well as the influence of other Russian thinkers (principally Soloviev) on him, merit separate monographic treatment. Also, his philosophy of science deserves to be studied in detail, although such a study is greatly hindered by the general inaccessibility of the relevant material to anyone in the West.

The first two chapters of this work have appeared separately in a slightly different form in the first two issues of *St. Vladimir's Theological Quarterly* for 1982. These chapters as given here, however, are to be given precedence.

Finally, we would like to express our gratitude to the following people. First, warm thanks are due to the Rev. Gustav A. Wetter, S.J., who guided this study to completion. Though perhaps not sharing all the views of this author, his helpful observations and scrupulosity for detail certainly aided the author in bringing forth the final product. Next, appreciation must be expressed to the Rev. Msgr. Robert Senetsky, J.C.D., who made useful, stylistic suggestions concerning part of the manuscript, to Sig. Giuseppe Baldacci, who assisted in the production of the final copy of the original manuscript, and to both the administration of the Pontifical Russian College, Rome, and the Rev. John Sekellick, J.C.L., pastor of SS. Peter and Paul Church, Elizabeth, N.J., for providing conducive environments for this study to be written. Lastly, a special word of gratitude must be addressed to the Most Rev. Michael J. Dudick, D.D., Bishop of Passaic, who sponsored the graduate studies of the author, and lent him inestimable moral support and encouragement. It is to him that this study is filially dedicated.

Robert Slesinski
Feast of the Annunciation
Rome, 1982

provided

Postscript. The allowance of a brief passage of time until this publication proved helpful to the author. Not only was there the possibility to correct some errors in detail in the original manuscript, but also to incorporate some of the suggestions of others to improve it. More important, the additional time made it possible for us to take due note of the latest bibliographical entries on Florensky published by official Orthodox organs within the Soviet Union during 1982, the year marking the centenary of Florensky's birth.

R.S.

Feast of the Holy Transfiguration

White Plains, N.Y., 1983

LIST OF ABBREVIATIONS

FTH   *Iz bogoslovskogo naslediya svyashchennika Pavla Florenskogo* (From the theological heritage of the priest Pavel Florensky), in *Bogoslovskie trudy* (Theological studies—TS), 17 (1977): 85-248.

JMP   *Zhurnal Moskovskoi Patriarkhii* (Journal of the Moscow Patriarchate).

PFT   *Stolp i utverzhdenie istiny—opyt pravoslavnoi feoditsei v dvenadtsati pismakh* (The pillar and foundation of truth—an essay in Orthodox theodicy in twelve letters). Moscow, 1914.

TM   *Bogoslovskii vestnik* (Theological messenger).

TS   *Bogoslovskie trudy* (Theological studies).

Vestnik   *Vestnik russkogo khristianskogo studencheskogo dvizheniya* (The messenger of the Russian Christian student movement). The word *studencheskogo* is omitted in all issues from 112 (1974) on.

E me alo. (I feed myself.)

Part One

GENERAL INTRODUCTION
TO FLORENSKY'S LIFE
AND THOUGHT

CHAPTER I

Rudiments of a Biography

Pavel Alexandrovich Florensky was unquestionably one of the most gifted personalities ever to appear in Russian intellectual history. He was not only a celebrated priest and a genial philosopher-theologian of the Russian Orthodox Church, but was also an outstanding humanist of encyclopedic interests, running the gamut from mathematics, physics, and electrical engineering to linguistics and art history. Indeed, the strength of his personality and the profundity of his philosophical, religious, and scientific intuitions deserve a keener appreciation and a more objective scrutiny on the part of scholars not only in his homeland, but especially abroad where his name has not been sufficiently known nor his thought extensively elaborated upon by commentators. Many Russian thinkers, in fact, have likened him to Leonardo da Vinci due to his acumen and scientific prowess, although it is doubtful that Florensky himself would have accepted the comparison without serious reservations.[1]

[1]Authors who have likened Florensky to Leonardo da Vinci include: Nicholas O. Lossky, *History of Russian Philosophy* (New York: International Universities Press, 1951), 176f; F. I. Udelov (a pseudonym for S. I. Fudel'), *Ob o. Pavle Florenskom* [Of Fr. Pavel Florensky] (Paris: YMCA Press, 1972), 10; Boris Filipoff, "O. Pavel Florenskii" [Fr. Pavel Florensky], in N. P. Poltoratzky, ed., *Russkaya religiozno-filosofskaya mysl' XX veka* [Russian religious-philosophical thought of the 20th century] (Pittsburgh: University of Pittsburgh, 1975), 356, 370; Sergius Bulgakov, "Svyashchennik o. Pavel Florenskii" [The priest Fr. Pavel Florensky], *Vestnik russkogo khristianskogo studencheskogo dvizhenia* [The messenger of the Russian Christian student movement], 101-102 (1971): 127. (Hereafter listed as *Vestnik.*)

Florensky's philosophic speculations and religious meditations were written against the background of nineteenth-century positivism, materialism, and nihilism with its morbid, monoideistic preoccupation with the abolition of autocracy and the propagation of socialism in its stead and that of twentieth-century ethical idealism with its championing of social betterment according to deeply rooted Russian religious convictions.[2] The new age was indeed, according to many intellectuals, a time of religious renaissance in the intellectual life of Russian society, whose avant-garde had all too often been openly antagonistic to the Church and opposed to its claims to a central position and role in Russian society.[3] Florensky's masterwork, *The Pillar and Foundation of Truth,* has been judged to be the most characteristic work of this renascent movement, and indeed its most original and influential philosophical and theological composition.[4] It has, moreover, a special relevance for today. Its treatment of the perennial problems of critical philosophy, cosmology, anthropology, and theology not only has an intrinsic interest in itself, but

Starting with issue 112 (1974), the word "student" has been dropped from the title to indicate a new, wider orientation.

For himself, Florensky speaks of Leonardo da Vinci in somewhat negative terms. Citing Freud's critical study of da Vinci's personality (see *The Standard Edition of the Complete Psychological Works of Sigmund Freud,* vol. 11 [London: Hogard Press, 1957] 57-137), he seems to cast aspersions on the motivations behind his creative work. In fact, Florensky states that Mona Lisa's smile is nothing other than a smile of sin. See *Stolp i utverzhdenie istiny* [The pillar and foundation of truth; hereafter referred to in footnotes as PFT] (Moscow, 1914), 174, 697 (n. 267).

[2]Lossky, *History of Russian Philosophy,* 171f.

[3]For a concinnous treatment of this renaissance, see Nicolas Zernov, *The Russian Religious Renaissance of the Twentieth Century* (London: Darton, Longman & Todd, 1963).

[4]Zernov, *Russian Religious Renaissance,* 101ff; Georges Florovsky, *Puti russkogo bogosloviya* [The ways of Russian theology] (Paris, 1937), 493; Sergius Bulgakov, *The Wisdom of God* (London: Williams & Norgate, 1937), 25; and Lossky, *History of Russian Philosophy,* 179. Berdyaev also agrees with this assessment, but in a negative way. To his mind, this new movement, of which he sees Florensky at the head, is little more than a "decadent aestheticism." See Nicholas Berdyaev, "Tipy religioznoi mysli v Rossii" [Types of religious thought in Russia], *Russkaya mysl'* [Russian thought], 31, no. 6 (1916): 1-31. These pages include part one of his extended study on this topic, entitled "Vozrozhdenie pravoslaviya" [The renaissance of Orthodoxy]. For our assessment of Berdyaev's position, see sec. 2.2, 46 below.

enjoys particular significance for our own era, itself absorbed
in the existential questions of the meaning of human life and
existence and preoccupied with the search for nonephemeral
value and enduring importance. In contemporary Soviet
society this has been verified in a unique way; Florensky's life
and work have drawn, apart from the limited and slanted
notice of official Soviet publishing circles, the serious attention
of the *samizdat* press.[5]

No one less than the Nobel laureate Alexander Solzhenitsyn, the dean-in-exile of Soviet dissidents, has been intrigued
by the figure of Father Pavel. He notes with distress and
evident indignation in his novel, literary investigation, *The
GULAG Archipelago*,[6] of the imprisonment of Florensky in
a camp on one of the Solovetsky Islands in the White Sea
with thousands of other priests and religious and other nota-
bles, and bemoans his ultimate fate. With other like-minded
Soviet intellectuals, Solzhenitsyn also strives to perpetuate
Florensky's memory in a collection of essays, written in the
spiritual tradition of *Vekhi* (Landmarks) of 1909 and *Iz
glubiny* (Out of the depths) of 1918, under the title of *Iz-pod
glyb* (From under the rubble).[7] *Vekhi* was penned by concerned intellectuals, newly converted to religion, to indicate
the decay of the intelligentsia of czarist Russia and to isolate
its causes, while *Iz glubiny* was written by a similar group,
which included most of the original authors of *Vekhi*, in the
aftermath of the Bolshevik Revolution, noting the tragic and

---

[5]Filipoff, "O. Pavel Florenskii," 370. The above-cited work of Udelov
(Fudel') is itself a *samizdat* publication. The Soviets, on the other hand,
for the most part treat Florensky in their typically jaded way. P. Palievsky,
for instance, in his introduction to "Pristan' i bul'var" [Quay and boulevard;
an excerpt from Florensky's autobiography of his childhood years], *Prometei*,
9 (1972): 138-48, implies, citing *The Encyclopedia-Dictionary of the Russian
Bibliographical Institute Granat* (7th ed.; in Russian; see vol. 44, p. 144),
that Florensky's conception of integral knowledge is identical with that of
dialectical materialism. Cf. Lossky, *History of Russian Philosophy*, 188.

[6]Alexander Solzhenitsyn, *Arkhipelag GULag, III-IV* (Paris: YMCA
Press, 1974), 42 (n. 17), 627, 656. Eng. Trans., *The GULAG Archipelago
Two* (New York: Harper & Row, 1975), 44n, 641, 670f.

[7]Alexander Solzhenitsyn, M. S. Agurskij, *et al.*, *Iz-pod glyb* (Paris:
YMCA Press, 1974). Eng. trans., *From Under the Rubble* (Boston-Toronto:
Little, Brown & Co., 1975). See also, N. A. Berdyaev, *et al.*, *Vekhi* [Land-
marks] (Moscow, 1909), and S. Askol'dov, *et al.*, *Iz glubiny* [Out of the
depths], 2nd ed. (Paris: YMCA Press, 1967).

untimely fate of a society that failed to heed the prophetic
warnings of 1909. *Iz-pod glyb,* which, as has been noted, is
itself a phonetic echo of *Iz glubiny,* for its part, laments the
curtailment of free thought and the intimidation of independent thinkers in contemporary Soviet society. One of its essays
in particular, that by F. Korsakov (a pseudonym), entitled
"Russkie sud'by" (Russian destinies), is specifically dedicated
to the memory of Father Pavel Florensky.[8]

1. BIOGRAPHICAL SKETCH

1.1 Basic Data

Considering that Florensky was such a towering intellectual
figure in his time, and his influence so widespread, it is somewhat surprising that no full-length biography on him has yet
appeared. Until now only brief sketches of his life, work, and
personality have appeared in print, unfortunately meaning
that many lacunae in his life story have perforce remained,
not the least of which have been the place, date, and exact
circumstances of his death.[9]

Pavel Florensky was born in Yevlakh, Azerbaijan, in
Transcaucasia on January 9, 1982, the son of an engineer.
His father was Russian, his mother Armenian, and he may
have had some Georgian blood in him.[10] His secondary school
studies were done in Tiflis (Tbilisi), Georgia, during which
time he displayed an exceptional talent for mathematics.

[8]F. Korsakov (a pseudonym), "Russkie sud'by" [Russian destinies], in
Iz-pod glyb, 159-76; Eng. ed., 151-71.

[9]Official Soviet sources list Florensky's date of death as December 15,
1943, and the place of death as the Solovki concentration camp in the White
Sea. The accuracy of both of these official notices has been questioned. For
a discussion of this issue, see "V kakom godu umer o. Pavel Florenskii?"
[In what year did Fr. Pavel Florensky die?], *Vestnik,* 115 (1975): 151-54.
Zernov, *Russian Religious Renaissance,* 101, lists his date of death as
occurring in 1952. Alexander Schmemann conditionally agrees with this
information; see his *Ultimate Questions: An Anthology of Modern Russian
Religious Thought* (New York: Holt, Rinehart & Winston, 1965), 135.
L. Ganchikov lists a probable 1946 death date in his encyclopedia notice on
Florensky in the *Enciclopedia Filosofica,* 3, 698, while J. Papin in a similar
notice in the *New Catholic Encyclopedia,* 5, 974, says it is unknown.

Upon their completion he not surprisingly matriculated in the Physics and Mathematics Faculty of Moscow University in order to pursue his interest in mathematics. While a university student, his chief mentor was the noted mathematician, Nikolai Vasilevich Bugaev (1837-1903), the father of the famous symbolist poet, Andrei Belyi (1880-1934).[11] At the same time he studied philosophy under Sergei Nikolaevich Trubetskoy (1862-1905) and Lev Mikhailovich Lopatin (1855-1920) in the Philosophy Faculty of the same university.

During the years 1904-1905, together with his close friends, Valentin Pavlovich Sventsitsky (1879-1939), Vladimir Frantsevich Ern (1881-1917), and Aleksander Viktorovich Elchaninov (1881-1934), Florensky formed the *Khristianskoe bratstvo bor'by* (The Christian brotherhood of the battle) with the aim of radically renewing the social sphere in the spirit of Solovievian theocracy with the free subjugation of the state to the Church.[12] This fraternal union was too utopian in orientation, and, not without the influence of the revolutionary events of 1905, was soon disbanded.

After his university graduation in 1904, Florensky decided not to accept the university's offer of a research scholarship in mathematics but rather to enroll in the Moscow Theological

[10]Udelov, *Ob o. Pavle Florenskom*, 13-17, and German Troitsky, "In Memory of the Reverend Pavel Florensky," *The Journal of the Moscow Patriarchate*, no. 11 (1972): 74-80 (hereafter referred to as JMP). Interestingly enough, there is no corresponding article in the Russian edition of this issue.

[11]For Florensky's interesting correspondence with Boris Nikolaevich Bugaev, who wrote under the pseudonym of Andrei Belyi, see *Vestnik*, 114 (1974): 149-68.

[12]Cf. the editor's note regarding Florensky's correspondence to B. N. Bugaev (A. Belyi), *Vestnik*, 114 (1974): 150, and S. A. Levitzky, *Ocherki po istorii russkoi filosofskoi i obshchestvennoi mysli* [Outlines for the history of Russian philosophical and social thought] (Frankfurt am Main: Posev, 1981), 2:140. From other correspondence, especially that of Archimandrite Serapion Mashkin to Florensky (see *Voprosy religii* [Questions of religion], 1 [1906]: 174-83), we learn of the former's bitter disapproval of the Moscow Theological Academy's lack of social and civic consciousness in not speaking out as an institutional body against the Russo-Japanese War of 1904-5, which he considered unjust. In this letter, dated February 3, 1905, he writes that he presumes that Florensky shares his opinions in this matter. This same issue of *Voprosy religii*, 143-73, contains Florensky's own personal portrait of his mentor, entitled "K pochesti vyshnyago zvaniya" [To the honor of a higher calling].

Academy for religious studies and seminary training. This decision he made after consultation with his spiritual director, the noted hierarch, Bishop Antony (Florensov) (1847-1918).[13] He finished his spiritual and theological formation in 1908, at which time he was elected to the Faculty of the History of Philosophy at the academy. Having married Anna Mikhailovna Giatsintova on August 17, 1910, he was ordained to the holy priesthood on April 24, 1911, by Bishop Feodor (Pozdeevsky) of Volokolamsk. On May 19, 1914, he defended his master's thesis,[14] *Of Spiritual Truth,* which with several modifications and amplifications would become *The Pillar and Foundation of Truth.*[15]

1.2 *Autobiographical Remarks on His Childhood*

Before proceeding with Florensky's life story and career, it is worthwhile to backtrack for a moment in order to con-

[13]A. Elchaninov, "Episkop-starets'" [Bishop-staretz], *Put'* [The way], no. 4 (1926): 159, 164; also cf. Hierodeacon Andronik, "Episkop Antonii (Florensov)—dukhovnik svyashchennika Pavla Florenskogo" [Bishop Antony Florensov—spiritual director of the priest Pavel Florensky], JMP, no. 9 (1981): 71-77; no. 10 (1981): 67-73.

[14]A confusion concerning *Of Spiritual Truth* should be dispelled at this time. Sometimes, as in Lossky, *History of Russian Philosophy,* 179, we find it inexactly labeled as a doctoral dissertation. According to the Russian university system then in effect, the master's thesis would indeed be what we would consider a doctoral dissertation. The true doctoral dissertation according to this same system would, strictly speaking, be what is known as a work of habilitation, as found in German universities, i.e., in effect a second doctorate, qualifying one for a professorship at the university level.

[15]Pavel Florensky, *O dukhovnoi istine* [Of spiritual truth] (Moscow, 1913). This edition lacks the first and eighth letters of PFT, entitled "Two Worlds" and "Gehenna." Also there are no vignettes in this preliminary edition. Lastly, it contains no notes (though, oddly enough, their numeration is given in the text proper!), and lacks the explanatory appendix on various symbols and drawings. Udelov, *Ob o. Pavle Florenskom,* 13, and Bishop Feodor (Pozdeevsky), the rector of the Moscow Theological Academy at that time, in his review of this work in *Bogoslovskii vestnik* [Theological messenger; hereafter referred to as TM], 2, no. 5 (1914): 141-81, both refer to a 1912 edition of *O dukhovnoi istine* containing only seven chapters (letters) of what would become PFT. In addition to the preface and the notes, the chapters included are those entitled: "Doubt," "Triunity," "Light of Truth," "The Comforter," "Contradiction," "Sin," and "The Creature." Lacking, therefore, are the chapters on "Two Worlds," "Gehenna," "Sophia," "Friendship," and "Jealousy."

sider his autobiographical essays concerning his childhood in the Caucasus, which have only relatively recently found their way into print[16] after having been virtually lost in obscurity from the time of their being penned in the early twenties. According to editorial indications in *Vestnik*,[17] these memoirs consist of four parts, respectively entitled, "Religion," "Nature," "Poetry," and "Family." A three-part serialization of these childhood recollections has appeared in *Vestnik*. The aforementioned first two parts, "Religion" and "Nature," have been printed in their entirety, while the third selection is apparently only an excerpt from the remaining portion of these memoirs. The information contained in them is truly most valuable for making a more adequate assessment of Florensky's moral and intellectual greatness and, indeed, for properly appraising the true nobility of his personality.

Reading the first installment of these memoris reveals, rather surprisingly, that Florensky did not come from an overtly religious family. It was not, however, an antireligious one either; it was merely indifferent to all religious matters, although Florensky says they did observe conventional, religious practices.[18] With a touch of humor, he specifically remarks that Great Lent was not as such observed in the Florensky household, but still the best traditional Caucasian lenten specialties were served them for their culinary qualities during this penitential season. Similarly, the annual preparations for Easter were always joyful to him, but, of course, were devoid of any properly religious significance. Florensky claims that he simply loved to decorate *pisanki,* the traditional Easter eggs. Not only Easter, but also Christmas and Pentecost were moments of unstinted celebration in the household, when his father, who normally frowned upon any misconduct or slight of manners during mealtime, even encouraged a festive disorder at the dinner table. But all this, Florensky repeats, was done not out of any religious conviction, but only

---

[16]P. A. Florensky, *Vospominaniya detstva* [Reminiscences of childhood], *Vestnik*, 99 (1971): 48-84; 100 (1971): 230-54; and 106 (1972): 183-200. The latter entry is also to be found in *Prometei,* 9 (1972): 138-48 (cf. n. 5, p. 23 above).

[17]*Vestnik*, 99 (1971): 48.

[18]Ibid., 51, 71-78.

to observe and promote the more cultural and ethnic vestiges of an ignored and forgotten religious heritage. It was this same attitude that governed all the family's outward religious practices. Baptisms, mere conventions as far as his parents were concerned, for instance, were so arranged as not to involve any outsiders.

Florensky candidly admits that he was given no formal religious instruction, was never taken to church, and did not even know how to bless himself. Nonetheless, Florensky claims he always felt a hidden, mysterious power in life; indeed, he frankly acknowledges that his first religious impulses and reasonings were clearly pantheistic in character.[19]

Speaking of his parents,[20] Florensky observes that while his mother seemed more open to religion and more inclined to affirm the existence of God and the importance of religion and the clergy, his father was of the opposite tendency. His father always avoided the word "God," although at times he would speak of the "Higher Being" or of the "Divinity" or of "that One whom people call God." But he did so, according to Florensky, only to indicate the incommensurability of the Higher Being with human knowledge and the human word. Florensky further writes: "This abstinence from the name [of God] was not for motives of reverence, but for cognitive conscientiousness, on the one hand, and for social carefulness, on the other."[21] His father's basic attitude was that if all humanity has professed religion, it cannot not be. However, to his mind, it was a futile endeavor to try to decide in favor of any one religion. In sum, Florensky concludes, his father bore no enmity towards any religion, but adhered to none. In fact, if he had any "religion," it was solely towards humanity. His favorite word and battle cry, indeed, as Florensky informs us, was *"chelovechnost' "* (human-ness/humanity).[22]

His father's relativistic and agnostic stance toward religion did, however, have a positive influence on his son, even if,

[19]Ibid., 78f.
[20]Ibid., passim.
[21]Ibid., 52.
[22]Ibid., 56.

Florensky concedes, it was not the effect his father would have desired for him. A later, fundamental conviction of Florensky was that at the root of all religions, there is one Religion.[23] Florensky does not from that conclude the relativity of all religions, but only that there is one transcendent God and one transcendent Truth lying at the base of all the religions of the world.[24]

Another inadvertently positive influence his parents had on his future religious views was their rejection of the idea of ethnic or, more precisely, nationalistic Churches. The mixed marriage of his parents did not set well with his mother's Armenian family, and Florensky remarks how his mother subsequently rejected not only her family, but even her nation and race. She absolutely refused to speak Armenian, attend the Armenian Church, or have anything else to do with things Armenian. She maintained ties only with her sister, and apart from her evaded all other questions about her family when speaking with her children. Though Florensky chides his mother for her unyielding stance towards her own Armenian culture, he scores the Armenian Church for its hopeless conservatism, abstention from all proselytizing activity, and refusal to accept converts from outside its midst. The Russian Orthodox Church was, in Florensky's opinion, more open in this regard, though he adds it was prone to the same dangers, whenever slavophilism received an undeserved attention. Florensky, however, was no less a convinced Orthodox in view of the expanded horizons of his religious vision. He only resolutely rejected any exclusively nationalistic understanding of the Church.

Besides his confessions concerning his family's religious practices, his recounting of his first, genuine, metaphysical experiences are of special import insofar as Florensky himself retrieves for us the germs of his own later thought. But once again, these particular experiences, all experiences with nature, reveal to us the pantheistic overtones of his thought. Already

[23]Ibid., 53.
[24]A further implication of this understanding of religion, one not explicitly elaborated upon by Florensky, is that in order to decide on the proportionality of truth in religions, one must necessarily appeal to revelation.

in the second published installment of his memoirs, Florensky notes that as a child his one true love was nature.[25] More
telling, however, is the third installment, dedicated to his
memories of Batum, a seaport in Russian Georgia. In his
experience of the vastness of the sea lying before him, we see
hints of his subsequently articulated experience of the pan-
unity of Being. He writes:

> . . . I remember my childhood impressions, and I do not
> err in their regard: at the seashore, I felt myself face
> to face before a dear, solitary, mysterious, and endless
> eternity, from which all flows and in which everything
> revolves. It called me, and I was with it.[26]

He comes back to the same basic point, but from another
direction, when he describes his general impressions of the
trader-contrabandists who flourished in the Turkish quarter
of Batum. Commenting specifically on the traders who dealt
in handmade, Venetian glass beads, Florensky remarks how
to him there was always a great difference between handmade
and machine-made products. The latter evoked his suspicions,
and invariably seemed to be "without soul."[27] The former,
on the other hand, brought him before the face of Being and
all its transcendental properties of unity, truth, goodness, and
beauty. In his own words:

> Through these glass beads, by means of them, the
> substance of the world learned to love itself and to
> delight in itself. And I loved it—not the matter of
> physicists, not the elements of chemistry, not the proto-
> plasm of biology—but the *very* substance, *with its*
> truth and *its* beauty with *its* moral goodness. I felt with
> trepidation, that the glass beads of this Venetian
> contrabandist were not only beautiful, but, indeed,
> were splendid, just as the perceived depth of being is,

[25]*Vestnik*, 100 (1971): 231.
[26]Ibid., 106 (1972): 188.
[27]Ibid., 198. Cf. PFT, 295f, for Florensky's analogous remarks critical of
the artificiality of the Age of Enlightenment.

in general, splendid, and just as everything genuine is splendid.[28] (Emphasis his)

To sum up this brief commentary on Florensky's auto-biographical memories of his childhood, attention should be drawn to two facets of his thought in development. First, there is a definite, pantheistic timbre to Florensky's first metaphysical stirrings and a similar coloring to his juvenile, conceptual formulations of this experience. But we have also seen that Florensky fully owns up to having passed through a pantheistic stage, and in no way tries to hide it or to explain it away. More important, however, we can see the makings of a real metaphysician in him, one deeply sensitive to the true fullness of being under all its articulated, transcendental formalities. And possibly, we can even see in his tender and responsive soul the seeds of a calling to serve at God's altar.

1.3 *Professional Activity*

Upon successful defense of his dissertation *ad lauream, On Spiritual Truth,*[29] he remained on at the Moscow Theological Academy as a professor. During this same period, from 1911-1917 to be exact, he also served as the editor of the journal, *Bogoslovskii vesnik* (Theological messenger), in which numerous of his own studies appeared. It should also be noted that during all this time as well as before, from the time of his graduation from Moscow University, Florensky never let his mathematical and scientific interests wane, but rather continued in their research and elaboration. The fruits of his endeavors in these fields are his published articles on mathematical topics, which date from 1904.[30] In addition, his early keen interest in linguistic concerns remained in full force at the same time. Never a mere casual observer of any

---

[28]Ibid., 200.

[29]See p. 26 above, especially nn. 14 and 15, for our previous discussion of this dissertation.

[30]A modest example is his review of Jules Tannerie's *Kurs teoreticheskoi i prakticheskoi arifmetiki* [A course of theoretical and practical arithmetic], TM, 3, no. 12 (1913): 864-72.

intellectual domain to his liking, Florensky likewise published in the camp of general linguistics.[31]

As a priest he never held a formal pastorate, though he did serve as a pastoral assistant in the chapel of the Red Cross Society at Sergiev Posad (now Zagorsk), and conscientiously pursued any pastoral duties that came his way.[32] He was above all else a zealous priest, under whose spiritual leadership certain prominent intellectuals like the learned Sergius Bulgakov (1871-1944) and Nicholas Lossky (1870-1965), as well as the dissolute and bigoted Vasily Rozanov (1856-1919), returned to the Church and the faith of their fathers. Bulgakov, who himself was to become an archpriest of the Orthodox Church, very movingly notes that the very spiritual center of Florensky's personality was his priesthood, and that his greatest creation was not his writings, but his own life, formed and nourished by the grace of holy orders and the Eucharist.[33]

Rozanov, on the other hand, would probably jump at the opportunity to offer a prompt and unsolicited rejoinder to Bulgakov, and, gadfly that he was, attempt a counterbalance to his highly favorable assessment of Florensky's personality. Most likely, he would draw into focus the aspect of Florensky's apparent pride, which even Lossky mentions in his otherwise very complimentary and endearing remarks about Florensky,[34] and flaunt his adamant refusal to receive the last sacraments from Father Pavel, the very one who was instru-

[31]Cf. his review article, "Novaya kniga po russkoi grammatike" [A new book about Russian grammar], TM, 2, no. 5 (1909): 138-45.

[32]Cf. Bulgakov, "Svyashchennik," 131.

[33]Ibid., 129ff. According to their own testimony, both Bulgakov and Lossky attributed their own hard-won conversions to Christianity to Father Pavel. See Sergius Bulgakov, *Avtobiograficheskie zametki* [Autobiographical notes] (Paris: YMCA Press, 1946), 158, and Lossky, *History of Russian Philosophy*, 177. On Rozanov's conversion, see Andrei V. Stammler, "V. V. Rozanov" (in Russian) in Poltoratzky, *Russkaya mysl'*, 313; Lossky, *History of Russian Philosophy*, 344; and Paolo Leskovec, S. I., *Basilio Rozanov e la sua concezione religiosa* [Basil Rozanov and his religious conception], *Orientalia Christiana Analecta* 151 (Rome: Pontificium Institutum Orientalium Studiorum, 1958), 47.

[34]Lossky, *History of Russian Philosophy*, 177.

mental in his own moral reawakening to Christianity, so as not to flatter this alleged pride.[35]

Whatever the final, full assessment of Florensky's personality may be—and the best indications certainly point to a highly laudatory one, especially as Florensky neared the end of his sojourn on earth—we need only underscore the complexity and outright enigma of his character. No commentator is silent on this issue, and the verdicts on the man and his life, whether temporary or final, recognize a truly entriguing personage of immense stature in Pavel Florensky.[36] Some might prefer to agree with Leonid Sabaneeff's highly personal portrait of his very close friend, and maintain that "Lucifer was closer to him than Christ,"[37] but others surely would avouch only for a genuinely mystical presence in him, that could only draw people, even if seemingly hypnotically in some cases,[38] to the Church and its Bridegroom.

1.4 *The Untimely End of Florensky's Career*

With the closing of the Moscow Theological Academy and Seminary after the Bolshevik Revolution, Florensky's life

[35]Leskovec, "Rozanov," 57, and Levitsky, *Ocherki po istorii*, 63.

[36]This point is borne out in the recollections of various famous Russian intellectual figures who give a place to Florensky in their writings. See N. O. Lossky, *Vospominaniya* [Reminiscences] (Munich: Wilhelm Fink Verlag, 1968), 197f; Zinaida Nikolaevna Gippius-Merezhkovskaya, *Dmitrii Merezhkovskii* (Paris: YMCA Press, 1951), 134-37, 193, and her *Zhivye litsa* [Living portraits] (Munich: Wilhelm Fink Verlag, 1971), 74-76, 81, 88-92. See in particular the biographical study of Evgenii Modestov, *P. A. Florenskii i ego sovetskie gody* [P. A. Florensky and his Soviet years], *Mosty* [Bridges], 2 (1959): 419-34, esp. 420ff.

[37]Leonid Sabaneeff, "Pavel Florensky—Priest, Scientist, and Mystic," *The Russian Review*, 20 (1961): 316f. The Russian-Soviet writer, Marietta Shaginyan, would appear to align herself with Sabaneeff. In her memoirs, in the section dealing with her association at the end of the first decade of this century with various "renegades" from the intelligentsia, like Berdyaev, Bulgakov, and Florensky, she remarks that Florensky impressed her as being "a fanatic with the face of a Savonarola, the likes of a severe ascetic." See "Chelovek i vremya" [Man and time], *Novyi mir* [New world], no. 4 (1973): 113-31; no. 5 (1973): 160-86; no. 6 (1973): 128-53. See in particular no. 5 (1973): 165.

[38]V. V. Zenkovsky, *Istoriya russkoi filosofii* (Paris, YMCA Press, 1950), 1:437; Eng. trans. (New York: Columbia University Press, 1953), 895;

changed directions. His cherished plans to establish a special philosophical academy in Moscow dedicated to the scientific study of religion and religious phenomena had to be abandoned,[39] and now most of his professional energies were to be rechanneled back into his original mathematical interests and research in physics and electrical engineering. Owing to his reputation and value as an outstanding research scientist Florensky was not exiled from the Soviet Union with other like-minded intellectuals in the famous banishment of 1922,[40] but was to remain in his official scientific posts in which he had found work. From 1920 to 1927, he lectured on the theory of perspective in the Higher State Technical-Artistic Studios (the VKHUTEMAS), and at the same time was a leading collaborator in the Commission for the Electrification of Soviet Russia (the GOELRO). He also was an editor of the Soviet *Technical Encyclopedia* to which he himself contributed many articles. He even made a number of important scientific discoveries and inventions of notable benefit to the Soviet economy. One worthy of special note is his 1927 invention of an extraordinary noncoagulating machine oil, called "dekanite" by the Soviets in commemoration of the tenth anniversary of the Bolshevik Revolution. In addition, one of his scientific works, a book on dielectrics, even became a standard textbook.

But all was not, at last, to fare well for Florensky.[41] He

and also Levitsky, *Ocherki po istorii*, 147. These authors specifically describe Florensky's influence of Bulgakov in these exact terms.

[39]Florensky stated his intentions regarding this matter already on June 12, 1917, in Sergiev Posad. See Pavel Florensky, *Iz bogoslovskogo naslediya* [From the theological heritage], *Bogoslovskie trudy* [Theological studies; hereafter referred to as FTH and TS respectively], 17 (1977): 86.

[40]In total, over one hundred intellectuals were exiled by Lenin in this most unexpected, yet providential, move, which spared these figures from a worse fate. Some of the personages included in this noteworthy banishment were Nicholas Berdyaev, Sergius Bulgakov, Simeon L. Frank, Lev Platonovich Karsavin, Nicholas O. Lossky, and Pyotr B. Struve.

[41]A good indication of the turn in Florensky's fate is given in E. Kol'man, "Protiv noveishikh otkrovenii burzhuaznogo mrakobesiya" [Against the latest revelations of bourgeois befuddlement], *Bol'shevik*, no. 12 (1933): 88-96. The author specifically criticizes Florensky for trying to ground logic in intellectual intuition and not sensual intuition (p. 92), a pointed criticism of his article, "Fizika na sluzhbe u matematiki" (Physics in the service of mathematics), published in 1932 in the *Review of Socialist Reconstruction*

refused to renounce his priesthood, and even dared to don his priest's cassock, pectoral cross, and cap while attending to his official scientific duties. This, of course, only earned the enmity and scorn of Soviet authorities, who, as Levitzky notes,[42] feared the figure of a "scholarly *pop*"[43] and the influence he would have on young Soviet scholars, and who, in consequence, finally deprived him of all his professional capacities and had him imprisoned in 1933.

The exact details of Florensky's remaining years now become sketchy and subject to dispute. Florensky apparently was at first sent to the Skovorodino labor camp near Lake Baykal in Siberia. Still refusing to renounce his faith, he was sent to another, more bleak camp, the Solovki Island concentration camp, where, according to official information, he died on December 15, 1943.

Solzhenitsyn traces Florensky's years in exile somewhat differently in his admittedly provisional but certainly credible accounting.[44] He lists his exiles as in Siberia, then Solovki, and lastly the Kolyma (the area in eastern Siberia around the river Kolyma which hosted numerous concentration camps), where Florensky seemingly managed to study flora and minerals. This information, at any rate, corroborates some of the conjectures offered in the previously cited *Vestnik* piece on the same subject.[45]

Not even the Soviets, however, have been able to deny the importance of Florensky's thought nor the outstandingness of his achievements. The Soviet *Philosophical Encyclopedia*, indeed, speaks of him and his contributions to thought and to Soviet society in favorable terms. But as to his ignominious fate, this encyclopedia entry has no comment; it just tersely states: "In 1933 he was repressed. He was posthumously rehabilitated (1956)."[46]

and Science. He calls on editors to show "revolutionary vigilance" (p. 96) in regard to Florensky's writings.

[42]Levitzky, *Ocherki po istorii*, 141.

[43]The word *pop* is a derogatory Russian expression for a priest.

[44]See *Arkhipelag GULag*, 656; Eng. ed., 670f.

[45]115 (1975): 151-54.

[46]*Filosofskaya entsiklopediya* (Moscow, 1970), 5:377.

2. THE SCOPE OF HIS PHILOSOPHIC-THEOLOGICAL CORPUS

Until very recently, a relatively complete bibliography of Florensky's literary corpus has not been available. Indeed, only within the past year, in conjunction with the centenary year of Florensky's birth, has one appeared in print.[47] It, however, lists only those works of Florensky published in Russia or the Soviet Union, and thus omits mention of those published abroad in Russian émigré and other publications. For years much of Florensky's work remained unedited in virtually forgotten manuscripts. Fortunately, within the past decade or so these pieces have begun to resurface in published form, chiefly in the *Vestnik* of the Russian Christian Movement, in the Moscow Patriarchate's *Bogoslovskie trudy* (TS) and its official monthly journal, and in some Soviet periodicals.[48] Florensky's publications in mathematics, physics, and engineering also comprise a formidable corpus, but we prescind from a consideration of these works here.[49]

[47]For this bibliography, cf. Hierodeacon Andronik (Trubachev), "K 100-letiyu so dnya rozhdeniya svyashchennika Pavla Florenskogo. Ukazatel' pechatnykh trudov" [The centenary of the birth of the priest Pavel Florensky. Index of published works], TS 23 (1982) 264-309. Up until this bibliography, the most complete one was found in Udelov, *Ob o. Pavle Florenskom*, pp. 134-41. Our own bibliography takes account of not only Florensky's work published in the West, but also the secondary studies on him published both in Russia and the Soviet Union and abroad. It does not, however, pretend to be exhaustive, as it contains *only* those materials that were accessible to the author. Of those inaccessible studies which would be of a philosophic-theological nature, most are of an apparently minor or secondary importance. The bulk of the other inaccesible works treat scientific and technical topics not in the purview of the present study.

[48]For instance, "Vospominaniya detstva," in the *Prometei* issue cited above (9 [1972]). Florensky's last known article, "Itogi" [Summations] is contained in *Vestnik*, 3 (1974): 56-65. In TS, we find *Ikonostas*, 9 (1972): 80-148; *Ekkleziologicheskie materialy* [Ecclesiological materials], 12 (1974): 73-183; FTH, 17 (1977): 85-248. In JMP, no. 4 (1969): 72-77, we find Florensky's "Dukh i plot'" [Spirit and flesh], an apparent extract from the ninth letter of PFT ("The Creature").

[49]Probably the best synopses of Florensky's work in these fields are the previously cited studies by Troitsky, "Reverend Pavel Florensky" (n. 10) and Modestov, *Florenskii* (n. 36).

2.1   Initial Work

Already while a student at Moscow University and especially at the Moscow Theological Academy, Florensky began
to write and publish extensively. His first published articles,
"O sueverii" (On superstition),[50] "Spiritizm, kak antikhristianstvo" (Spiritualism as anti-Christianity),[51] and "O simvolakh bezkonechnosti" (On symbols of infinity),[52] appeared
in the short-lived Novyi Put' (The new way), a monthly
issued in 1903-1904 by the Religious-Philosophical Society of
Writers and Symbolists, which soon dissolved owing to both
internal and external pressure.[53] From his seminary years date
some student homilies, a lengthy monograph on the concept
of the Church in Sacred Scripture, and several preliminary
studies exploring themes subsequently treated and developed
in his master's thesis. The homilies have an interest, apart
from their content and devotional value, from the stylistic
point of view. Florensky's literary style has been both praised
and sharply criticized. In the opinion of S. A. Volkov,[54] one
of his former students, Florensky's literary and oral style
exhibited "magical charm." Contrary evaluations, however,
are uttered by others. Father V.V. Zenkovsky, for instance,
laments his "pretensiousness,"[55] While Nicholas Berdyaev, in
a similar vein, objects to his excessive stylization and aestheticism.[56] In these published homilies we witness a contrast of

[50]Novyi put' [The new way], no. 8 (1903): 91-121. In PFT, p. 751
(n. 565), Florensky notes that the editors of this journal redacted part of
it in a Kantian spirit, and to that extent he disclaims the work as fully
his own.
[51]Ibid., no. 3 (1904): 149-67.
[52]Ibid., no. 9 (1904): 173-235.
[53]Cf. editor's note, Vestnik, 114 (1974): 150. See also n. 11 above, and
Lossky, History of Russian Philosophy, 337. This society, organized with
the intent of bringing intellectuals into the Church, was chaired by Dmitry
Merezhkovsky and his wife Zinaida Gippius. The group met the sharp dis-
pleasure of the government, since they criticized the autocratic hold of the
state over the Church.
[54]Cf. Udelov, Ob o. Pavle Florenskom, 9.
[55]Zenkovsky, Istoriya, 2:415; Eng. trans., 876.
[56]Nicholas Berdyaev, "Stilizovannoe pravoslavie" (Stylized Orthodoxy),
Russkaya mysl', 29, no. 1 (1914): 109-24, and his Russkaya ideya [The
Russian idea] (Paris: YMCA Press, 1946), 238ff.

styles which discloses not only his unquestionable literary talent, but also a certain proclivity toward manneristic writing. A first, his paschal Bright Week homily, *"Nachalnik zhizni"* (The Author of life),[57] which alludes to St. Peter's remarks about the crucified Savior in Acts 3:15, highlights the cosmological dimension of Christ's victory over evil, death, and sin. It is written in a rich, rhetorical style, exuding an air of pretentiousness, thus bearing out the unfavorable critiques by Zenkovsky and Berdyaev. Such is not the case, however, with another published sermon, *"Radost' na veki"*[58] (Joy unto ages), a moving panegyric on man, which uses the Cherubic Hymn from the Byzantine Divine Liturgy as its point of departure. Unlike the former homily, it is written with an even-paced, awe-inspiring simplicity, that highlights both Florensky's connatural sensitivity to the religious sphere and his innate ability for spiritual and devotional writing.

Attention must be drawn to another published student homily, but from an entirely different point of view. On March 12, 1906, the Sunday of the Veneration of the Holy Cross, Florensky preached a sermon entitled *"Vopl' krovi"* (The cry of blood), in which he criticized the execution six days prior of Lt. Pyotr Schmidt (1867-1906), one of the leaders of the Sevastopol Insurrection of 1905. For this sermon he received an immediate three months prison sentence. Due to the efforts of G.A. Rachinsky, however, he was released before Easter.[59]

Although this is not the place to give a detailed commentary on Florensky's youthful philosophical and theological works, it is important to call attention to these juvenilia as they indicate the paths his thought was to follow, and thereby assist us in coming to terms with his profound thought and novel ways of communicating his ideas. Two points in particular merit highlighting. The first concerns his philosophical orientation; the second the focus of his theological concen-

---

[57]Published in pamphlet form (Sergiev Posad, 1907) as an extract from *Khristianin*, 1 no. 4 (1907): 705-9.

[58]Also in brochure format (Sergiev Posad, 1907) and similarly an extract from *Khristianin*, 1, no. 2 (1907): 248-57.

[59]For this information, see Hierodeacon Andronik, "Episkop Antonii," p. 72, n. 10. The homily itself, unfortunately, was not accessible for review.

tration. Florensky was interested in disclosing the Platonic and idealist background of European philosophy. In his *"Obshchechelovecheskie korni idealizma"* (The universally human roots of idealism),[60] he traces philosophy back to magic and occultism by means of which man tries to exert influence and control over the forces of nature. Plato's search for integral knowledge[61] is, according to Florensky, nothing more than an offshoot of this same basic yearning to penetrate into the depths of reality and learn its inner secrets. Florensky writes: "The yearning of Plato for integral knowledge, for the unbroken unity of a world-presentation, finds its precise answer in the all-embracing and organic unity of a primordial world-contemplation."[62] In "The Cosmological Antinomies of I. Kant,"[63] Florensky turns his attention from Platonic to Kantian idealism and considers another aspect of integral knowledge, that is, its attainment through the antinomic structure of the mind. Here he analyzes the foundations and structures of thought and reason, disclosing their intrinsic limitations and the need to appeal to antinomies in order to extricate and explain the full mystery of man's cognitive experience. To his mind, Kant's chief merit lies in his teaching concerning the antinomies of the mind, which, he adds, "only open the doors behind the scenes of the mind."[64] Florensky concludes this particular study with the notice that his prospective work, *The Pillar and Foundation of Truth*, will attempt to address the problem of how reason itself is possible.[65]

We can, of course, guess the form Florensky's own answer to his epistemological quest will take from the very title itself of his famous book, which clearly alludes to St. Paul's first

[60]TM, 1, no. 2-3 (1909): 284-97, 409-23.

[61]By using "integral knowledge" in this context, Florensky is enlarging upon the strict meaning this *terminus technicus* carries in Russian philosophy. We shall return to this point in our discussion of Florensky's methodology. See ch. 2, sec. 2, below.

[62]"Obshchechelovecheskie," 420.

[63]"Kosmologicheskie antinomii I. Kanta," TM, 1, no. 4 (1909): 596-625. Florensky virtually repeats pp. 623-25 word for word in PFT, 484-87.

[64]Ibid., 625 (PFT, 487).

[65]Ibid.

letter to Timothy.[66] We can conclude from the context of
1 Timothy 3:15 that somehow the Church will figure into the
solution. And if this is so, his earlier monograph on the
Church, written while he was only a third year theology student and entitled *Ecclesiological Materials*,[67] takes on special
importance. In it, however, we should not expect to find an
overabundance of original insights, as his own views were
yet to mature, but it does, nonetheless, show that the Church
enjoys a central place and pivotal role in his speculations and
vision of reality. It also proves that some of the key concepts
of his later thought, like "antinomy," "consubstantiality," and
"numerical identity,"[68] were already germinally present in his
student thinking.

2.2 *Florensky's Magnum Opus*

Florensky's searching study for the foundations of ultimate
truth led him to the Church, which in his view constitutes at
once the means for the attainment of truth and the environment for an encounter with it. *The Pillar and Foundation of
Truth* represents the fruits of this quest, and, considering his
intent, the title chosen for this investigation, his *magnum
opus,* is indeed most felicitous. The work was a labor of love,
and judging from bibliographical indications, was moreover
a work of many years of student labor. The first traces of
the definitive edition[69] of *The Pillar and Foundation of Truth*
is a monograph, bearing the same title and published in 1908
in the short-lived *Voprosy religii* (Questions of religion).[70]

[66]"I hope to come to you soon, but I [Paul] am writing these instructions
to you [Timothy] so that, if I am delayed, you may know how one ought
to behave in the household of God, which is the Church of the living God,
the pillar and bulwark of truth" (1 Tim 3:14-15).

[67]Cf. n. 48 above.

[68]See *Ekklesiologicheskie materialy,* 81, 116, 130, respectively, for these
notions.

[69]The definitive edition of PFT contains a preface, twelve letters
(namely, "Two Worlds," "Doubt," "Triunity," "Light of Truth," "The
Comforter," "Contradiction," "Sin," "Gehenna," "The Creature," "Sophia,"
"Friendship," and "Jealousy"), a postscript plus sixteen appendices, notes,
and an explanation of some of the symbols and drawings in PFT.

[70]*Voprosy religii* [Questions of religion], 2 (1908): 223-384. Only two

The product of his years as a seminarian, the work contains eight chapters, all but the first being called "letters" as in his definitive study. The first chapter contains the first half of the preface (also given as a first chapter) in the 1914 edition. The letters, all noticeably shortened versions of their later equivalents, are entitled "Two Worlds," "Doubt," "Triunity," "Light of Truth," "The Comforter," "Contradiction," and "Gehenna." Right up to and including the next to last letter here given, he follows the order of the final rendition of his argument in the 1914 text. The lacking letters include those on sin, creation, Sophia, friendship, and jealousy. It also does not have the afterword, appendices, and extensive footnoting of the definitive edition.

The next item of interest is the fairly lengthy review in the February 1909 edition of *Bogoslovskii vestnik* by Sergii Glagolev, an ordinary professor of the Moscow Theological Academy, of a student composition by P. Florensky, entitled *Of Religious Truth*.[71] Although this work was not available for our personal inspection and may not even be extant, Glagolev does give a detailed description of it, thus making it possible for us to compare it with the previously cited work published in 1909 but entitled *The Pillar and Foundation of Truth*. He notes in the first place that part of the composition was submitted in a printed format, most likely the *Voprosy religii* monograph or at least a hefty part of it, and part only in manuscript form, a fact clearly indicating that it was still being composed.[72] Furthermore, he says it contains ten chapters or, more exactly, letters addressed to a friend. Excepting the second chapter about which he does not comment, he gives a brief summary of the respective contents and salient points of the other chapters, and moreover, with the exception of the first and eighth letters, states their individual titles. The preface of both the earlier and later redaction of *The Pillar and Foundation of Truth* may not be present in this particular composition, but then again it may be present as the first part

editions of this journal ever appeared, one in 1906 and the other in 1908. Florensky contributed to both. Cf. n. 12 above.
[71]TM, 1, n. 2 (1909): 129-35.
[72]Ibid., 132.

of the first chapter, which from Glagolev's comments would
appear to treat much, if not all, the problematic contained
in the letter "Doubt" which is included in the 1908 published
monograph. The second chapter, which is not afforded any
special notice by Glagolev, could well be the letter "Two
Worlds," and the letter "Jealousy," which would appear at
first sight to be entirely lacking, may in point of fact be
attached as an excursus at the end of the letter on "Friendship." Florensky did indeed publish his letter, "Friendship"
separately as a contribution to *Bogoslovskii vestnik*,[73] and
appended a special reflection, entitled "Jealousy,"[74] which
upon examination is shown to be what becomes a separate and
last letter to *The Pillar and Foundation of Truth*. Only the
letter on sin, the diffusive notes, and appendices appear not
to play any particular role in this composition.

The already cited *Of Spiritual Truth*,[75] which was submitted as Florensky's master's thesis, is virtually the same
text, only with certain omissions and one noticeable addition.
In this text, the one reviewed by Bishop Feodor (Pozdeevsky),
then rector of the Moscow Theological Academy, and given
a 1912 publication date, the seventh, ninth, and tenth
chapters of *Of Religious Truth*, respectively entitled, "Gehenna," "Sophia," and "Friendship," are left out, but an
entirely new chapter, bearing the title "Sin," included. This
particular edition, unfortunately, also was not available for
our personal inspection. Only its 1913 edition was accessible
for review, and it is clearly a considerably expanded edition
of the dissertation, including much of his original student
composition omitted from the defended 1912 edition. Still,
it too is only a work approaching the final, definitive text.
The only puzzle is why it was published at all. *The Pillar
and Foundation of Truth* was to appear in 1914, and considering the relatively minor elements missing from this
second edition, we may justly ask: why the expenditure of the
time and money? Though an answer to this particular ques-

[73]TM, 1, nos. 1, 3 (1911): 151-82, 467-94.
[74]Ibid., 494-507.
[75]Cf. p. 26 above, especially n. 15, for the discussion contained in this
paragraph.

tion may never be forthcoming, we have, nonetheless, ascertained beyond a doubt that Florensky's masterwork had a convoluted and checkered history, marked by various redactions with both irregular omissions and augmentations along the way.[76] We may also reasonably conclude that there is a need for a new critical edition of *The Pillar and Foundation of Truth*, indicating the various stages of redaction it underwent.

No less revealing than the title of Florensky's work is its subtitle, "An Essay on Orthodox Theodicy in Twelve Letters." Having so designated his work, Florensky lets us know that he does not aim at completion, but only wishes to sketch outlines for us to fill in by our own experience and meditation. His major concern, in other words, is to initiate us into the Orthodox ecclesial experience, and not to satiate our innate need to know. His study, however, is much more than a theodicy in the strict sense of the word, as its topics, which are presented in an organic series of provocative essays, touch upon the grand themes of criteriology, cosmology, anthropology, and theology.

Indeed, Florensky's understanding of the term, "theodicy" merits special notice. He does not use it in the strict sense of a vindication of divine justice in permitting evil to exist. Rather he uses it somewhat apologetically, to denominate his attempted justification of the mind's claims to know Truth. Florensky does not explicitly explain this usage in his book as such, but specifically clarifies his meaning of the term in the public address he delivered before the defense of his dissertation.[77] Unless this discourse is examined in detail, it is doubtful that one can understand why he would label his study a "theodicy."

[76]Mention also must be made of the preparatory studies anticipating PFT. For example, cf. "Kosmologicheskie antinomii," referred to in n. 63 above. Also Florensky's letter on "Sophia," which appears as the ninth chapter in *Of Religious Truth* and as both the eleventh chapter and tenth letter of PFT, appeared separately in TM, 2, nos. 5, 7-8 (1911): 135-61, 582-613. Then, of course, there is the separate publication of the letter "Friendship" in TM, 1, nos. 1, 3 (1911). Parts of Florensky's letter "The Creature" also appeared separately in "Dukh i plot'," JMP, no. 4 (1969).

[77]P. Florensky, "Razum i dialektika" (Mind and dialectics), TM, 3, no. 9 (1914): 86-98. Florensky dedicated this address to his spiritual father, Bishop Antony (Florensov).

Florensky begins his discussion of the meaning of theodicy with an observation on the nature of religion. The role of religion, he stresses, is to save, and its focus is nothing other than the soul.[78] Having thus delineated the purpose of religion, he further adduces two additional determinations of it. Ontologically speaking, he states that "religion is our life in God and God's in us,"[79] while in a phenomenological perspective it is rather a "system of those actions and experiences, which provide for the salvation of the soul."[80]

To foster this life of God in us, Florensky states that religion has two mutually conditioning ways before it, the theoretical way of theodicy, which promotes our ascension into the life of God under the impulse of grace, and the practical way of anthropodicy, which underscores Christ the Savior's condescension into our midst and our loving embrace of Him as the unique means to salvation.[81] Christology is, accordingly, central to this latter way of religion.[82] The former way, on the other hand, highlights the human mind; it begins with the mind, and then proceds to go behind the scenes and transcend the mind. Its point of departure, in other words, is an analysis of the mind in action. Florensky says he is less concerned about the nature or existence of the mind than he is about its activity.[83] The question, "Is there a mind?," is, to his thinking, a poor formulation of the problem, suggesting as it does a static conception of the mind. He prefers to ask: "How is the mind possible?" In his subsequent analysis of the mind's activity in his book, Florensky finds that unless there is some ultimate foundation sustaining it, it is lost to absolute scepticism. Thus, he can rightly affirm: "The mind

[78]Ibid., 87.
[79]Ibid.
[80]Ibid.
[81]Ibid., 88ff.
[82]That Florensky conceives the task of Christology to be a dimension of anthropodicy, and not of theodicy, is one explanation of why he skirts any protracted christological discussion in PFT. This is a good beginning for a rebuttal of the sharp critism of Georges Florovsky, *Puti russkogo bogosloviya*, 495f, that PFT is deficient from the christological point of view. Cf. also his view of PFT in "Tomlenie dukha" (The pining of the spirit), *Put'* [The way], no. 20 (1930): 104.
[83]"Razum i dialektika," 91.

thirsts after salvation,"[84] meaning stability of mind. "And if
religion promises this stability," Florensky claims, "then the
business of theodicy is to show that this stability can indeed
be given to the mind, and just how."[85] This is his first formulation of the task of theodicy. His second formulation is a
restatement of his answer to the problem of how to assure the
reliability and stability of the mind. Florensky holds that the
mind transcends the inherent limitations of reason only once
it acknowledges the presence of Truth. In his own words, "the
mind ceases to be sickly, i.e. to be reason, when it acknowledges Truth; since Truth makes the mind reasonable, i.e. an
intellect, and it is not the mind which makes Truth truthful."[86]
Thus, to his original question, "How is the mind possible?"
Florensky answers that the mind is possible through Truth,
and, accordingly, conceives the task of theodicy to consist in
demonstrating that "Truth itself makes itself Truth."[87]

Considering the ingenuity of Florensky's framing of the
nature and task of theodicy and the key role it plays in the
development of his argument, it is rather surprising that his
commentators have all seemed to ignore this matter. It is,
indeed, their chief omission. Without a clear understanding
of what Florensky means by theodicy and how he envisions
its task, it is impossible to come adequately to terms with
him in analyzing and expounding on his work, a masterwork
addressing many major issues and having an extremely com-
plex and varied problematic.

Considering that his work is so expansive, however, we
may rightfully question the advisability and appropriateness
of having such an explorative work, even in an abridged form,
as a master's thesis or doctoral dissertation.[88] It treats many
themes, and indeed it does so profoundly, but none of them
in the systematic and exhaustive way we may expect to see
in this ultimate kind of academic exercise. Its central point is
not always clear, and, in fact, we may object that Florensky
handicaps his own work. Simply speaking, the book is too

[84]Ibid.
[85]Ibid.
[86]Ibid., 92.
[87]Ibid.
[88]Cf. the comments of n. 14 above.

long. A hefty, eight-hundred-page tome, it is unwieldy, and overburdened with needless, even if in themselves interesting, digressions, excursuses, appendices, and labored footnotes, which serve only to clutter the way towards understanding him and to exasperate the reader, who may unfortunately despair of following him to the end of his investigative journey. Often too many arguments seem to be going on simultaneously, only serving to obscure his general line of reasoning and to give the impression that he himself lacks a clear idea of what he is, in the last analysis, trying to communicate. From his own comments, however, Florensky does not appear to be entirely oblivious to these difficulties.[89]

The boldness and striking novelty of his presentation could not have failed to have evoked the spirited response, which was indeed immediately forthcoming. Unfortunately, the criticism it generated was restricted primarily to the psychological point of view. Florensky's personality and style no doubt lent themselves to this psychological scrutiny, but the unilateral attention afforded this dimension precluded a more adequate account and appreciation of his true genius as objectively manifested in the fruits of his inquiries.

This lack of critical balance is especially evident in Berdyaev's unduly harsh review of Florensky's work.[90] According to him, one can detect in every word of Florensky the decadence of an aesthete, and, he bluntly states that, apart from the teaching concerning the antinomic character of religious truth, the book "is not needed by anyone," as it is "only a document of a soul fleeing from itself."[91] Years later, Father Georges Florovsky makes a similar evaluation in his review of *The Pillar and Foundation of Truth*, and further adds that Florensky has more of a liking for theologoumena than for dogma.[92] Elsewhere, he will echo these same critical comments, and note that the book is merely the work of a "writer

[89]Cf. Florensky's comments, PFT, 785 (n. 773), in which he explains why he frequently interjects etymological digressions into his argumentation.

[90]Oddly enough, V. N. Il'in, in his critical review of PFT, lumps Berdyaev together with Blok, Ivanov, Rozanov, Bulgakov, and Florensky, and chides them all for being "gnostics." See *Put'*, no. 20 (1930): 116-19.

[91]"Stilizovannoe pravoslavie," 109, 118, 125.

[92]"Tomlenie dukha," 102-7, esp. p. 102.

enclosed within himself,"[93] its importance lying more in its being a psychological document and historical testimony to the romantic movement in Russian theology than a representative account of traditional Orthodox thought. Rather severely, and indeed unjustly, Florovsky writes: "It is the book of a Westernizer who dreamily and aesthetically seeks salvation in the East."[94] Prince Evgeny Trubetskoy, on the other hand, is more sympathetic to Florensky's aims, and for this reason concentrates less on the author himself and more on the labors of his pen.[95] He makes many positive remarks, and offers a good, constructive criticism of some of the book's points. He does not, accordingly, refrain from negative observations when necessary, and in no way lionizes him, as some contemporary commentators like Udelov had a tendency to do. As to Florensky's Orthodoxy, Bishop Feodor (Pozdeevsky), the rector of the Moscow Theological Academy at that time, upholds the fully Orthodox character of Florensky's master's thesis in his review of the contents of the work, and he maintains that the uniqueness of its style is merely a question of the individualism of its author.[96]

The movement for renewal in Russian religious thought at the beginning of this century was indeed intertwined with romantic threads, and it accordingly displays all the typical features of romanticist exposition. Florensky's masterwork, with its melancholic imagery and somber modality, with its lack of logical precision and the meandering accounting of its problematic, admittedly is of this nature, so there is little point in faulting his critics on this score. Florensky himself would not deny the stylistic difficulties of his own work. To his friend, the famous symbolist poet, Andrei Belyi, he despairingly wrote:

As far as my "written work" is concerned, it is here that I so often hit upon complications that I am

[93]*Puti russkogo bogosloviya,* 494.

[94]Ibid., 497.

[95]E. P. Trubetskoy, "Svet favorskii i preobrazhenie uma" (The Taboric light and the transfiguration of the intellect), *Russkaya mysl',* 29, no. 5 (1914): 25-54.

[96]Bishop Feodor, "Review," 180f in particular.

beginning to see in this a sign, an acknowledgement that is coinciding with my secret desires. A publisher is decidedly not to be found: for one it is too scholarly, for another too much "in the new style"; for one it is too mathematical and so forth, to another the mystical and theological elements are loathsome. In a word, I cannot please anybody, and to change that method, which for me seems to be my present path (the investigation of concepts and the synthesis of heterogeneous materials), I cannot do in conscience. As a result, you prefer more to think than to write. Still the question arises: "For what? At any rate it remains in the portfolio."[97]

But to stop only at his style and go no further, as his critics have frequently done, would seem to be a falling short of the true mark of Florensky's adventure in ideas—the initiation into the experience of Orthodox theodicy. In this respect at least, Florensky does succeed in accomplishing what he sets out to do. His work is a veritable seminal work, that has yielded fruits in other thinkers, for instance in Bulgakov and Karsavin.[98] Accordingly, when the chief historian of this movement Zernov notes that this work of Florensky "marked the beginning of a new era in Russian theology,"[99] he in no way overstates his case.

2.3 The Philosophy of Cult

The final stage of Florensky's known philosophical development is notably shaped by his relentless desire to sound the depths of religion in its essence and manifestations. As

[97]*Vestnik*, 114 (1974): 166. This extract is from a letter dated January 31, 1906.

[98]Zenkovsky, *Istoriya*, 2:382, 437; (Eng. ed., 843, 895), notes Florensky's clear influence on Karsavin and Bulgakov respectively.

[99]Zernov, *Russian Religious Renaissance*, 101. B. Jakovenko in his *Ocherki russkoi filosofii* [Outlines of Russian philosophy] (Berlin: Russkoe Universal'noe Izdatel'stvo, 1922), 11, compares PFT to St. Augustine's *Confessions*, and likewise affords it a formidable place in recent Russian thought.

religion in his view enjoys a central place in human thought and activity, Florensky accordingly maintains that religious cult, itself the point of encounter between the two spheres of man's being, between his heavenly and terrestrial dimensions, should be a special, the central point of philosophical inquiry and indeed the axis around which all philosophical reflection revolves.[100] He is true to his own position, and in a series of lectures and other studies written intermittently from 1918 to 1922,[101] pursues a philosophical investigation of the foundations and implications of religious cult.

There are, of course, many points Florensky makes along his way to the understanding of cult, but of special note are his exposition of the sacramental system as integral to man's anthropological structure and his attempted deduction of the seven sacraments,[102] his consideration of personal witness as the foundational concept of all Christian philosophy,[103] and his elaboration of the phenomenon of prayer according to the classical, Aristotelian scheme of material, formal, efficient, and final causality.[104] Elsewhere in a lecture[105] on the poet Blok, Florensky goes so far as to claim a genetic dependence of culture on cult. In this context, he bluntly states:

[100]P. Florensky, "Kul't i filosofiya" [Cult and philosophy], FTH, 119-35, esp. 132. Analogous remarks he makes in his "Molennye ikony prepodobnogo Sergiya" (Prayer icons of the venerable Sergius), JMP, no. 9 (1969): 80-90. Specifically drawing attention to the icon corner in Sergius' room, he says that the icon there was "the living soul of the home, its spiritual center, the perceived axis around which the whole house revolved" (p. 81).

[101]These investigations have been collected under the heading of the above mentioned FTH (see nn. 39 and 48 above). For a survey of this collection as well as his monograph, *Ikonostas* (see below, n. 107), cf. our "Filosofiya kul'ta po ucheniyu o. Pavla Florenskogo" [The philosophy of cult according to the teaching of Fr. Pavel Florensky], *Vestnik*, 135 (1981): 39-53.

[102]Deduktsiya semi tainstv" [The deduction of the seven sacraments], FTH, in TS, 17 (1977): 143-47.

[103]"Svideteli" [Witnesses], FTH, TS, 17 (1977): 156-72. "Personal testimony" would also become a key concept in the thought of the French existentialist, Gabriel Marcel.

[104]"Slovesnoe sluzhenie. Molitva" [Vocal service. Prayer], FTH, TS, 17 (1977): 172-95.

[105]"O Bloke" [On Blok], *Vestnik*, 114 (1974): 169-92. This talk was written in 1931 as a result of an agreement with friends to rediscuss Blok after a disappointing conference on him in January of 1931.

"The creativity of culture uprooted from cult is, in essence, only PARODY."[106] Lastly, in one final monograph of great merit entitled *Iconostasis*,[107] Florensky ferrets out the true metaphysical nature of iconography, and at the same time, develops a concrete metaphysics of the icon and an original aesthetics of Christian experience with special reference to the veneration of icons.

[106]Ibid., 170. Emphasis his.

[107]*Ikonostas*, TS, 9 (1972): 80-148. An integral Italian translation exists under the title *Le porte regali* [The royal doors] (Milan: Adelphi, 1977). An apparently abridged version was first published in the *Vestnik russkogo zapadno-evropeiskogo patriarshego ekzarkhata* [The messenger of the Russian western European patriarchal exarchate], 65 (1969): 39-64. The work itself was, according to present documentation (cf. FTH, 85), written from June 17, 1921, to July 8, 1922, and apparently was Florensky's last lengthy treatment of a religious topic. An English translation of the latter variant may be found in *Eastern Churches Review*, 8 (1976): 11-37.

CHAPTER II

Methodology in Florensky

Nicolas Zernov attributes the fundamental importance of *The Pillar and Foundation of Truth* for Russian religious thought to the fact that its author therein breaks with the traditional western or scholastic modes of theologizing which prevailed in Orthodox thought at the turn of this century.[1] If this is indeed true[2] and Florensky does in point of fact attempt to open up new horizons for Russian philosophical and theological speculation with this work then it is of the first order of necessity to examine the formal methodology that lies at the basis of the material contents of the book. That Florensky does in truth view his task in this light becomes evident in a reading of the preface and first letter of the work, which form a methodological introduction to it. Accordingly, our present concern is to set forth the salient features of Florensky's new and unconventional methodological point of view.

1. THE PRIMACY OF EXPERIENCE

Florensky opens his book postulating: "Living religious experience [is] the sole legitimate method for understanding

[1]Zernov, *Russian Religious Renaissance*, 101.

[2]We must, nonetheless, bear in mind that Florensky himself—despite all his innovations—sprang from a certain tradition, namely Slavophilism, and that in Kireevsky and especially Khomyakov, not to mention Soloviev, we find precursors of his own patterns of thought.

dogma."[3] Thus, he gives us a novel, axiomatic restatement of the classical methodological rule, *lex orandi lex credendi,* which now on every page of *The Pillar and Foundation of Truth* will enjoy full thematicity. According to Florensky, in other words, the great dogmatic themes of the Christian religion cannot be grasped in abstraction from the lived situation of man in two worlds the terrestrial and the divine but rather must be considered as resultant symphonic presentations of this joining of these worlds.

Favoring this requisite experiential contact with religious truth, Florensky expressly avoids writing formal articles or chapters that propose "to prove." Instead, he presents his views in the form of congenial letters[4] to us, his friends in the dialogue for truth, with the hope that we may be led in true maieutic fashion to a *prise de conscience* of the great spiritual truths of religious faith. Similar thoughts he was to repeat several years later[5] while commenting on the nature of the "lecture" as a formal mode of presentation of thought. In this work, his chief point of concern is not just the imparting of knowledge but the *process* of learning and the acquisition and development of a taste for concrete experience. He writes:

> For the one who is strolling it is necessary *to go,* and not merely *arrive,* and to proceed at an unhurried pace. Finding an interest in some stone, tree, or butterfly, he stops so as to study them closer and more attentively ... In a word, he strolls in order to breathe fresh air and pass time in contemplation, and not just in order to arrive all the more quickly, out of breath and dusty, at the designated end of his journey.[6]

Applied to the religious field in particular, the cognitive process seeks to develop our taste for concrete experience and existential contact with spiritual reality. In no way, however,

[3]PFT, 3.
[4]PFT, 129.
[5]*Pervye shagi filosofii* [First steps of philosophy] (Sergiev Posad, 1917), 3, 5.
[6]Ibid., 3. The emphasis is the author's.

can this contact ever be exhaustive—the spiritual domain simply transcends the capacities of human reason to encompass it in its totality. A fully integral knowledge, accordingly, is beyond man's reach.

The inner mechanism of Florensky's experiential methodology is dialectics, as explained in his introductory discourse at the defense of his dissertation. The title of this address, *"Razum i dialektika"* (Mind and dialectics),[7] is most revealing, and ably draws attention to two critical junctures in his thought. The mind, with its experience of truth and its inherent weaknesses in sounding the depths of truth, is the focal point of Florensky's essay in theodicy, and at the same time serves as the point of departure for his investigation. Florensky tags his intellectual pursuit dialectics, without however intending this kind of inquiry to be a merely disengaged exercise in logic. Dialectics, in his broader understanding of it, is "lived and living, unmediated thought in contraposition to schooled thought, i.e., to that which is rationalistic, analyzing, and classifying."[8] For him the mind's grasp of reality, its impassioned pursuit of it, is never total, and a residual tension always continues between them, giving rise to dialectics. Without this interplay, thought becomes immobile, and restricted to a sum of definitions and theses. Living thought, on the contrary, Florensky maintains, is essentially dialectical and always in the process of greater approximation and differentiation.[9] It proceeds not in a line, but more in a mesh, as intricate in detail as lace.[10]

Having expressed his thoughts on the mind's precariousness in arriving at truth and on dialectics, Florensky frankly admits his inability to penetrate the full depths of the spiritual order. Indeed, he asks himself in true humility: "Who am I to write about the spiritual?"[11] In one sense, Florensky inquires, is it not best for us to turn only to the Church and her treasury of venerable tradition for our guidance and spiritual enrichment? While fully agreeing with this point, he hastens

[7]In TM, 3, no. 9 (1914): 86-98.
[8]"Razum i dialektika," 93.
[9]Ibid., 94.
[10]Ibid., 98.
[11]PFT, 5.

to add that possibly there is still a certain, even if meager, value that can be attributed to his reflections, if they can lead others to the same ecclesial experience that inspired him to write in the first place. In this case, however, they enjoy value solely for those in the catechumenate,[12] waiting for full initiation into the Church and the realm of sacramental mystery. And being written in love, they stand for catechumens as veritable "lessons of love."[13]

2. INTEGRAL KNOWLEDGE

Florensky expressly states that he envisages his investigation as a search for integral knowledge.[14] He thereby places his own researches and speculations in the general context of the Slavophile tradition[15] in Russian thought, which fashioned this particular conception of knowledge, and gave it its technical, if not always uniform, sense. Since the term, as first coined by Ivan Vasilevich Kireevsky and subsequently developed by Aleksei Stepanovich Khomyakov and Vladimir Soloviev,[16] knows various shadings and developments in meaning, it warrants an explicit consideration and exposition of its connotative outreach. As a basic principle, however, it appears to maintain a constant, operative significance. In brief, it states that the knowledge of truth is not the affair of only one human faculty, namely, the mind, but is a matter of the whole man, of man in his totality, that is, of all man's faculties and strivings.

[12]On this score, however, Bishop Feodor (Pozdeevsky) wonders whether Florensky presupposes too much knowledge, both philosophical and theological, on the part of his readers. See his "Review," 160.

[13]PFT, 14.

[14]See pp. 39, 53 for previous indications of this point.

[15]Jakovenko, *Ocherki*, 109, in point of fact places Florensky at the head of twentieth-century "neo-Slavophilism."

[16]For a good, synthetic treatment of these thinkers' views, cf. E. Radlov, "Teoriya znaniya slavyanofilov" [The theory of knowledge of the Slavophiles], *Zhurnal Ministerstva Narodnogo Prosveshcheniya* [The Journal of the Ministry of Public Education], no. 2 (1916): 153-65, and also his *Ocherk istorii russkoi filosofii* [An outline of the history of Russian philosophy] (Petrograd: Nauka i shkola, 1920), 30-42.

2.1 Ivan Vasilevich Kireevsky

Ivan Vasilevich Kireevsky (1806-56) is the first Russian intellectual associated with the theory of integral knowledge. This particular acounting of cognition occupies a predominant place in his explicitly speculative thought. In his chief philosophical essay, "*O neobkhodimosti i vozmozhnosti novykh nachal dlya filosofii*" (Of the necessity and possibility of new principles for philosophy),[17] he contrasts the abstract-logical thinking, which has characterized western, rationalist systems of thought, with the integral thinking he claims is the hallmark of eastern thought, and chides the rationalist position for its pretentious claims to having arrived at a full knowledge of truth and for its failure which bespeaks its arrogance to acknowledge its own inherent limitations. "If it would only recognize its own limitations, and see that, in itself, it is only one of the instruments by means of which truth is known, and not the sole way to knowledge," Kireevsky writes of rationalism, "then it would also view its conclusions as only conditional and relative solely to its limited point of view, and would expect other, supreme and most truthful conclusions from another, supreme and most truthful mode of thinking."[18] This supreme mode of thinking, according to Kireevsky, is thought flowing from belief, that "higher spiritual vision, which is acquired not by outward scholarship, but by inward integrality of being."[19] As he notes, "in integral thinking, at every movement of the soul, all of its strings

[17]Ivan Vasilevich Kireevsky, *Polnoe sobranie sochinenii* [Complete collected works] (Moscow, 1861) 2: 283-325. An English translation may be found in James M. Edie, James P. Scanlan, *et al.*, eds., *Russian Philosophy* (Chicago: Quadrangle Books, 1965) 1: 174-213. We do not, however, quote from his translation here, because it sacrifices technical precision for literary elegance. Although the stylistic demands of good translations at times require more than an exact, literal rendition of a text, this same procedure at other times can obscure or at least give the impression of overlooking, certain characteristic themes that would be evident were exact terminology to be used. This is the case, in the present context, in the translations of "*sushchestvennost'*," "*tsel'noe znanie*," and "*tsel'nya zhizn'*," respectively meaning "essentiality," "integral knowledge," and "integral life."
[18]Ibid., 318.
[19]Ibid., 311.

must be heard in full accord, blending into one harmonious sound."[20] This supreme form of thinking, the goal of all true philosophy, is not a matter of the theoretical life alone, but entails praxis as well, itself a necessary condition of a genuinely integral life, which alone guarantees the integrality of the mind.[21] This means that a moral dimension is necessarily at stake in the search for and attainment of knowledge.

Man, he adds, can attain the plenitude of the real only if he is faithful to his own inner constitution, which requires collaboration with others in a joint pursuit of truth. This idea he captures in his concept of *"sushchestvennost',"* a word not given to easy translation, but possibly best rendered as "essentiality," though at other times as "the essential" or "reality," and which carries the additional connotations of lived contact with reality and responsibility toward society and the world. Elaborating on this point, Kireevsky writes:

> . . . all that is essential [*sushchestvennoe*] in the soul of man grows in him only socially. Thus, it is essential that personal convictions do not occur in a hypothetical, but in a real encounter with the questions of the surrounding formative ambience [*obrazovannost'*], since only from actual relationships with the essential [*sushchestvennost'*] are the thoughts, which illuminate the intellect and warm the soul, enkindled.[22]

Elsewhere, he cryptically states: "The essential [*sushchestvennoe*] in general is inaccessible to abstract thinking alone. Only essentiality [*sushchestvennost'*] can touch the essential [or the real *sushchestvennoe*]."[23] Essentiality is one with the integral life, and is given, he avers, only in belief, that awareness of the relation of living, divine personality with human personality, which alone grasps the integrality of man, and alone is fully commensurate with his plenitude.[24] Faith or "believing thought" is characterized by a "striving to collect

[20]Ibid., 310.
[21]Ibid., 311.
[22]Ibid., 315.
[23]Cf. "Fragments" in *Sobranie*, 2:335.
[24]Ibid., 336.

all the separate parts of the soul into one power, to find that inner center of being where mind and will, and feeling, and conscience, and the beautiful, the true, the wonderful, and the hoped for, and the just and merciful, the whole range of the intellect, are fused into one living unity, thereby restoring the essential personality of man to its primeval indivisibility."[25] Seemingly unaware of his equivocal use of the word "belief"—using it, as he does, interchangeably both in the sense of strict, theological faith and in that of natural belief, founded on intuition—the general thrust of his position nonetheless seems to be that integral knowledge is obtained by essentiality, steeped in faith and engrafted into the life of the Church.[26]

2.2 *Aleksei Stepanovich Khomyakov*

Aleksei Stepanovich Khomyakov (1804-60) continues in the line of Kireevsky, and, in an article devoted to a clarification of Kireevsky's posthumously published fragments,[27] similarly distinguishes abstract-rational knowing from the thinking of the integral mind, and like Kireevsky before him also considers the fundamental task of philosophy to consist in the harmonization of belief and the mind.[28] Khomyakov, however, is unlike Kireevsky in that, even though he employs the same basic terminology, he tries to delineate his terms more precisely and to give them greater coordination.

There are three constitutive elements to Khomyakov's conception of integral knowledge: reason, will and belief.[29] Reason as such does not put us into direct contact with reality, but is, he says, limited to the formal side of our knowledge

[25]Ibid., 336f.

[26]A full treatment of Kireevsky's position lies beyond the scope of this study.

[27]A. S. Khomyakov, "Po povodu otryvkov naidennykh v bumagakh I. V. Kireevskogo [Concerning the fragments found in the papers of I. V. Kireevsky], in *Polnoe sobranie sochinenii* [Complete collected works], 3rd ed. (Moscow, 1900), 1:263-84.

[28]Cf. Radlov, *Ocherk*, 55, and Kireevsky, *Sobranie*, 2:313.

[29]Radlov, "Teoriya znaniya," 155-58.

of reality.[30] And its inability to grasp the reality of the known itself thereby manifests its fundamental insufficiency. To the will belongs, Khomyakov maintains, the function of establishing a difference between the merely depicted and the real object, between an imaginary and an actual object.[31] In Khomyakov's own unique words, it pertains to the will to judge between the imaginary representation, or the *ya i ot menya* (the I and from me), and the actual perception of a real object, the *ya, no ne ot menya* (the I, but not from me).[32] The content to which the mind in an act of the will assents is given by belief, which he denominates the *zryachest' razuma* (vision of mind) or *razumnaya zryachest'* (intelligible vision).[33] This visibility of mind is nothing other than intuition, and, in this conception, belief thus becomes the organ or faculty of the mind, which grasps concrete reality in itself. Belief can be either natural or supernatural, depending on whether it grasps sensual and intellectual reality or suprarational, mystical reality. It furthermore enjoys a double moment. From the side of the knowing subject, it brings the will before an actual reality, which serves to activate its assent. On the side of the object, it is the immediate apprehension of an object in its actuality, thus contributing what Khomyakov labels the "mystical element" in knowledge. It is precisely this element of immediacy that distinguishes belief from reason, the one differing from the other as matter from form.[34] Radlov succinctly summarizes Khomyakov's view on the operations of the integral mind, noting that "belief gives the living content to the mind, the will divides the domain of fantastic representation from the domain of the objective world, while reason finds abstract law in the content of knowledge."[35]

---

[30]Khomyakov, *Sobranie*, 1:278.
[31]Cf. Radlov, "Teoriya znaniya," 155.
[32]Khomyakov, *Sobranie*, 1:278.
[33]Ibid., 280. Khomyakov speaks only of "*zryachest' razuma*," while Radlov renders it "*razumnaya zryachest'*" (see "Teoriya znaniya," 156) in his treatment of Khomyakov's position.
[34]Radlov, "Teoriya znaniya," 157, and Khomyakov, *Sobranie*, 1:343.
[35]Radlov, "Teoriya znaniya," 156f.

2.3 *Vladimir Sergeevich Soloviev*

One of the chief heirs to the early Slavophile tradition, as bequeathed to Russian thought by Kireevsky and Khomyakov, is clearly Vladimir Sergeevich Soloviev (1853-1900), who not only incorporates their teaching into his own, but, in expanding upon it, makes it the very cornerstone of his subsequent speculative system. In his major epistemological monographs, *Filosofskie nachala tsel'nogo znaniya* (Philosophical principles of integral knowledge)[36] and *Kritika otvlechennykh nachal* (Critique of abstract principles),[37] he clearly follows the lead of Kireevsky and Khomyakov, contrasting integral knowledge with abstract, logical thinking, the one characteristic of the East the other prevailing in the West. Furthermore, he states that the former type of thinking belongs to the primordial intellect, owing to its intuitive character, while reflective or abstract thought arises only subsequently in the mind's act of self-affirmation.[38]

In his development of this position, however, Soloviev patterns an original conception of integral knowledge according to his novel synthesis of free theosophy (*svobodnaya teosofiya*),[39] which is the primary focus of his speculative attention in his early thought. Examining the various forms of human knowledge, he reduces them to three: material, formal, and absolute knowledge, which respectively give rise to empirical science, philosophy, and theology. Theology, according to Soloviev, is the harmonization of the formal and positive disciplines, that it, philosophy and empirical science providing, as it does, that absolute principle which frees material knowledge from indistinct matter and formal knowledge from empty form. The resultant harmonious blend of cognitive form is free theosophy, which is nothing other than "an organic synthesis of theology, philosophy, and

[36]*Sobranie sochinenii V. S. Solov'eva* [Collected works of V. S. Soloviev] (Brussels, 1966), 1:250-406.
[37]Ibid., 2:xiii-397.
[38]Radlov, "Teoriya znaniya," 159.
[39]Cf. ch. 1 of *Filosofskie nachala* in *Sobranie*, 1:250-90.

experimental science."[40] Soloviev adds that "only such a synthesis can contain the integral truth of knowledge: outside of it science, philosophy, and theology are only single parts or sides, fragmented organs of knowledge, and thus not in any way adequate to integral truth itself."[41]

Taking a different turn now in his argument, Soloviev maintains that free theosophy is the only true philosophy, since both empiricism and rationalism, the only other two types of philosophy,[42] are internally flawed. The object of empiricism is only the world of appearances as reduced to our sensations, while the object of rationalism is merely the world of ideas as reduced to our formal thoughts,[43] with neither, therefore, arriving at true, objective reality independent of ourselves and our own subjective constitution.[44] Thus taken in themselves, they can only ultimately lead to absolute scepticism. The only way out of this impasse is via free theosophy, which manages to transcend the difficulties of empiricism and rationalism by rooting itself in "mystical" knowledge, whose object is the "living reality of beings in their internal, lived relationships."[45] "Mysticism"[46] of itself, however, as Soloviev notes, does not give a system of true philosophy, but serves only as its necessary, but insufficient,

[40]Ibid., 290.
[41]Ibid.
[42]Ibid., 290-308.
[43]Ibid., 304.
[44]In this synopsis of Soloviev's epistemology, it is impossible to treat all of its problematic aspects directly. For instance, Soloviev appears to reduce empirical and rational knowledge to merely subjective, psychical processes, and we dissent from this position. Unfortunately, however, the scope of this present study does not permit us to enter into a discussion with Soloviev on this and other points.
[45]Soloviev, Sobranie, 1:304.
[46]We must score Soloviev for his equivocal usage of terms here. He appears to use the terms "theology" and "mysticism" as if they were entirely interchangeable, and, furthermore, he is inexact in his usage. Indeed, in the contexts in which these terms are employed, it would seem that "intuitivism" or "intuitive knowledge" would have been the better, more precise choice. In addition, when he speaks of "theology," he sometimes seems really to mean "true philosophy," in contrast to the rationalist knowledge given in mere "philosophy" (cf., e.g., Sobranie, 1:260). At any rate, Soloviev's bottom-line position appears to be that the integral knowledge of true philosophy or free theosophy is the synthesis of the particular knowledges given in mysticism (i.e., intuitivism), rationalism, and empiricism.

basis. The reflex of reason or the justification of rational thought must be added, plus the confirmation of the empirical factors, as provided by empirical knowledge. Radlov aptly summarizes this view as follows: "mysticism determines the superior principle and ultimate aim of philosophical knowledge; empiricism serves as its external base; and rationalism is the mediator or general bond of the whole system."[47]

From this discussion it becomes clear that Soloviev's "mystical knowledge," i.e., intuitive knowledge, is closely linked to, if not virtually the same as, Kireevsky's "belief" ("faith") and Khomyakov's variant usage of this term.[48] This correspondence is unmistakably evident once we turn to Soloviev's *Kritika otvlechennykh nachal,* and confirm that here, in his analysis of the constitutive elements of objective knowledge ("object-knowledge"), he specifically considers three, namely, "sensation," "thinking," and "belief."[49] Soloviev writes: "We *sense* the known action of the object, we *think* its general characteristics, and *are convinced* of its proper or absolute existence."[50] Sensation and thought, however, are only relative or conditional in their respective givennesses as real, factual actions and ideal relations. An absolute note with respect to the being of the known object is had only in the "mystical," intuitive element or belief, in which its unconditionality as an existent is perceived as *credible,* and, therefore, evocative of conviction.[51] "This belief," Soloviev maintains, "is the testimony of our freedom from everything and, along with this, the expression of our internal bond with everything."[52] Without it, that is, were we to have no credible assurance of the being of the object, then all we would remain with would be the mere, subjective states of our consciousness, and only absolute scepticism could obtain.

[47]Radlov, "Teoriya znaniya," 160.

[48]For Kireevsky, "belief" is integral thinking itself, although sometimes he uses it in the sense of the teaching of the Orthodox Church. With Khomyakov, "belief" is only one of the three elements constitutive of integral knowledge. His usage of the term shows he intends "intuition," which is what Soloviev signifies by the term "mysticism."

[49]Soloviev, *Sobranie,* 2:324-42.

[50]Ibid., 325.

[51]Ibid., 331.

[52]Ibid., 330.

Soloviev does not despair before the complexities of knowing that we truly know. On the contrary, objective knowledge
becomes for him a primary instance of man's fundamental
freedom and call to creativity. In this type of knowledge,
man truly acts creatively by giving unity to his otherwise
chaotic impressions. The triad, "sensation-thinking-belief" is
now subject to a fundamental transformation by Soloviev,
and comes to read "belief-representation-creativity,"[53] which
clearly parallels Khomyakov's triad, "belief-reason-will."[54] In
belief we confess our intuitive grasp of the real and find the
matter of our knowledge; in the formal representation of the
real we find a synergy or mutual, concertive activity of man
as a constituting and knowing subject and of the object as a
constituted and known object; and in the creative act, we
witness man's free "yes," his affirmative, judicative response
before the real.

Soloviev adds another important point to his conception
of integral knowledge, namely, the element of the pan-unity
of the entire created order, which entails man's own integral
bond with creation, and which, in his view, is also the ontological condition making all knowledge possible.[55] It is precisely the weakness of merely abstract knowledge, Soloviev
maintains, that it dissolves the "bond of the knower with the
all, with the all-one," thereby "pulling the knowing subject
away from his true relationships"[56] and precluding any truly
integral knowledge for him.

Also like Kireevsky and Khomyakov, Soloviev upholds
the view that a truly integral knowledge is ultimately impossible apart from the integral life, in which one finds an active
harmonization and synthesis of man in his totality, of man's
reason, will, and sentiment, that is, in other words, that
coalescence of the elements of man's personality which alone
guarantees man's openness to the depths and plentitude of
the real. The *animus* of this integral life is none other than
love. It is, accordingly, in love that one must center one's life
in order to chart the way to integral truth.

[53]Ibid., 324-42.
[54]Cf. Radlov's observation in "Teoriya znaniya," 163.
[55]Cf. ibid., 161, 163, and Lossky, *History of Russian Philosophy*, 97.
[56]*Sobranie*, 2:298.

2.4 *Further Developments in Florensky*

That Florensky is firmly implanted in the Slavophile tradition is evidenced by the many themes he treats in common with Kireevsky, Khomyakov, and Soloviev. This is especially true in the case of the theory of integral knowledge, whose overtones are heard on virtually every page of *The Pillar and Foundation of Truth*. This particular epistemological interpretation of human cognition, which highlights belief as an independent source of knowledge, is an original feature of Russian thought. It is, however, marred by a basic equivocation concerning the meaning of belief and a failure to demarcate clearly the realm of natural reason from the supernatural realm of gratuitous grace and infused knowledge. Though he himself never directly treats the theories of Kireevsky, Khomyakov, and Soloviev, in his *magnum opus* Florensky does much to bring greater clarity to this discussion, as will become evident during the course of this study.

Without going into further detail in regard to what his critique of them might have been were he to have embarked upon such a review of their teaching, it suffices at this point just to indicate the apparent additions he contributes to the theory of integral knowledge. First of all, he extends the application of the term "integral knowledge" (*tsel'noe znanie*) to other thinkers besides those in strictly Russian and eastern traditions. This *terminus technicus* of Russian philosophy now is applied to describe the philosophical strivings of all philosophers who abjure, and forthrightly reject the unilaterality of rationalism. Florensky makes this application for the first time in his previously cited study on the Platonic and idealist roots of European philosophy.[57] He specifically draws attention to Plato as an example of one who searches for integral knowledge. Secondly, Florensky underscores that integral knowledge is attained only via the antinomic structure of the mind, a position first maintained in his examination of Kantian antinomism[58] and subsequently much enlarged upon in *The Pillar and Foundation of Truth*.

[57]Cf. p. 39, esp. nn. 60 and 62 above.
[58]Cf. p. 39 above.

3. ECCLESIALITY

Florensky develops the concrete articulation of his methodological axiom concerning the primacy of experience in religious speculation—a consideration by no means extraneous to his position on integral knowledge as an offshoot of the integral life—in conjunction with his understanding of "*ecclesiality*" (*tserkovnost'*).[59] Ecclesiality, to his mind, is none other than the stance that religious truth is graspable only in the context of ecclesial life, or, more specifically, in the experience of divine worship, which is the heart and pulse beat of this life.[60] Here Florensky harks back to Khomyakov, whom he cited in his earlier, youthful study, *Ecclesiological Materials*, as follows: "Only he understands the Church who understands the Liturgy."[61]

An introspective view into the human soul, however, reveals that man has a natural inability to grasp immediately and fully the totality of divine revelation, or to give a fully adequate response to it in all its diverse aspects. The ecclesial life at the root of all truly spiritual, and not merely biological, vitalistic existence,[62] essentially transcends man at the same time that he participates in it. He does not have an integral vision of it, but only apprehends partial truths concerning it. However, from his real experience of categoreal truth in the depths of his soul, he is led to affirm as the basis and norm of this assertory truth an all-embracing, transcendental Truth, that is at once eternal, one, and divine. Simultaneously, he becomes fully cognizant of his need for an unfailing wellspring and support to sustain him in his search for truth, whence his appeal to the Church of the living God as the pillar and foundation of truth.[63]

---

[59]PFT, 5.

[60]PFT, 118. In PFT, 299, Florensky, using another analogy, writes that "divine worship is the *flower* of ecclesial life and, along with this, its root and seed."

[61]*Ekkleziologicheskie materialy*, 94.

[62]Florensky makes an important observation in regard to precisely what kind of life he means. Distinguishing spiritual life (ζωή) from biological life (βίος), he identifies ecclesial life with the former, thus indicating its transcendent, suprarational source. Cf. PFT, 608 (n. 2).

[63]Florensky's first reference to 1 Tim 3:15 comes on PFT, 12.

Ecclesiality as a life-concept, however, by nature is not fully accessible to human reason. This thought, previously developed by the Slavophiles, Kireevsky and Khomyakov,[64] follows from the fact that the phenomenon of life as such is an irreducible datum, and therefore one incapable of strict definition and logical formulation. Being itself an ultimate reality, it is not analyzable into smaller components.

A problem immediately presents itself, however. If life indeed is ultimately unanalyzable, how then does one determine the quality of life in general and of ecclesiality in particular? What criterion or criteria can be applied to determine their authenticity? If life as such, and more specifically, ecclesial life, is inaccessible to human reason, how can we answer these questions without begging them? These are, indeed, most valid questions, and merit close attention and consideration.

Florensky's proffered resolution to this problematic is only partially successful.[65] In particular, his treatment of what he considers the Catholic and Protestant criteria for determining the validity of ecclesial life is both unfair and injudicious. Most likely it is owing to his otherwise laudable confessional loyalty that Florensky imputes a lack of spiritual life and depth to Catholicism and Protestantism. This view, however, has justly elicited the stern dissent of his critics and admirers, both Orthodox and non-Orthodox alike.[66] His discourse, based as it is on a distinction between external and internal criteria of ecclesiality, seems especially misplaced. He tries to show that the respective Catholic and Protestant juridical and scientific understandings of ecclesiality are restrictively confined to the domain of the concept, to which ecclesial life by its very nature cannot be confined. Catholicism with its appeals to the hierarchy and magisterium and Protestantism with its *sola Scriptura* doctrine, apply, according to Florensky, solely extra-life criteria for determining ecclesiality,

[64]PFT, 5, 608 (n. 2).
[65]PFT, 6f.
[66]Cf., e.g., Berdyaev, "Stilizovannoe pravoslavie," 115, and Elémire Zolla, "Introduzione" of the Italian edition of PFT (*La colonna e il fondamento della verità* [Milan: Rusconi, 1974], 26). For examples of Florensky's disparaging remarks, see PFT, 6f, 58, 266f, 404, 765 (n. 639).

which as such demands internal, life criteria for determining viability. Orthodoxy, on the other hand, takes no recourse, in Florensky's opinion, to spheres beyond life itself. From the Orthodox perspective, since life is undefinable, so also is ecclesiality incapable of conceptual determination and beyond the scope of criteria restricted to the conceptual plane.

Insofar as no concept can ever be fully commensurate with the phenomenon of life, Florensky is justified in stressing the indeterminate character of ecclesiality. He is also correct in regarding the very indeterminateness of ecclesiality as a decisive proof of its vitality. But is he entirely justified in his distrust of extrinsic valuations of ecclesiality? And does not Orthodoxy also employ them? Does it not have a hierarchical, organizational structure? And does it really relegate Sacred Scripture to only a secondary, supporting role and not to a foundational and normative one? And do Catholics really consider all free stirrings of the Spirit as "uncanonical," or Protestants as "unscientific"? On the basis of Florensky's own experiential criterion his judgments here seem to defy the facts. Granted that the experience of Christianity in Catholicism and Protestantism is different from that in Orthodoxy, and granted that one might rightly question, depending on one's point of view, whether all Christian denominations possess all the desired, divinely willed ecclesial structures and elements for the full breadth and depth of ecclesial experience, it still would definitely be an extreme position to declare that non-Orthodox bodies are deficient in vital, spiritual life. But considering the age Florensky was writing in, his position probably is not all that surprising, though he would appear nonetheless to be reverting to positions previous to the daring genius of Vladimir Soloviev, who signaled new horizons for ecumenical *rapprochement,* and would even seem to be at odds with his own subsequently detailed views concerning the transcendental oneness of all religions.

The very indeterminateness and fluidity of ecclesiality indicate the need for some extrinsic points of reference such as hierarchical approbation and scriptural conformity for guidance in determining true viability in its regard. These considerations are not extraneous but are directly relevant since from the viewpoint of faith they are equally revealed by God and willed by Him to guide us in this matter. Florensky's basic point, nonetheless, remains unchallenged and retains its poignant validity. For a faithful description, ecclesial life *qua* life needs dynamic, experiential concepts, ones which are also somewhat indeterminate in themselves, so that no aspect of its authentic vitality may be obscured or stifled, or its full import in any way be underestimated. He suggests that the best we can do is to resort to concepts borrowed from biology and aesthetics. Some possible examples, admittedly ambiguous, could be "new life" and "life in the Spirit."

In an attempt to decide upon some acceptable criteria for determining the authenticity or truth-value of this "new life" and "life in the Spirit"—his chosen concepts for shedding light on the nature of ecclesiality—Florensky, continuing in the same general line of reasoning that they should be of the internal order, that is, not extrinsic to life, proposes spiritual beauty as the best criterion of ecclesiality and the surest indication and gauge of its authenticity and truthfulness.[67] We might, of course, immediately enquire whether Florensky does not thereby confuse conceptual orders. Simply put, how can a primary notion from aesthetics like beauty be employed as an epistemological criterion for determining authenticity in ecclesiality?

An answer to this difficulty is hinted at in the objection Bishop Feodor raises in regard to Florensky's proposal of beauty as the most suitable criterion of ecclesiality.[68] If the needed criterion must be, like ecclesiality, indeterminate, why, this hierarch asks, should we restrict ourselves to beauty? Can we not find other equally indeterminate criteria? Would not "goodness" or even "truthfulness" itself equally suffice? The answer to this basic query concerning the possibility of other criteria is, of course, yes. Florensky's criterion of beauty and Bishop Feodor's criteria of truthfulness and goodness all witness to the existence and bearing of spiritual life for man. But do they share a common feature? Is there something that

[67]PFT, 7f. Cf. also Adriano Dell'Asta, "La bellezza splendore del vero" [Beauty, the splendor of the true], *Russia Cristiana*, 174 (1980): 32-53.
[68]Bishop Feodor, "Review," 146f.

can unite them as well as distinguish them? And if so, in what does this factor of commonality and distinction consist?

Looking carefully, we can see that each—beauty, truthfulness, goodness—corresponds with one of the traditional, transcendental properties of being. These properties are different formalities from under which we can articulate the plenitude of being. They are properly transcendentals, because they are of absolutely unlimited extension, and are both convertible and coterminous with being itself. They do not as such add something to being that it does not already have, but only a relation of reason to being itself.[69] The mind before being sees it as truth in relation to the intellect, as good in relation to the will, and as beauty in relation to itself as a whole. Accordingly, truthfulness, goodness, and beautifulness, themselves, serve as transcendental criteria of being.

But what, it may be objected, is the precise relevance of this discussion? Its point is simply to make clear that Florensky and Bishop Feodor are asking for *transcendental* criteria for determining the existence of spiritual life and for measuring its intensity. Neither of them make this explicit in their reasonings however. Bishop Feodor, moreover, who is on the right track with his initial objection, veers off it when, after suggesting the transcendental criterion of truthfulness, cites instead only a determinate one, the Nicaean Creed, for making an actual determination in any one case, thus literally switching discourses in mid-sentence[70] and reverting back to the very extrinsic type of criterion that Florensky is striving to supplant. It is not that Florensky would say that the Nicaean Creed should not enter into the picture, since it most assuredly does express those faith convictions we would expect to find in anyone professing to live a Christian existence and spirituality. It is only that Florensky would object that it is inadequate in its very conceptual character, and cannot, in the final analysis, fully attend to its purpose, as the

---

[69]We prescind from a consideration of the other remaining, classical transcendental, namely oneness or unity. This property adds only negation to being, insofar as it excludes all that is other than being. For a succinct treatment of the transcendentals, see E. Coreth, *Metaphysics* (New York: Herder & Herder, 1968), 120-46.

[70]Bishop Feodor, "Review," 146f.

reality it seeks to indicate is much broader, and, indeed, lies beyond its conceptual grasp.

Florensky himself, however, has still to address and resolve all the issues. We may grant that he can resort to beauty to settle accounts with truth, at least on the transcendental level. But we may rightly object that in concrete circumstances this criterion, or any other transcendental criterion for that matter, is not too helpful. Can we not point to famous heretics who in their own way were also masters of the spiritual life? And what about those who may expound the right truth but are deficient in the spiritual life? In their very indeterminateness, in their very transcendentality, these criteria appear almost empty, and, indeed, give the impression of being decidedly inoperable. Just to cite them as deciding factors is to beg the question. But to make them work we must enter into matters of proportionality, and determine the proportions of truth, goodness, and beauty at stake in any given case. And that means appealing to external sources of judgment like conformity to creedal statements, authentic teaching, and revelation—all considerations Florensky wants to avoid in order to come to a final determination.[71] There is, however, no other alternative open to us and no other avenue of appeal.

Florensky does, indeed, have an important point to make and a profound insight to convey. Ecclesiality, the life of the Church in the Spirit, cannot be fully captured by any concept, nor can conflicts concerning it be resolved by conceptual apparatus alone. In this sense, his favoring transcendental criteria for describing and discussing ecclesial life is most appropriate and entirely correct. His analysis is weak only insofar as he does not delve into and treat the crucial problem of proportionality in religious truth, goodness, and beauty, a problem which his own position implies, but which he himself never appears to consider. He may not have been oblivious to it, but in bypassing it, he neglects to place in proper relief the legitimate role extrinsic criteria of judgment have to play in resolving cases of conflict.

He is also most trenchant when he stresses that we come

[71]For a similar discussion, see p. 29, esp. n. 24 above.

to the spiritual life and begin to confess its truth only with existential contact, and not by any form of discursive reasoning. This new life is a primary, irreducible datum accessible only in experience, which can mean nothing to those who have not shared in it. In this light, his dictum: "Orthodoxy manifests itself; it does not prove itself,"[72] which otherwise might have the dull ring of a slogan, indeed resonates a profound and irrefutable truth of the spiritual life. In other words, to know Orthodoxy, or for that matter any religion, is to have an immediate experience of it. Without this indispensable experience, the spiritual quest of the naturally religious soul becomes little more than what Sartrean logic reduces to a vain and futile passion of the mind.

Florensky's emphasis on the primacy of experience, especially in its conjunction with the Church and ecclesial life, has, most unfortunately, occasioned charges of subjectivism against him by some of his critics. M. Tareev, to cite a good example, upbraids Florensky for not pursuing a truly Christian philosophy, but only an excessively personal, spiritualist one.[73] Zenkovsky criticizes Florensky in a similar vein, stating "Florensky places too much emphasis on 'personal religious experience,' seeking to draw from it everything necessary for his theological and philosophic system."[74] But, to our mind, both Tareev and Zenkovsky are too severe in their judgments. Florensky may give the appearance of being an eclectic at times, yet his underlying motivation, insofar as he is seeking experiential corroboration of his theses, seems basically above reproach. He is merely striving to show the broad range of possible experiences in some way or other touching upon his

[72]PFT, 8. Years later, Sergius Bulgakov would reecho Florensky's thoughts concerning the ultimate indefinability of the Church and ecclesial life and the primacy of experience in deliberations about their nature, when in The Orthodox Church (New York and Milwaukee: Morehouse Publishing, 1935; a translation of the 1932 French original), he writes (p .12): "There can thus be no satisfactory and complete definition of the Church. 'Come and see'—one recognizes the Church only by experience, by grace, by participation in its life. This is why before making any formal definition, the Church must be conceived in its mystical being, underlying all definitions, but larger than them all."

[73]M. Tareev, "Novoe bogoslovie" [The new theology], TM, 2 (1917): 3-53; 168-224. See esp. p. 214.

[74]Zenkovsky, Istoriya, 2:417; Eng. ed., 878.

problematic and therefore meriting mention, if not complete accounting.[75] Florensky himself goes to great length to disavow any subjectivistic moment to his conception of philosophy. To his mind, it is not enough to philosophize *about* religion—one must rather philosophize *in* religion.[76] Without such an approach to religion "from within," the religious sphere as a datum for philosophical *prise de conscience* remains foreign to the philosopher's ken.

This particular fashioning of the philosophical enterprise, Florensky emphasizes, is anything but subjectivistic. It only stresses the fact that philosophical thought must needs be *personal* thought, "thought characteristically correlating a given object with a *given* subject."[77] "Thinking," he maintains, "is an unceasing synthesis of the known with a knower, and, consequently, is deeply and through and through penetrated by the energies of the knowing personality. As such, it cannot be abstract, colorless, and impersonal, 'an acknowledgment in general,' since I know that it is I who takes careful stock of reality."[78] Only a person can dialectically concert with reality, penetrate into its secret recesses, and derive meaning for himself from it. It is this thinking subject who becomes Florensky's "methodological I," the inquiring ego at the heart and focus of dialectical thought in search of meaning in life.[79] Its task is eminently personal, and is radically misconstrued if imputed to be solely psychologistic. This "methodological I," however, Florensky maintains, does not do its work all by itself. The discovery of meaning in life is a collaborative effort of man in relationship with others, the project, therefore, of a

[75]In this discussion, it is well to recall Florensky's words to Belyi, that his method is "the investigation of concepts and the synthesis of heterogeneous materials" (*Vestnik*, 114 [1974]: 166).

[76]"Razum i dialektika," 95.

[77]Ibid., 96.

[78]Ibid. These themes of Florensky are, interestingly enough, the very cornerstones of Gabriel Marcel's conception of philosophy. However, in all probability, there was no direct influence of Florensky on Marcel, as Florensky's thought is relatively unknown in the West. Indeed, it is often unknown in the East.

[79]Ibid., 97.

"methodological we" conspiring in its proper "methodological environment" for the attainment of authentic insight.[80]

4. The Language of Metaphysics

Florensky, as we have seen, views method in philosophy as dialectics. But he also would not disagree with Alfred North Whitehead, who says the epigraph of John Henry Cardinal Newman's *An Essay in Aid of a Grammar of Assent*, itself a citation from Saint Ambrose, should be every metaphysician's motto.[81] This epigraph reads: *"Non in dialectica complacuit Deo salvum facere populum suum."* (It was not by dialectics that God vouchsafed to save His people.) Florensky's understanding of dialectics is not that of its usual sense of sheer, logical disputation, but centers around a lived contact with reality which transcends man's powers of conceptualization. Man's dialectical exercises are necessarily inadequate and cannot salve his intellectual unrest nor bring him the final happiness he so ardently seeks. Without any qualms about transgressing the proper bounds of philosophy, Florensky candidly acknowledges the inherent deficiencies of dialectical thought, and confesses faith in the living God and life in the Church as the sole means for overcoming these limitations and for bringing man to his proper end, life in God.

The very titles of Florensky's letters, "Doubt," "Light of Truth," "Contradiction," "The Creature," "Sophia," "Friendship," indicate that throughout his masterwork he treats of ultimate, irreducible realities and mysteries beyond the full conceptual powers of man. The inherent insufficiencies of dialectics and language to express these phenomena in a completely adequate manner obviously entail that his elaborations can never be final in themselves, and can, at best, be only suggestive. Florensky's philosophical and religious speculations accordingly remain open-ended, as evidenced in the very fact of his "letter-writing."

[80]Ibid.
[81]Alfred North Whitehead, *Adventures in Ideas* (New York: Free Press, 1967) 295.

That his chosen form of philosophical exposition is a more informal, essay style, however, does not mean that his speculations are any less profound. Quite the contrary; penetrating insights abound on his pages, and often they are expressed by means of a difficult and baffling conceptual apparatus that can be both technical and poetic at the same time. Indeed, such is the nature of his sophiological speculations, and precisely on this account they lend themselves to the charge of Gnosticism. Florensky frankly admits this, but rejoins that he intends them only as "wretched schemata for what is experienced in the soul."[82]

The intrinsic deficiencies of language notwithstanding, Florensky observes that man still undergoes a compelling urge to bring to light and express his lived experience of a more foundational and transcendent truth, conceived to be at the root of his very existence in space and time. By spontaneous, religious instinct, he naturally appeals to the Godhead for divine assistance and illumination in this endeavor. For the Christian Florensky, this means taking special recourse to the Holy Spirit as the Light of Truth and eternal source of our enlightenment. With a restrained yet evident stir of emotion, Florensky expresses this central thought as follows: "All the perplexities, difficulties, and torments of our life are gathered around the Holy Spirit; yet all our hopes are found in His revelation."[83]

5. The Work of Ascesis

If the search for a criterion of ecclesiality leads us to the domain of the beautiful and that of spiritual beauty in particular, it becomes apparent that ultimately we must turn our attention to the masters of spiritual beauty to clarify our understanding of ecclesiality. These masters, the holy fathers and confessors of the faith, the venerable martyrs, and all other saintly men and women, indeed, are the best evidences of a truth transcendent to themselves, as their heroic virtue

[82]PFT, 324.
[83]PFT, 140, and Schmemann, *Ultimate Questions*, 170.

and sanctity can never be fully explained on a purely natural basis alone. These are the ones, who, according to the Sermon on the Mount (Mt 5:8), have been blessed with the vision of God owing to their purity of heart. Florensky picks up this biblical teaching which is also a recurrent theme in patristic literature,[84] and in his search for the foundations of truth, develops a unique epistemological point of view highlighting integral knowledge as a fruit of ascesis and as a concomitant feature of spiritual beauty. If integral knowledge and, moreover, the vision of God itself await only those who are pure of heart, it is not surprising that Florensky, in his analysis of the cognitive process, concentrates his interest not so much on the intellect as such but more on the heart as the organ of spiritual perception.[85] "The purification of the heart," as he states elsewhere, "gives communication with God, and communication with God puts straight and organizes the entire personality of the ascetic [*podvizhnik*]."[86]

In his first letter, "Two Worlds," Florensky attempts to justify this position further with an analysis of a gospel passage, Matthew 11:27-30, which in his view has a predominantly cognitive meaning.[87] Indeed, he states that the entire eleventh chapter of Matthew represents a marked contrast between two types of knowledge, "labored" and "spiritual" knowledge,[88] the one burdened and handicapped by the inherent insufficiencies of natural reason, the other loosed from these bonds owing to the victory of the Spirit, the fruit of the synergy or working together of human ascesis and divine grace. Though a careful examination of this chapter, especially its last four verses (vv. 27-30),[89] would not appear to

---

[84]Tomás Spidlík, S.J., *La spiritualité de l'Orient chrétien* (Rome: Pontificium Institutum Orientalium Studiorum, 1978), 141.

[85]Florensky notably makes this point in his philological analysis of the Russian word, *tselomudrie*, which translates "chastity," and which he in turn understands as "purity of heart." Its two roots, *tselo-mudrie*, literally mean "whole-wise," therefore indicating that in the traditional Russian consciousness "purity" carries the sense of "integral wisdom." Cf. PFT, 268f, 534-39.

[86]PFT, 271, and "Dukh i plot'," 73.

[87]PFT, 12f. The gospel passage in question is the one prescribed for the moleben (prayer) service for a venerable man in Byzantine ritual.

[88]PFT, 609f.

[89]Mt 11:27-30 reads:

bear out this view, and would seem more to indicate that Florensky is giving not so much an exegetical, as an eisegetical interpretation of the text, this does not mean that his accommodation of the passage is without merit. On the contrary, he gives valuable new indications for its possible applications to the troubled human situation, especially as it refers to questions of doubt and intellectual despair. His epistemological point is both clear and opportune. The Divine Word alone reveals to us the mystery of the Holy Trinity and all heavenly truth, and alone takes upon Himself our doubts and despairs. Burdened down with a "labored," limited and imperfect knowledge, we find our sole consolation and intellectual relief, that is to say, our true spiritual beautitude and knowledge, in the fiducial abandon of faith, animated by sincere love of God.

The point of Florensky's discussion of Matthew 11 is the underscoring of the fact that human reason, if left to its own devices and resources, cannot lighten its own intellectual burdens and resolve its own doubts. It may struggle in earnest, but without opening up to the workings of divine grace in moral and ascetical struggle, its inquietude continues unabated. One may readily agree with this basic point but still seriously question whether Florensky can readily draw support for his thesis on ascesis and the intellectual life from this text. As an exegesis his analysis is strained and implau-

(27) All things have been delivered to Me by My Father; and no one knows the Son except the Father, and no one knows the Father except the Son and any one to whom the Son chooses to reveal Him.
(28) Come to Me, all who labor and are heavy laden, and I will give you rest. (29) Take My yoke upon you, and learn from Me; for I am gentle and lowly in heart, and you will find rest for your souls. (30) For My yoke is easy, and My burden is light."
It is apparent that we are here dealing with two different pericopes. The former (v. 27), which has been described as "a meteor from the Johannine heaven," is, we may say, more directly of an epistemological nature. However, the latter pericope (vv. 28-30), it would seem, does not directly deal with knowledge as such. Florensky accommodates its meaning when he distinguishes "labored" from "spiritual" knowledge. The weary and burdened in the text are the poor who have the good news proclaimed to them; the yoke and burden of our Lord refer to personal submission to the reign of God. Cf. John L. McKenzie, S.J., "The Gospel according to Matthew," *The Jerome Biblical Commentary* (Englewood Cliffs, NJ: Prentice-Hall, 1968), 2:83.

sible, though it may, from an eisegetical point of view, be an acceptable accommodation of its literal meaning.

When we turn to the religious sphere and spiritual domain, questions of praxis, of moral struggle, and of ascetical exercise are not irrelevant to the quests of the intellect. Indeed, the role of moral conversion in sharpening spiritual vision and expanding its horizons is of central importance.[90] The religious life—Christianity's in particular—is not a mere system of ideas, logically proved and systematically expounded. Precisely as *life*, to know it as true requires, as Florensky's close friend, Alexander Elchaninov, as a respected priest serving the Russian émigré community in France would one day advise youth,[91] more than intellectual effort alone. It demands moral living, ascesis, purification of heart and mind, and prayer.

[90]For a discussion of the role of conversion in thought, cf. Bernard J. F. Lonergan, S.J., *Method in Theology* (London: Darton, Longman & Todd, 1971), passim, esp. p. 131.

[91]Alexander Elchaninov, *Zapisi* [Jottings], 3rd ed. (Paris: YMCA Press, 1962), 113, 119f. An English translation exists under the title of *The Diary of a Russian Priest* (London: Faber & Faber, 1967).

His ornari aut mori.   (Be crowned of these or die.)

Part Two

FLORENSKY'S ANTINOMIC CONCEPTION OF TRUTH

CHAPTER III

The Experience of Truth

To pose the problem of truth for Florensky means to inquire into the *experience* of truth.[1] Apart from experiential contact with data to be known there can be no knowledge, since all knowledge essentially is a knowledge of an objective datum as given only in experience. Quite clearly, Florensky refers not to the subjectivistic experience of mere egotistical feeling, but to experience in its intentional dimension as a coordination of the subjective pole of a thinking subject and the objective pole of a known object. Intentional coordination does, nonetheless, entail *feeling* in the knowing subject. In the experience of truth, this feeling may be either positive or negative. If positive, it is called *certitude,* and if negative, it gives rise to *doubt.* The problem of truth, thus, becomes one with the problem of doubt and certitude in our knowing, and it is around them that all probings and yearnings for authentic contact with the real revolve. Indeed, the mark of truth is certitude, and as long as doubt persists the grasping of truth eludes and unsettles us.

1.   THE POLYVALENCY OF TRUTH

True to his methodological principle which stresses concrete experience as the necessary point of departure for philo-

[1] The problematic of this chapter is found in Florensky's second letter, which treats the phenomenon of doubt. Cf. PFT, 15-50.

sophical reflection,[2] Florensky begins his discussion of doubt and certitude with an etymological digression on the word, "truth" as found in various languages.[3] His excursus is by no means beside the point, because he tries to illuminate the fact that the manifold modes in which truth has been experienced by diverse peoples throughout the course of time are uniquely expressed in the particular words themselves for truth.

1.1 *The Ontological Moment*

The Russian word for truth, *istina,* clearly highlights what Florensky labels the ontological moment of truth. Literally, *istina* means "that which is," and is the substantive form of the verb, *est',* meaning "is." Truth in the Russian consciousness accordingly is an existent. Yet, it needs a further determination if all misunderstandings are to be avoided. Since not all that exists is true, *istina* must more specifically correspond with *real* being, just as a figure to its type. Figments of the imagination and lies also exist, but not truly. They have only a simulated, would-be being, and do no more that mimic and mock the reality of true being, of the truly existent.[4]

This understanding of truth as the really existent receives additional support, Florensky adds, if we dig deeper into the roots of the Russian verbal form, "is." *Est',* according to Florensky and other linguists, contains the Sanskrit root, *as,* which equally connotes the concepts of "breathing" and "being alive." Thus, from an etymological point of view, the Russian word for "to be" carries the additional meanings of "to breathe" and, more abstractly speaking, "to be alive." That "truth," "life," and "existence" are connected in primitive Slavic consciousness is a fact of no little import. Indeed, Florensky avers that the conjunction of these three concepts in the depths of Russian consciousness constitutes the originality of Russian philosophical intuition, which has largely

---

[2]Cf. pp. 51-54 above.
[3]Cf. PFT, 15-22.
[4]Soloviev gives a detailed discussion of this point in *Kritika otvlechennykh nachal,* in *Sobranie,* 2:192-95.

been absorbed in the search for "living," integral knowledge
and in the exposition and interpretation of the world as an
organic whole.[5]

1.2   *The Gnoseological Moment*

The Greeks, on the other hand, concentrated their attention more on the gnoseological or epistemological moment
of truth. Their word for truth, *aletheia,* has a possible, twofold meaning, depending upon one's preferred interpretation
of its root-structure. The word definitely has for one of its
elements the privative particle, "a," thus rendering it *a-letheia.*
Two possible etymologies of *letheia* are offered by Florensky.
It could come from the verb, *lanthanein,* meaning "to be
hidden" or "concealed," or from the substantive, *'e lethe,*
signifying "forgetfulness" or "unconsciousness." *Aletheia,*
accordingly, connotes the ideas of "unconcealedness" and
"unforgottenness."

At the same time, the word calls attention to the fact of
"memory" as the special locus of truth, insofar as truth,
a-letheia, persists on in the mind against the current of forgetfulness, and is therefore something which overcomes time,
being at once something not flowing but eternally remembered. Truth in this way bears the sense of "eternal memory,"
and is, accordingly, most amenable to the Christian dogmatic
teaching concerning Christ as the Eternal Logos or Word of
the Father. The fact that the verb, *lanthanein* in its middle
mood also acquires the special sense of "to drop from
memory" or "to forget" Florensky further adduces to substantiate his interpretation, since the addition of the privative
particle alters its sense to "not to drop from memory" or
"not to forget."

1.3   *The Juridical Moment*

The Latin word for truth, *veritas,* highlights still another
[5]PFT, 17, 614f.

indispensable element in the experience of truth. The primordial meaning of its Sanskrit root, *var*, refers to the cultic sphere, as indicated in the Sanskrit word, *vratam*, which means a "sacred action." Unmistakable remnants of the original sense of this root remain in both dead and modern languages. The Russian word for "faith," *vera*, for example, testifies to this, as well as the title, "Reverend," which is common to so many languages. The Latin language's multiform use of the root *var* is of particular interest and relevance. Three type-words which demonstrate this multiformity include *vereor*, *verdictum*, and *veritas* itself, meaning "to fear" or "to respect," "verdict," and "truth," respectively. The juridical application of the root is especially relevant, since it points the way to the central philosophical insight that truth and falsity are formally contained in the judgment, that is, in the act of affirmation or negation. For this reason, the juridicial or judicative moment is by no means a dispensable feature of truth, but is rather an intrinsically necessary dimension of the truth experience.

1.4 *The Historical Moment*

The ancient Semites in general and the Hebrews in particular stressed, in their turn, the historical, or more precisely, the theocratic moment of truth. To the Hebrew, truth was always the Word of God, and, as God is always faithful to His word, the experience of truth becomes one of fiduciality. The Hebrew word for truth, *emet*, is cognate with the verb for "to support" and with the substantive for "column," among others. Thus, the sense of reliance and security and, more abstractly, that of trustworthiness are evoked. The frequently encountered biblical exclamation, "Amen," which can be variously translated as "my word is sturdy," "in truth," "so it be," etc., itself is an obvious derivative of this word. In fine, we can, in Hebraic consciousness, rely on truth and be assured of it, because it is the faithful word of God.

1.5   *An Aside on Heidegger*

Florensky's penchant for etymologies and "etymological proofs" is not an entirely unique feature of his thought. Other philosophers also resort to them in their philosophical speculations. In the case of truth, one immediately thinks of Martin Heidegger, who is also well-known for his partiality to the etymological argument. Indeed, his discussion of truth as *aletheia* is particularly relevant.

While for Florensky, the Greek word *aletheia* highlights the gnoseological moment of truth insofar as it points to "memory" as the locus of truth, for Heidegger it would appear primordially to make the ontological dimension of truth manifest. *Aletheia* he variously etymologizes as "uncoveredness"[6] or as "unconcealment."[7] To him, truth is nothing other than "the manifestness of the essent,"[8] which can otherwise be defined as "the disclosure of what keeps itself concealed."[9] This concept of truth as a "being-uncovered," Heidegger maintains in *Being and Time,* primordially undergirds the traditional concept of truth as an *adaequatio intellectus et rei,* which is merely derived from it.[10] Indeed, as he notes elsewhere, "the original essence of truth, *aletheia* (unconcealment) has changed to correctness. For unconcealment is that heart and core, i.e. the dominant relation between *physis* and *logos* in the original sense."[11]

This Heideggerian interpretation of the etymological significance of *aletheia* does not, however, invalidate Florensky's own analysis as such, nor negate its import for the discussion of the experience of truth. It only evinces *aletheia's* own basic ambiguity and its multiple, possible applications in the attempt to elucidate this problematic.

[6]*Being and Time* (New York: Harper & Row, 1962), 256-73, passim.
[7]*An Introduction to Metaphysics* (Garden City, NY: Anchor Books, 1961), 86f, 159.
[8]Ibid., 17.
[9]*What Is Called Thinking?* (New York: Harper & Row, 1968), 19.
[10]For this discussion see *Being and Time,* 256-73.
[11]*Introduction to Metaphysics,* 159.

1.6   Final Summations

Florensky synthesizes the results of his etymological digression by categorizing the various terms for truth as found in
the four cited languages according to two criteria: whether
the relation which obtains between truth and reality is an
immediate one or is mediated through society; and whether
they refer to the content or the form of truth. He thus indicates the inherent polyvalent character of truth.[12] Four possible shadings of meaning concerning truth are obtained. The
Russian and Greek terms, *istina* and *aletheia*, refer to an
immediate contact with the given or datum by the knowing
subject, but with *istina* underscoring the material content of
truth and *aletheia* the formal side of this content. These two
shadings highlight the more properly philosophical aspect of
the problem of truth. Indeed, in technical terms, the Russian
istina refers to *ontological* (or *ontic*, as some would have
it) truth or the truth of existence. The Greek *aletheia*, on
the other hand, concerns *logical* truth, i.e., the truth of knowledge, which properly belongs to the judgment. The socio-
logical dimension, on the other hand, is more fully put into
relief by the Latin and Hebrew terms for truth, *veritas* and
emet, which both indicate the mediating role of society and
social forms in the process of knowing truth. Since truth for
the Hebrew is God's faithful word, he points to the material
content of truth, whereas the Roman emphasizes the formal,
judicative dimension of the problem of truth. The immediate
conclusion to be drawn from this discussion of Florensky is
clear. The fact of truth eludes easy articulation, and, indeed,
with its wealth of meaning and suggestive multidimensionality, essentially transcends the capacities of human reason to
capture its essence in any one, determinate concept.

Nonetheless, care must be taken not to overstress the
importance of Florensky's etymological digression.[13] It is

---

[12]Cf. the discussion of this point in Altissimo Costante, *Gli elementi
tradizionali della contemplazione nell'interpretazione filosofico-teologica di
Pavel Florenskij* [The traditional elements of contemplation in the philosophic-
theological interpretation of Pavel Florensky] (Vicenza, Italy: 1979), 43.

[13]Cf., once again, Florensky's comments, PFT, 785 (n. 773), which
parallel these remarks. See p. 46 (n. 89) above.

useful insofar as it is a means for indicating the various, intrinsic dimensions of the experience of truth, but the etymology cannot replace philosophical insight. Etymological considerations may aid, and even occasion, the intuitive grasp of a state of affairs, but intuition as such can never be reduced to such a consideration.

Etymologies, moreover, never guarantee the attainment of philosophical insight, let alone necessarily elucidate present meanings on the basis of either the remote or the immediate past significance of a term. In the present instance, as we have seen, the etymology of *aletheia* can give rise to insights into both the ontological and gnoseological dimensions of truth. But it cannot be appealed to in order to favor absolutely either one of these aspects. For that matter, it does not necessarily entail any philosophical *prise de conscience* at all.

2. TRUTH AS JUDGMENT

Truth, as Florensky clearly shows, is experienced as certitude,[14] and only on the basis of this particular feeling of truth are we in the position to make an affirmative judgment concerning its existence[15] and to appropriate it, as it were, to ourselves. Indeed, apart from the formal judgment concerning it, the question of truth does not arise, inasmuch as, formally speaking, the locus of truth is in the act of judgment. Such a judgment, however, as Florensky notes, need not be of one set type alone. Judgments, on the contrary, can be broadly classified according to whether their apprehension of truth is achieved immediately in direct contact with a given or mediately through other intervening judgments.

---

[14]Cf. sec. 2.5, pp. 106f below.
[15]PFT, 23.

2.1   Immediate Judgment or the Self-Evidence of Intuition;[16] Mediate Judgment of Discourse[17]

In immediate judgment, according to Florensky, there is an intuitive contact with reality that can be of three basic types: sense, intellectual, and mystical, depending on the type of givenness at issue. In sense intuition we are presented with the self-evidence of the external, empirical world, while in the case of intellectual intuition[18] we are dealing with the knower's own internal experience, the experience of his own consciousness, and his experience of necessary essence, which likewise present themselves for immediate judgment. Mystical experience, on the other hand, refers to the suprarational, metalogical sphere, and is accessible only to the person presented with a special vision of it, the mystic, who can, accordingly, perceive its particular self-evidence. Thus presented, Florensky says these three types of intuition may be respectively labeled: objective, subjective, and objective-subjective.

The mark of intuition is the self-evidence of the given that finds its acknowledgment in the immediate envisagement and judgment of the knowing subject who cognizes it. All intuition, be it sense, intellectual, or mystical, on the other hand, is, according to Florensky, likewise flawed by a common element. Its most basic weakness, he stresses, is its "naked" or "unjustified givenness."[19] Accordingly, the fact of its immediateness has, he claims, solely the character of external necessity, which lends it the air of forced inevitability. It lacks a grounded basis because its internal necessity is not given to human reason.[20] Accordingly, it is only a conditional givenness

[16]PFT, 24-30. It goes without saying that in the present discussion, the term "intuition" is always used in its technical, philosophical sense of "immediate apprehension," and not in the sense it is often given in popular parlance as a "presentiment," a sort of intellectual counterpart to biological instinct. This popular meaning is what is intended by the expression, "woman's intuition." Cf. PFT, 30, for Florensky's tripartite division of intuition as objective, subjective, and objective-subjective.

[17]PFT, 30ff.

[18]Cf. the following subsection, pp. 91-100 below.

[19]PFT, 25.

[20]In the case of necessary essence, however, we immediately grasp its

that does not qualify as *episteme*, the classical Aristotelian designation for the "grounded knowing" of true philosophical and scientific knowledge. All it can state is blunt facticity. In terms of the principle of identity, it merely states "A is A"; it does not at all address the issue why A must be A. Thus, as a criterion of givenness, it is ultimately inadequate, since it cannot per se occasion certitude. Or, more simply, from its "is" no "ought" can be derived.[21]

Ironically, the principle of identity, which aims for, and indeed pretends to have achieved, absolute universality, can never decide the question of certitude. It is merely the "spirit of death, emptiness, and nothingness."[22] and provides nothing more than an "empty schema of self-affirmation,"[23] that is incapable of synthesis, that is, of affirming or conjoining into real, integrative unity other elements distinct from itself. As such, it is essentially the "cry of unmasked egoism."[24]

Florensky gives his reasoning in a dense and enigmatic passage. He writes:

> The principle of identity, which pretends to enjoy absolute universality, is found to obtain decidely nowhere. It justifies its claim in its factual givenness, but every givenness, *toto genere*, in fact confutes it, always and everywhere infringing upon it both in space and in time. Each A, by excluding all other elements, is excluded by *all* of them; indeed if each of them for A is *only* non-A, then also A in respect to non-A is only non-non-A. From the point of view of the principle of identity, all being, though wishing to affirm itself, in point of fact only annihilates itself, making itself an aggregate of such elements, whereof each is a center of negation and *only* of negation. In

internal necessity, and its very self-evidence is its justification. A detailed discussion of this problematic will follow immediately in the next subsection (sec. 2.2.) in connection with our presentation of the thorny problem of intellectual intuition.

[21]PFT, 26. Again, the qualifying remarks given in n. 20 above should be borne in mind. Cf. also, sec. 2.4, pp. 103-5 below.

[22]PFT, 27.

[23]PFT, 28.

[24]Ibid.

such fashion, all being is sheer negation, one grand "No."[25]

What is baffling is that Florensky conceives the principle of identity only in the negative terms of emptiness and nothingness. How can this be? As perplexing as his stance may at first approach seem, it is, in fact, rather traditional, even if his argumentation is not. What it presupposes is a developed, metaphysical understanding and appreciation of the full meaning and import of the principle of identity. This principle only formalizes the metaphysical insight into the transcendental unity of all being. Being, insofar as it is, is essentially one. But what does this unity add to being? Florensky, in line with traditional philosophy, answers straightforwardly: It introduces negation to being. "A" is identical to itself by a negation of a negation, by its "not-being-other" than itself. Further, it is marked by outer unity insofar as it is divided from all other than itself, and is, accordingly, determined by its negative relation to this all other than itself.

Identity as an essential negativity, Florensky claims, cannot serve as a proper criterion of truth. To quote his exact words:

> If *immediate givenness* is the criterion, then it is so absolutely everywhere and at given times. Therefore, all mutually excluding A's, insofar as they are givens, are true, and everything is true. But this reduces the force of the principle of identity to zero, because it then turns out to contain an internal contradiction.[26]

In other words, what Florensky is saying is that the principle of identity cannot of itself successfully address the problem of truth, because it cannot synthesize other elements into itself. Indeed, he notes, it is only in synthesis that we truly come before the question of truth, for only in the conjoining of disparate elements does an increase in knowledge and truth really occur. Florensky is thus most correct in his obser-

[25]PFT, 27.
[26]Ibid.

vation that "where there is no diversity there cannot be union,"[27] and hence no truth. What rather obtains is only egoism, the fact of each A being just an isolated monad in space and a "naked '*now*' "[28] in time, a "pure *zero* of content."[29]

All this, above all, holds true for fully personal reality, in which instance the principle of identity is nothing other than an absolute monarch whose subjects do not protest its autocracy only because they are bloodless specters lacking any real, personal existence[30] and being only "rationalistic shadows of persons."[31] The flow of time, from the point of view of egotistic identity, consists solely of merely contiguous, atomic units in no way internally linked with one another. On the other hand, if persons, as well as all individual beings conceived on analogy with the person, are faithfully viewed as *living* entities, then their very *life* makes them phenomena which at any determinate point in time are in some way nonidentical with themselves,[32] as they necessarily flow from and toward what is other than their momentary selves.

Florensky thus maintains that there are two models of identity: the static, "rational" model of unconditional self-identity as not deriving its *reason* in being from its "other" and the dynamic model of self-identity viewed as *life* and, accordingly, conceived as having its reason in being in some greater flow of events. While in the former instance, we witness an A which pretends to be rational but which, in truth, is an "absolutely unintelligible, irrational, and blind A, which is opaque to the mind,"[33] in the latter, we encounter a truly rational A, one which is rational precisely owing to the fact that it is *life*, i.e., an entity *rooted* in something other than its blunt self-givenness, something which flows from something else and from which it enjoys its rational and intelligible consistency.

[27]PFT, 28.
[28]Ibid.
[29]Ibid.
[30]Ibid.
[31]Ibid.
[32]PFT, 29.
[33]Ibid.

It is at this juncture that we can understand why Florensky insists that the self-evidence of the immediate givenness of intuition as conveyed by the principle of identity, at least as this principle is traditionally formulated, is, both from the theoretical point of view of satisfying the hunger of the spirit and from the practical standpoint of convincingly demonstrating its pretensions, an unsatisfactory basis for grounding our certitude.[34] The principle of identity simply cannot account for the datum of life since it cannot provide an adequate articulation of its essential organicity. All it is capable of doing, Florensky claims, is to dissect life and reduce it to unconnected, inorganic, atomic units of experience accessible only to blunt perception or intuition.[35] The full reality of A thus lies beyond its conceptual grasp, and can only be accounted for within a more encompassing complexus of thought and explanation.

It is rather, Florensky stresses, in the mediate judgment or *discursus* that we find a truly grounded or justified judgment. Its justification lies in its being a resultant conclusion of the reasoning process in which the mind, having perceived two propositions as both true and in some sort of mutual relationship, grasps from this fact of mutuality between them the truth of a new, third proposition. The only problem is that the search for discursive certitude is never-ending. If one seeks to find the justification of the premises themselves from which a well-founded conclusion is drawn, one immediately finds oneself is a *regressus in indefinitum* in this pursuit of a truly rational explanation that will ground all our knowledge. No one *discursus* can be final. The mind, in its natural inquietude before immediate reasons, always pushes further

---

[34]PFT, 30.

[35]In a similar vein, Lev Karsavin, in the section of his *Poema o smerti* [Poem on death] (Kaunas, 1932) dealing with the discursive powers of reason, writes (par. 40, p. 18): "Is it not reason that corrupts life? Reason decides everything, even its very self, it dispassionately kills any desire. In the realm of reason, everything disintegrates, is dissipated; and it alone, coldly, slithers like a snake, enveloped in dust . . . It does not look at the heavens, and does not see the heavens, although the heavens are reflected in it: it creeps along. Anything living is inaccessible to it: it must destroy everything from the beginning. It feeds on dust; the tree of life makes itself a tree of knowledge and death."

back for more fundamental reasons, which, of course, can never be fully forthcoming. Thus, Florensky rightfully concludes that the quest for such a rational proof "only creates in time the dream for eternity."[36]

2.2 The Question of Intellectual Intuition: A Digression

At this point, we must interrupt Florensky in his argument and expressly address a problematic which his own presentation merely presumes but the explicit consideration of which is, nonetheless, of immediate relevance and, indeed, of decisive importance for arriving at any final, formal judgment concerning his views on the nature of truth. In his treatment of the nature and extent of man's intuitive experience of reality, Florensky does not enter into a discussion with those who would disagree with his position that man enjoys three specific types of intuition. In our immediate context the fact of sense intuition or sense perception does not appear to arouse a critical opposition, at least in respect to its basic existence, if not as to its exact nature. But the question whether man does indeed enjoy the other two types of intuition, namely, intellectual and mystical intuition, has been sharply contested in philosophical quarters. As far as mystical intuition is concerned, we may, however, at least for the time being, prescind from any direct consideration of it, insofar as it is a suprarational experience predicated upon the infusion of special divine grace, a point presently not at issue. The question of intellectual intuition, on the other hand, is of immediate interest. Florensky's acceptance of the fact of intellectual intuition in man clearly demarcates him both from Kantian idealism and from the immediate realism of neo-Thomism and the critical realism of contemporary, transcendental Thomism, all of which, in contrast, deny intellectual intuition to man and attribute only sense intuition to him by nature,[37] in accordance with the traditional principle: *Nihil*

---

[36]PFT, 32.

[37]Thomism, of course, does accept the possibility of mystical intuition as a concomitant feature of the supernatural order.

est in intellectu quod non prius fuerit in sensibus (There is
nothing in the intellect, which is not previously in the
senses).[38]

From the Kantian standpoint, apart from the pure intuitions of space and time, intellectual intuition has no role to
play in human knowledge. Kant expressly writes: "The understanding cannot see [intuit], the senses cannot think. By
their union only can knowledge by produced."[39] Knowledge
to him, accordingly, is nothing more than a synthesis of
sensation and understanding, of sense impressions, given
intelligibility by the *a priori* forms imposed by the mind upon
them. An intelligible, objective world, the world of the
so-called "noumena," however, is not given to him, just a
world of phenomena restricted to the senses, enjoying form
and intelligibility only insofar as it is a product of the mind.
Thomism, in both its varieties, on the other hand, overcomes
this subjectivistic, idealist perspective of Kant, and affirms
that in the immediate datum presented to the senses there are
in fact two aspects given, both a sensible and an intellectual
one. But in the Thomistic view, still only the sensible aspect
is given to us intuitively; the other, the intellectual moment
of the sense datum, is known merely through it in a non-
intuitive way by way of abstraction.[40] In this fashion, Thomism upholds that intellectual knowledge does indeed partake
of the intuitive character of sense knowledge, and truly does
attain the real as existing independently of the mind.[41]

Florensky's own stated point of view stands in marked
contrast to both these philosophical stances. Contrary to the
Kantian position, it asserts a realist conception of the world
and of intellectual knowledge, and maintains that there are
both objectively real and ideal states of affairs, independent
of man's mind and open to man's cognitive grasp of them.

[38]For a treatment and contrasting of these three positions, see Bernard
Lonergan, S.J., "Metaphysics as Horizon," *Gregorianum*, 44 (1963); 307-18;
also as an appendix in Coreth, *Metaphysics*, 199-219.

[39]Immanuel Kant, *Critique of Pure Reason* (Garden City, NY: Doubleday
& Co., 1966), 45 (A51, B75).

[40]L. Noël, *Le réalisme immédiat* (Louvain: Editions de l'Institut Superieur
de Philosophie, 1938), 275f.

[41]Ibid., 228, 230.

In opposition to the latter, it favors an entirely different conception of the workings of the intellect and its powers of understanding and of the origins and nature of intellectual knowledge in particular, while at the same time sharing the realist world-view central to Thomism.

Precisely because of this point in common between Florensky and the Thomistic tradition, namely realism, it is important that consideration be given to the bearing their parting of ways over intellectual intuition may have for the question of truth and, specifically, for Florensky's own position regarding the nature of truth. For the Thomistic school no intellectual intuition[42] is possible to man owing to his corporeal nature as an incarnate spirit, which restricts his vision to the world of bodies. Only pure spirits, divine Persons and angels, are capable of such intuition,[43] since they alone, unlike human persons, are not tied to bodily organs which limit the mind to a mere, opaque grasp of the real. They accordingly enjoy a transparent grasp of existing particulars in their concrete fullness. Man's intellectual knowledge, on the other hand, comes about only through abstraction from the corporeal presence of things given to his bodily senses. In other words, it is essentially an abstractive cognition based on sensual, material particulars.

One point in particular needs highlighting. The Thomist would appear to maintain that intellectual intuition necessarily entails an absolute "totalizing" or fully encompassing knowledge that captures every aspect of a given datum. As one author writes: "If we had an intellectual intuition of things, we should be able to seize upon, even to the last detail, all the differences which determine them to such and such a being. Such, however, is not the case. Our notion of *being* remains vague and indeterminate; intuition obtains only in

[42]Some neo-Thomists, e.g. Jacques Maritain, do indeed speak of an "intuition of being," but what is intuited is an *act* of existing as affirmed in the judgment of existence, and not an object or essence as at present under discussion. See Maritain's *Existence and the Existent* (Garden City, NY: Doubleday & Co., 1956), esp. 28-31.

[43]Cf. M.-D. Roland-Gosselin, "Peut-on parler d'intuition intellectuelle dans la philosophie thomiste?" [Can one speak of intellectual intuition in Thomist philosophy?], *Philosophia perennis*, 2 (1930): 708-30.

sensation."[44] If this is so, then Florensky must ask himself
whether his own conclusions regarding the ultimate, intrinsic
insufficiency of intuition alone as a sufficient basis for sustaining certitude in knowing, which give all appearances of coinciding with the very objection raised by Thomists against the
possibility of intellectual intuition for man, do not, indeed,
undermine and invalidate his own position that attributes
this specific kind of intuition to man. As we have already
seen,[45] Florensky claims that intuition is blunt in its givenness,
that it does not justify itself, and that, therefore, it ultimately
serves only to disappoint us. Is not Florensky, then, inconsistent in his theorization when he at once affirms the presence
of intellectual intuition in man and yet denies the possibility
of its proper actualization in him? In fine, does not this
apparent clash of opinions counsel Florensky to abandon his
own views regarding man's ability for intellectual intuition?

To ask what Florensky's own response to these questions
would have been had he asked them is perhaps only a vain
speculation. Certainly it is methodologically unfair to try to
speak for him when his own thought has left so many crucial
aspects of the problem of intellectual intuition unexplored.
But there are indications in his writings which offer us the
possibility of framing a coherent response on his own terms
to the theoretical difficulties posed by a stand in favor of the
presence of intellectual intuition in man, as well as to the
specific objections legitimately raised by the Thomistic school
against such a position.

Florensky himself sets the stage for a rebuttal to his
critics over the question of intellectual intuition in his subsequent treatment of the aporia of thought[46] and of the
internal dynamics of truth as intuition-discursion.[47] In order
to address the present difficulty, however, we must anticipate
these discussions, which are treated in the subsections immediately to follow, and offer a few comments in their regard at
least insofar as they are directly relevant for finding a way out

[44]Noël, Le réalisme, 276f. Also quoted in N. O. Lossky, "Intuitivizm,"
Grani [Frontiers], 78 (1970), 230f.
[45]See pp. 86f above.
[46]Cf. pp. 100-3.
[47]Cf. pp. 103-5.

of the apparent impasse in which Florensky finds himself.

Up until now, Florensky has maintained that the difficulty with intuition is that it is a blunt facticity, not furnishing us with the reasons for its own truth. But, confronted with the evident fact that we do experience and know truth, Florensky qualifies his remarks and notes that a "rational intuition," a paradoxical *coincidentia oppositorum* of intuition and discursion, of immediate givenness and founded judgment, would indeed offer this necessary foundation for truth and the knowledge of it. This is the crucial key for a final solution to the problem at hand. Unfortunately, what is lacking in Florensky is an analysis of the specific, intentional objects or states of affairs of the respective types of intuition, especially as regards the type of self-evidence or immediate givenness which is offered by them and which, more importantly, reveals their particular *ratio*.

For such an analysis, appeal must be made to phenomenology, in particular to the school of phenomenological realism, historically known as Munich phenomenology, which has focused on the question of gradations of essence, with special emphasis on the facet of "necessary essence." For synthetic purposes and for the sake of brevity, it suffices to highlight the thought of just one representative thinker of this school, namely, Dietrich von Hildebrand, who has pursued a phenomenological analysis of "such-being unities" notable for its clarity and simplicity in presentation.[48]

Von Hildebrand distinguishes three generic types of "such-being unity" in his investigation of essence. The lowest grade of unity is found in those chaotic and accidental unities, deprived of any real *eidos* or any genuine form.[49] Suggested examples would be of the order of a heap of stones or a mere group of random tones lacking any sort of melody. The next group is comprised by all those genuine unities[50] as verified in the animal, vegetable, and mineral kingdoms, which enjoy a meaningful nature, and which are the proper objects of

[48]See Dietrich von Hildebrand, *What Is Philosophy?* (Chicago: Franciscan Herald Press, 1973), esp. 97-140.
[49]Ibid., 100ff, esp. 101.
[50]Ibid., 102-10.

empirical study and research. The positive scientist, by inductive analysis, attempts to ferret out their hidden essences, in
order to formulate, among other things, adequate laws of
nature. The data are objectively meaningful, but, in present-
ing themselves for sense intuition alone, they lack a full
intelligibility, and elude a grasp "from within." Accordingly,
they yield only a probable knowledge, capable of grounding
solely an inductive certitude, on principle open to ultimate
disproof. The highest type of "such-being unity," on the other
hand, is that found in all instances of "necessary essence,"[51]
which enjoys full intellibility and can ground an absolute
certitude. Examples are data like a triangle, the color red, a
person, love, will, justice, and so forth,[52] and *a priori* propositions like "Moral values presuppose a person" and "A color
can never be present without extension"[53]; these are the true
intentional objects of intellectual intuition. They are fully
accessible to intellectual penetration, and also occasion absolute certitude in their regard.

To the specific Thomistic objections answers are also immediately forthcoming. First, sometimes the impression is
given that immediate experience is to be restricted to its
empirical dimensions alone. In the words of one writer: "The
term intuition is taken from sense experience . . . that a concrete *thing* is self-present and presented: this is the essence
of intuitive cognition"[54] (emphasis ours). The different strata
of "such-being unity" and the realm of necessary ideal being
in particular thus appear overlooked. But why should it be
presupposed that the object of intuition is restricted to blunt
sense data? Necessary essential unities like moral and aesthetic
values and geometric figures are no less given to us in immediate experience, and, indeed, are incomparably more accessible than the data of sense.[55]

Secondly, the claim that for intellectual intuition to hold

[51]Ibid., 110-31. In the case of "colors," however, we refer not to their
"intelligibility" as such, but to their "necessary unity."
[52]Ibid., 110.
[53]Ibid., 71.
[54]Rudolph Allers, "Intuition and Abstraction," *Franciscan Studies*, 8
(1948): 54.
[55]Cf. von Hildebrand, *What Is Philosophy?* 86-92.

for man necessarily entails a fully transparent knowledge on his part of a datum, in all its minute details, including all its foundations,[56] is also unjustified. Care must be taken to distinguish the epistemological issues at stake from the specific, metaphysical problem necessarily raised by it. It is one thing to ask whether we intuitively know necessary essential unities in our experience of reality with full certainty, but quite another to inquire into how we can do so or upon what metaphysical basis such knowledge rests. We may intuitively grasp the "such-being" of a triangle or of a moral proposition, but still not yet know of their exact metaphysical status in the realm of being.[57] In other words, we may indeed have, as Nicholas Lossky has stressed,[58] a limpid grasp of a datum that is still not a total knowledge of it.

To the further claim that a theory of abstraction offers the best accounting of the origins and nature of intellectual knowledge, the rejoinder may be made that, on the contrary, this type of theorization may be, in fact, missing the central point in the whole discussion, namely, that all our intrinsically necessary knowledge is based on a specific essence structure, and that no matter to what degree of abstraction[59] we may take recourse, as von Hildebrand avers,[60] one never arrives at apodictically certain knowledge prescinding from the question of specific essence structure.[61] Harking back to the Franciscan

[56]Cf. Noël's remarks, p. 103 above.

[57]Von Hildebrand, in particular, stresses this point (*What Is Philosophy?* 117). Josef Seifert's searching monograph, *Essence and Existence: A New Foundation of Classical Metaphysics on the Basis of "Phenomenological Realism," and a Critical Investigation of "Existential Thomism"* is specifically dedicated to laying the ground for pursuing such a study. This monograph has been published in *Aletheia*, 1 (1977): 17-157, 371-459.

[58]Cf. "Intuitivizm," 231.

[59]This meaning of abstraction should not be confused with the properly phenomenological procedure of reduction to the genuine *eidos*, that is the bracketing off of extrinsic elements, sometimes called an abstractive process. See von Hildebrand, *What Is Philosophy?* 113.

[60]Ibid., 113, 129-31, and cf. also Seifert, *Essence and Existence*, 93.

[61]As von Hildebrand notes, Husserl makes an analogous error with his "bracketing theory," in which he favors "putting existence into brackets," i.e., prescinding from the question of concrete, real existence in order to look at the essence of an object with the hope of arriving at *a priori* knowledge. Such a procedure is only a vain one, because not only do objects lose their interest for us apart from their real existence, but also no amount of

school in scholastic tradition[62] at least in this one respect, one might simply invoke the principle of economy, *"Entitates non multiplicandae praeter necessitatem"* (entities should not be multiplied beyond necessity), and apply Ockham's razor to the theory of abstraction,[63] contenting oneself with the fact of intellectual intuition in the process. It might even be asked whether the whole discussion is not predicated on a false anthropological assumption in the first place.[64] Is the limit of the soul's outreach the boundary of the body's skin? Or can the human mind truly arrive at ideal existence independently of the blunt observation of the senses?

Without upstaging the discussion to follow, we must, nonetheless, try to understand where Florensky fits into the present discussion. Florensky, as we shall soon see, softens his original tone and notes that intuition, insofar as it enjoys intelligibility, is more than a blunt given but is rather a true *ratio*. If we continue in this line of thought, we may easily give an accounting of sense intuition as a source of lesser intelligibility and intellectual intuition as a font of incomparable intelligibility which evidences a contact with necessary, essential unities.[65] Florensky himself may never specifically speak in these exact terms, yet he certainly gravitates towards this conception, a fact which becomes especially apparent in his subsequent lecture entitled "Cult and Philosophy,"[66] in which he expounds his own conception of philosophy

bracketing will provide this knowledge, if there is not the desired essence structure. It is this methodological move which, according to von Hildebrand, leads Husserl to transcendental idealism (*What Is Philosophy?* 99*n*, 128).

[62]Sebastian J. Day, O.F.M., *Intuitive Cognition: A Key to the Later Scholastics* (St. Bonaventure, NY: Franciscan Institute, 1947).

[63]Ibid., 189.

[64]Alfred North Whitehead, speaking of philosophic method (*Adventures in Ideas*, 255), in like fashion challenges the assumption that the five sense organs are the sole avenues of communication with the external world.

[65]Nonetheless, Florensky does not seem to have had a full *prise de conscience* of this discovery. At times, he gives the impression of restricting intellectual intuition to one's internal experience alone, thus appearing to overlook the realm of ideal being. Cf. PFT, 24f and esp. 30. That Florensky labels intellectual intuition as "subjective" intuition in particular evidences this weakness in his own understanding of the full nature and bearing of intellectual intuition.

[66]Cf FTH, 119-35, and also our discussion in "Filosofiya kul'ta," 42f.

as a "concrete idealism."[67] In this lecture, he offers a trenchant
critique of Kant, contrasting him with Plato, noting that they
"relate to one another as seal to impress."[68]
Without siding with Plato's metaphysical idealism, Florensky lauds his objectivist stance concerning knowledge, i.e.,
his epistemological realism,[69] in which it is maintained that
all genuine knowledge is a knowledge ("remembrance") of
an Idea, a rational essence. If Plato's theory of Ideas were
thoroughly revised, eliminating all non-genuine unities from
the realm of Ideal Forms and confining it to necessary, essential unities, it would become a viable "concrete idealism" in
Florensky's sense of the term, and, at the same time, a com-
plementary restatement of the position of phenomenological
realism.

Florensky himself conceives his "concrete idealism" in
radical opposition to Kant's subjectivistic idealism, which
claims man never knows "noumena" or things-in-themselves,
but only their appearances which are, in turn, reducible to
subjective events in the mind. Florensky scores this position,
holding that in Kant the only intelligible reality is himself,
effectively rendering his "self" the unconditional center of
the world.[70] Meaning and truth no longer know a transcendent source, but have their most radical origins in the human
mind itself. Kant having thus centered philosophy and the
knowledge of truth in the knowing subject and not around
objective reality, Florensky levels his own dissent:

> Whence the presumption of Kant, that there is no
> Mind apart from the mind, no Λόγος apart from our
> own λόγος? The presumption is from the will—the
> will to be *alone*, the will to *autonomy* and to onto-

[67]FTH, 126.
[68]Ibid.
[69]Epistemological idealism holds that every act of knowing terminates in
an idea, itself conceived as a purely subjective event. Epistemological realism,
on the other hand, maintains that our consciousness puts us in contact with
what is other than ourselves. Though Plato held that the "really real" world
is comprised only of Ideal Forms (an idealist conception), his theory of
knowledge is realist in outlook, since these Ideal Forms are objective realities, existing independently of our knowledge of them.
[70]FTH, 123.

logical independence. 'There is no mind outside of
myself' . . . this is the slogan of Kant. And, thus, he
prefers to enter the subjective and accidental into his
mind, rather than subjugate it to the objective and
essential. The mind is not from Truth, but truth from
the mind,—I am not from Truth, but it is truth that is
in me. This is the orientation that has determined the
course of Kantian philosophy."[71]

2.3   *The Aporia of Thought*

Returning to Florensky's explicit argument and prescinding for a moment from his own corrective to his views as has
already been indicated,[72] we may note that he is now at that
juncture where he can formulate the exact dilemma in which
he finds himself in his search for the ultimate foundation of
knowledge. A fundamental aporia is before him. On the one
hand, intuition, which gives us immediate, concrete access
to the real, is by nature "blunt" in its givenness. True, it
gives us a real "invision," so the speak, into phenomena, but
is, nonetheless, incapable of unveiling the reasons behind
this givenness. It stops short of telling "why" it is and "why"
it must be so. For this reason it can provide only a relative,
conditional knowledge, and accordingly can rightfully be called
"blind" and "awkward." Discursive reasoning, on the other
hand, even though it is naturally adept to pursue and descry
these reasons, is itself also unable to satisfy the longings of
the human spirit for unconditional truth. As an exercise of
demonstrative reasoning it is restricted to the abstract, logical
order, and notwithstanding its theoretical potency for attain-
ing absolute certainty, it per se concerns idealities and not
concrete realities. That is, it treats mere logical relations, and
cannot properly address the radical questions posed by determinate actualities, even less begin to solve the riddle of their
existence.

In an evident, even if not explicit, reference to Kant,

[71]Ibid., 128.
[72]See pp. 94f above.

Florensky aphorizes his view on the aporia, intuition-discursion, stating: "Blind intuition is a titmouse in hand, while discursive reasoning is a crane in the sky."[73] Behind these somewhat bizarre words lies a profound insight concerning the modes of human thought and their inherent limitations. Florensky here clearly harks back to Kant, and indeed offers us little more than a fanciful and rather extravagant paraphrase of Kant's famous, indeed classical, words: *"Thoughts without contents are empty, intuitions without concepts are blind."*[74] Intuition, with its percipient and cognitive grasp of the real, gives a certain, immediate satisfaction, but it falls short of providing full philosophic certainty. It grounds the simple assertory judgment, but cannot soar to the heights of the necessary judgment expressive of apodictic certainty, because the formal reasons needed to underpin this type of judgment are not given. Discursive reasoning, on the other hand, possesses the inherent, dialectical apparatus necessary for plumbing the depths of reason, and, in this very dialecticism manifests the mind's rational drive and undisputed capacity to execute infinite *discursus* in its search for the Reason of reasons ultimately grounding all true judgments. Yet, ironically, discursive reasoning is of itself little more than an ethereal exercise of the human mind. Its claims know no limits, but without an acceptance of a material premise it cannot deliver on its promises. Being itself purely formal, it is not within its competence, as such, to consign any material truth to the intellectual inquirer. It can do so only if before beginning its syllogistic exercise, it parts from an already existing, material entity, in which case its conclusions can obtain in material reality.

Accordingly, we seem to be caught between an unescapable Scylla and Charybdis. Florensky asks: "Is there not any way to rise above these obstacles?"[75] Can we not somehow find a way formally to ground our material certitude as obtained

---

[73]PFT, 32.

[74]Kant, *Critique of Pure Reason*, 45 (A51, B75). Kant's *Critique* was well known in Russian philosophical circles. It was variously translated into Russian in 1867, 1897, and 1907. The last translation was done by the renowned philosopher, Nicholas O. Lossky.

[75]PFT, 33.

in that "blunt first"[76] which constitutes evidence? Indeed, how do we know our evidence is truly factual and not fatuous? And if there is no way we can fully respond to these questions, is scepticism our only recourse and ultimate fate? Is the best that we can do merely to temporize with our judgments? In sum, does the natural incapacity of reason to lodge my apparent certitude on sturdier foundations counsel the aporetic life and the total abstention from all predicative activity?

The sceptic, of course, rests content with his *epoché* or withholding of judgment. But, Florensky pointedly asks, is his complacent attitude justified? Resolutely not, Florensky immediately rejoins, because, as both an intellectual stance and programmatic manifesto, scepticism is irremediably self-contradictory and incoherent. The sceptic is clearly inconsistent when he states that no truth is accessible to man, as this position itself is a claim to truth. Moreover, he can never maintain his own mere existence, if he truly abures all judgments and resolutely perseveres in this charge. His purported ataraxia, induced by his detached, noncommital attitude toward truth, is, likewise, illusory, and is little more than a languid and timorous recoiling from the anxious unrest of the human spirit for unconditional truth.

The very fact that we pine for truth and that we may even despair in our unavailing attempts to find it is, in Florensky's view, possibly the best indication that the spirit of truth is still alive in us, and that it can never really die in us—even before the relentless agonies of doubt. Florensky himself admits: "I do not have the truth in me, but the idea of it torments me."[77] In all this, we can truly glean a reason for hope, even if not a strictly logical declaration of hope,[78] that the foundation of truth may not forever elude us. The thematicity of truth is an indelible, omnipresent thread in the fabric of life. Without even looking for it, it is always and everywhere before us on the horizon. We may not see its foundations, but that it is there is incontrovertible. In fact, it presents

---

[76]PFT, 34. We have already shown, however, how Florensky qualifies this remark (see p. 95 above and p. 103 below).
[77]PFT, 38.
[78]PFT, 40.

itself to us as an unforeseen and unsolicited *gift*,[79] and possibly in this very gift-character we have the most propitious reason for subscribing to *probabilism*,[80] the doctrine that rational certitude is indeed possible for us to achieve even in our finite condition on this side of eternity. Citing the psalmist in an evident yet felicitous accommodation of his sense, Florensky sanguinely notes that "those who seek the Lord want for no good thing."[81] And in truth, it is in the Lord and the Triune Godhead that Florensky will find the final dissolution of the sceptic's *epoché*.

2.4 Truth as Intuition-Discursion[82]

Florensky now feels that he is in the position to take hold of both horns of the dilemma concerning truth and the foundations of certitude. He does so by proposing truth to be at once intuition and discursion, that is, simultaneously rational[83] or discursive intuition and intuitive discursion. Adopting the classical expression coined by Nicholas of Cusa, Florensky contends that truth is a *coincidentia oppositorum*, a unity of opposites.[84] In truth one finds, to Florensky's mind, both an intuition, which is not blind or limited but which rather contains within itself "a synthesized, infinite series of

[79]Ibid.
[80]PFT, 41.
[81]Ibid. The reference is from Ps 34:10.
[82]Cf. PFT, 42-46.
[83]The fact that Florensky claims that intuition discloses itself as a *ratio* and that intuition, accordingly, justifies itself, sets him off clearly from Bergson who, in defining intuition as "intellectual sympathy," maintains that it is "irrational." Cf. Henri Bergson, *An Introduction to Metaphysics* (Indianapolis: Bobbs-Merril Co., 1955), esp. 23f, 51, and Roger Baron, "Intuition bergsonienne et intuition sophianique," *Les études philosophiques*, 18 (1963): 439-42.
[84]PFT, 43. For the multiple possible applications of this expression, see Nicholas of Cusa, *De Docta Ignorantia* [Of learned ignorance], in *Opere Filosofiche*, ed. Graziella Federici-Vescovini (Turin: Unione Tipografico-Editrice Torinese, 1972), 53-202, passim. Noting the Cusanus' prevalent influence on Russian religious thinkers, Zenkovsky adds that these intellectuals have often surrounded his name with a kind of halo. See Zenkovsky, *Istoriya*, 2:383 (n. 8); Eng. trans., 844, n. 1.

its own foundations,"[85] and a discursion, which "in its turn must synthesize its whole indefinite series of foundations into finiteness"[86] and determinate unity. In a straightforward pronouncement Florensky states: *"Discursive intuition* is an intuition, differentiated to infinity, and *intuitive discursion* is a *discursio,* integrated to unity."[87] Intuition is, in sum, no longer a mere "blunt first" or dull facticity, but a *ratio* as well, from whose "is" an "ought" may well be derived.[88] A dialectical synergy between intuition and discursion is also involved. Intuition and discursion no longer stand in opposition with one another; they rather engage in intimate, mutual collaboration. Nicholas Lossky even goes so far as to consider discursive thought as one of the essential forms of intellectual intuition.[89] Whether one would want to accept this particular teaching of Lossky, the dynamics of intuition-discursion is a fact to which one can readily assent.[90]

But, it must be noted, Florensky does not as of yet actually declare *that* such a truth *is.* He merely states that "if truth *is,* then it is a real rationality and rational reality,"[91] or a "finite infinity and infinite finitude."[92] Up to this point, Florensky

[85]PFT, 43.
[86]Ibid.
[87]Ibid.
[88]The possibility, of course, rests on the essence structure at stake. If necessary, essential unities are not presented, only a probabilistic, inductive certitude can be obtained.
[89]Cf. "Intuitivizm," 232, and his *Chuvstvennaya, intellektual'naya i misticheskaya intuitsiya* [Sensual, intellectual, and mystical intuition] (Paris: YMCA Press, 1938), 1.
[90]The then Archbishop of Cracow, Cardinal Karol Wojtyla (Pope John Paul II) has admirably described the dynamics of intuition-discursion in his masterwork, *The Acting Person* (Dordrecht, Holland: D. Reidel Publishing, 1979). He writes (pp. 147f):
"Intuition and discourse are both involved, though in different ways, in the processes of cognition as a whole; sometimes it is intuition that lies at the origin of discursive thinking and sometimes it marks the end and is the indirect outcome of mental processes ... The important thing is the moment of truth, for it is the relation to truth that explains all choice and decision. The intuition lying at he origin of a discursive process seems to indicate that the intuitive truth needs to be further exfoliated. Intuition that comes as the fruition of discursive processes, on the other hand, is like a retrieval of truth and somehow like abiding in truth."
[91]PFT, 43.
[92]Ibid.

has remained solely on the hypothetical level, and has proposed merely—to use his own words—a "probabilistic-presuppositional construction"[93] concerning the essential structural features of truth. But if this truth is, Florensky adds, it is absolute truth, and within it a justification and foundation for the law of identity must be contained, though it itself would not be subject to its hold.

Pursuing this point, Florensky now submits his chief thesis: Truth is a Self-Proving Subject, one that is an absolute Lord to itself, and that "dominates the infinite series of *all* its foundations, synthesized into a unity, indeed into identity."[94] Such a Subject, observes Florensky, is *"qui per se ipsum concipitur et demonstratur*—which is known and proved through itself."[95] Of course, we cannot properly see, let alone concretely conceive this Subject, since it is utterly transcendent to us, and for this reason beyond all our intellectual powers to synthesize it in all its infinite aspects into one totality. Our knowledge itself is essentially finite and conditional, and, as such, is forever only on the way to the achievement of such an integral vision and synthetic grasp of this Infinite Unity and Unconditional Subject, which is not only known and proved through itself but is, as Florensky adds, its own proper cause.[96] This Self-Proving Subject could be rightfully compared, Florensky notes, to the sun in that it would not only serve to illuminate itself but also the entire cosmological order or universe.[97] As such, it would contain within itself the ultimate criterion of all truth, and indeed, constitute truth's very foundation and, at the same time, serve as the catalyst for the dissolution of all remnants of sceptical doubt and diffidence.

[93]PFT, 44.
[94]Ibid.
[95]Ibid.
[96]PFT, 45. Florensky cites with deference the canonized Scholastics Anselm of Canterbury and Thomas of Aquinas as corroborating authorities of his point.
[97]PFT, 43.

2.5 A Lacuna in Florensky?

Before proceeding on with Florensky in his argumentation, attention must be first drawn to an apparent lacuna in
his treatment of the experience of truth, at least in its elaboration up until this point. Truth, Florensky maintains, is
experienced as certitude. Yet he fails to mention that so is,
or can be, error. The question thus arises whether Florensky's
failure to take the experience of error into account has any
negative bearing on his analysis, indeed whether it may not
even invalidate it.

This objection, however, takes on much lesser importance
once the specific intent of Florensky's analysis as such is
clarified. He makes no claims of writing a treatise in criteriology, and therefore should not be expected to address all its
issues, either in regard to truth or in regard to error. His
specific criteriological problem at this juncture is only whether
we can ultimately ground our certitude in knowing, and if so,
how. He is not attempting to lay bare the sources of error,
even less to deny the fact that conviction often also accom-
panies an erroneous judgment.

As a subjective state, certitude is nondiscriminating, since
we can be just as convinced when we are in the right as in
the wrong. To determine its rectitude, on the other hand, our
only recourse is to inquire into the objective evidence upon
which it is founded. But prescinding from this additional
problematic, the fact still remains that the experience of
certitude is our first *felt* encounter with truth. And thus,
Florensky has ample vindication for his chosen point of departure.

It is in this same context that we may respond to Bishop
Feodor's objection that the feeling of certitude is too subjective and too deceptive a criterion for the determination of
truth and for the support of his probabilistic theory for the
existence of truth.[98] He appears to miss Florensky's point,
because Florensky does not found truth on certitude, but

rather certitude on truth.[99] Accordingly, he does not view the experience of certitude as a criterion of truth as much as a point of departure for determining its true ground.

At the same time, however, it must be noted that a theory of error would eventually have to be incorporated into his teaching in order to give a full accounting of the experience of truth. Later on, in his treatment of sin, Florensky does indeed bring up the question of error. But he then ties it in too closely with the concept of sin.[100] He writes: ". . . sin is the principle of unreasonableness, of incomprehensibility, and of an obtuse and desparate blockage of intellectual contemplation."[101] In this connection, he notes that the etymological origins of the Russian word for "sin" (*grekh*) are the same for the primitive infinitive for "to err" (*greshitisya*).[102] We shall return to this matter in our discussion of sin in Part III of this work.

3. THE TRINITARIAN RELATION

Returning to Florensky's basic argument, a question immediately arises. Just what is Florensky driving at in his last few pages of his letter on doubt, and where is he leading us? Without explicitly labeling his enterprise as such, to our mind, it would appear that Florensky is doing no more than mapping the way to a *heuristic* solution to the problem of truth and the foundations of certitude. In other words, he seems to be attempting to fashion a feasible solution to his stated problem by trying to determine antecedently what an

[99]Indeed, it would appear that Florensky would fully agree with Spinoza's maxim: veritas est index sui et falsi (truth is the criterion of itself and error).

[100]PFT, 179.

[101]Ibid.

[102]The etymological affinity of these two words is not without its grave consequences, especially in the dogmatic sphere. Due to a basic, morphological ambiguity, the dogmatic concept "infallibility," which has been traditionally rendered as *nepogreshimost'* in Russian, can easily be understood in the sense of "impeccability," the very denotation it does not carry in the Catholic dogma of papal infallibility. A more accurate rendering of this dogmatic term would be *bezoshibochnost'*.

adequate solution would have to entail in order for it to be both cogent and operative. Florensky states that a valid solution to the problem of truth and its concomitant problem, that of certitude, must account for all the foundations necessary to occasion, at once, full and transparent immediacy and absolute and necessary rationality, that is, to entail the full intelligibility of rational, discursive intuition. In negative terms, this solution must be able to avoid the contrary pitfalls of blind immediacy and empty possibility.

Specifically, Florensky inquires what could possibly be the "finite synthesis of infinity, actuated independently of us,"[103] that could found the rational immediacy necessary for apodictic truth. His answer is clear and readily forthcoming. He avers: Only a Self-Proving and Self-Authenticating Subject can sufficiently fulfill all the necessary conditions needed for this synthesis.

Unfortunately, however, our problems do not end here, as a new problematical issue immediately presents itself to us. If we accept this Self-Proving Subject as the apparent solution to the dual problem of truth and certitude, and embrace it as a "revelation,"[104] to use Florensky's exact word, how can we do so without clearly violating the first principle of all thought and being, the principle of identity or non-contradiction? How can we affirm as obtaining in this Subject the "infiniteness of the series of founded judgments, synthesized into finite intuition,"[105] and still maintain coherency? In forthright fashion Florensky admits this difficulty, but immediately places it in the perspective of eternity, where all apparent contradictions find their resolution and all opposites coincide. Indeed, it is in the metalogical order of eternity that Florensky tries to find a new foundation for the principle of identity which will allow us to reach that level—even if necessarily inadequate and partial—of insight from where we can legitimately conclude to an Intelligible Unity at the base of the manifest multiplicity found in the universe. In his reflections he clearly departs from and returns to philosophy's first

[103]PFT, 45.
[104]PFT, 46.
[105]Ibid.

problem, the question of the One and the Many, but in the process ventures a strikingly original restatement of the problematic in light of man's disconsolate dissatisfaction before doubt and his equally impellent quest for abiding truth and absolute certainty.

3.1 New Foundations for the Principle of Identity

Florensky maintains that the principle of identity as traditionally formulated has been given an inferior, rationalistic foundation that needs to be supplanted by a new superior formulation, or at least a more adequate justification, one more truly in accord with the demands of the mind. The common explanation of the principle which states "A is A," is, according to Florensky, "blind in its immediateness."[106] Its basis lies in exclusion alone. It holds that "A is A," merely because it absolutely excludes all other entities from itself. As such, Florensky insists, it is "dead as a *fact*."[107] If, on the other hand, we are to find a better warrant for its exercise, we must somehow construe it as a living *act*.[108] In this perspective, "A is A," because it affirms itself as non-A, that is, through the dynamic *adoption* (*usvoenie*) and *assimilation* (*upodobenie sebe*) of all other than itself.[109]

When Florensky opens his discussion of the principle of identity with the simply, seemingly innocuous question: "How is it possible that every A is A?"[110] one would hardly expect that in a few short verses he would be articulating one of his most penetrating and truly radical philosophical discoveries. Indeed, Florensky's uncanny insight comes so fast and is so limpidly expressed that many, unless they are truly attentive, may pass it by without notice, not at all attributing any special significance to it.[111] Few may have the sufficient

[106]PFT, 47.
[107]Ibid.
[108]Ibid.
[109]PFT, 48.
[110]PFT, 47.
[111]Florensky's insight, in point of fact, has never received from Russian thinkers, apart from possibly Bishop Feodor (cf. "Review," 154-58), the

perspicacity to grasp that in the very formulation of the question of how "A is A" possible lies its thought-reverberating answer.

Just to ask this question appears to undermine the principle of identity, because it carries the necessary implication that the principle of identity cannot stand by itself, that it needs the principle of sufficient reason for its support and ultimate justification. More simply expressed, "A is A," Florensky affirms, only because "A is also non-A," this other than "A" being the crypto-dynamism and latent sustenance of "A," that is, the radical condition of the possibility of the affirmation of "A's" existence. The principle of identity alone in sublime isolation indicates only the surface and external face of being. To know the hidden depths of being, on the other hand, means to activate the principle of sufficient reason, which states that every being has its sufficient reason, and which provides the necessary mechanism for fathoming these reasons. The problematic thus stated, what we actually find here is the intuition-discursion synergy revisited. Reechoing his thoughts concerning the dialectical process which brings us to truth Florensky writes: "Blind in its givenness (*dannost'*), the law of identity can be intelligible in its createdness (*sozdannost'*), in its eternal being-createdness (*sozdavaemost'*); carnal, dead and deadening in its static-ness, it can be spiritual, alive and life-creating in its dynamic-ness."[112] Contrasted, therefore, are the principle of identity viewed exclusively from the formal point of view, evincing only an empty and lifeless self-identity, and the same principle taken as a real self-identity, full of content and life, as it were "eternally denying itself and in its very self-abnegation eter-

attention it deserves. Florensky himself, however, does not seem to have grasped its fullest significance until the end of his work. Cf. PFT, 485ff. He actually attributes his insight to Archimandrite Serapion Mashkin (cf. PFT, 47), of whom we do not know much beyond what Florensky has written about him. Cf. p. 25 above, and also Florensky's *"Dannyya k zhizneopisaniyu arkhimandrita Serapiona (Mashkina)"* [Data for a biography of Archimandrite Serapion (Mashkin)], TM 1, no. 2-3 (1917): 317-54. Cf. also PFT, 23, 619ff. Florensky specifically refers to Mashkin's *Sistema Filosofii: Opyt nauchnago sinteza* [A system of philosophy: the experience of scientific synthesis], 2 parts, 1903-4.
[112]PFT, 47.

nally receiving itself."[113] The profound point Florensky is trying to make is that nothing can stand by itself, and be totally independent from the rest of being. Truly to understand a being means to delve into its ground of being.

The principle of identity by itself, that is, considered in abstraction from the principle of sufficient reason, is nothing more than an articulation of the transcendental property of the oneness of being at the level of principle. It says that all being is one with itself. No being can be, and not be itself. If it were not itself, it would not be; it would be nothing. But insofar as it is, it is undivided in itself, or, in other words, is simply one. Every "A" not only is "A," but is necessarily "A."[114] It is merely this insight into the nature of being as unity that the principle of identity purports to express. And what it states positively, the principle of noncontradiction only phrases in negative fashion: "A being cannot at the same time and under the same respect be and not be."

But Florensky cannot content himself with a metaphysical reflection on the essential unity of being that is restricted to a mere affirmation of self-identity. The principle of identity, to express more than mere equality and really evince the dynamic unity of being, must, in Florensky's view, be integrated with the principle of sufficient reason, which underscores the fact that it is the inquiring mind that stands before being.[115] The hunger of the mind for truth remains unsatisfied until it scans the full expanse of being and articulates its coexistensive intelligibility, adequating it to itself. In principle understandable, being has its sufficient reason only in being, its necessary ground. It is this ground, both as a background and an underground, that Florensky's revised prin-

[113]PFT, 47f. Florensky is clearly alluding to Mk 8:34ff.

[114]Florensky overlooks the aspect of necessity in his treatment of the principle of identity. He views it as a mere tautology (cf. PFT, 26): "A is A." More profoundly, it states: "A is *necessarily* A." This is rather a *synthetic* statement of the principle of identity. On this point, cf. Coreth, *Metaphysics*, pp. 95f.

[115]Cf. especially Florensky's concluding remarks, PFT, 485ff, for a pointed statement of this thesis. Florensky only expressly states his insight into dynamic identity in the strict terms of the principles of identity and sufficient reason in his conclusion. This leads us to surmise that even he had great difficulty in finding apt articulation for his discovery.

ciple of identity tries to take into account and assimilate into its own operations.

All of this, of course, to have any sense and bearing, must be directly applied to the hypothetical Self-Proving Subject, which has been seen to be necessary for absolute truth to exist. How does this Subject affirm itself? How does the principle of identity apply in its instance?

In response, Florensky begins with a non-personalist, symbolic explanation of what almost immediately is transformed into an eminently personalist thesis, namely, that the Subject of Truth is the Holy Trinity.[116] He asks that we designate this Subject of Truth as "A." According to his principle of dynamic identity, however, A can be A, if and only if it is also non-A, which, for the sake of clarity, he in turn labels "B." In order that B, for its part, enjoy dynamic identity, it also must have its respective non-B. But, then, does this not mean that non-B is simply A? Florensky, to the contrary, postulates that it must be "C." The question thus arises why there is a need for this third term, C. Cannot A and B suffice, each respectively being the "non-A" and the "non-B" for the other? Florensky responds, however, that non-B for B needs be C, if A and B are to maintain their full, respective *realities*. Otherwise, they actually are the same and only *modally* distinct. The lack of a third term, when applied to the Holy Trinity, Florensky maintains, gives rise to the heresy of Modalism or Sabellianism. Indeed, it is the third term that ratifies the dynamic existence of the other two, and serves as the guarantee against their mutual absorbtion.

Translating this presentation into the personalist terms of "I," "Thou," and "He." Florensky proceeds to offer a series of progressively daring affirmations.[117] In a first formulation, we read that the Subject of Truth is an "I" in relation to a "He" through a "Thou," that the subjective "I" is made an objective "He" through a "Thou." In other words, the "I" assimilates its ground, that is, receives its consistency, its being as a *living, personal* Subject and concomitant objectivization as a "He," only in its relation with a "Thou," who

[116]For this symbolic presentation, cf. PFT, 48.
[117]Ibid.

responds and interacts with it. The "He" is nothing other than the "I" revealed. Elaborating further, Florensky more simply says: "Truth contemplates Itself through Itself in Itself."[118] And in more theological terms, "Truth is the contemplation of Itself through Another in a Third: Father, Son, and Spirit."[119] The net result, Florensky affirms, is that the "Subject of Truth is a *relation of Three,* indeed, a relation, manifesting itself as a substance, as a relation-substance."[120] Accordingly, for Florensky the essence of Truth is an "infinite act of Three in Unity,"[121] or more radically still, *"one substance in three hypostases."*[122] His point, of course, may seem obscure, but possibly, upon reflection, it is more evident than one might at first think. A truly *living* Subject must also be viewed in terms of dynamic identity, that is, in relational terms, and specifically in the triadic terms of I-Thou-He, Father-Son-Spirit.

The central point that needs further clarification is why a specifically triadic structure is necessary for the Subject of Truth. Florensky claims that no less than three structural elements can resolve the difficulties at hand for guaranteeing certitude, and that more than three are unnecessary. The former holds true, Florensky suggests, because if there were only two elements they would end up being undistinguishable from one another. If A is A and B, and B is B and A, then A and B would be the same and not distinct, independent realities. Only C permits one to break out of this circle, since in non-C alone can A find itself as A again.

Although this symbolic explanation may not seem entirely cogent, the profound truth of personalism, however, can be gleaned once A, B, and C are translated into I, Thou, and He. If the I is solely constituted by the Thou, and the Thou by the I, what keeps them from dissolving into one another? Only a third Other, a He or an It, can, as Florensky interjects, ensure the maintenance of their distinct existences, that is, the preservation of a real, dynamic identity between them.

[118]Ibid.
[119]Ibid.
[120]PFT, 49.
[121]Ibid.
[122]Ibid.

Granted that to two lovers, it may seem that they alone exist, it is, nonetheless, rather the outside world beyond their mutual relationship that guarantees that they do not absorb one another, and, accordingly, eliminate their dynamic, mutually constituting relationship.

Further, Florensky observes that no more than three terms are needed, since the circle necessary for guaranteeing dynamic identity can be closed with three members. Other members, he adds, can of course exist—and, in reality, do exist—but they are only ancillary to the three essential elements. In the precise terms of trinitarian theology, this means that only the three heuristically required constituents are full Hypostases of the Subject of Truth, while all other terms or hypostases are only conditional. They may exist, but need not. As such, Florensky says that they are, at best, only "deified persons"[123] that introduce a new order among the Three Hypostases in relation to themselves. The Three Hypostases, Florensky however maintains, enjoy no order among themselves.[124] This is why the number three, in his opinion, is an apt symbol of eternity. Admittedly, no fully satisfactory explanation of this point is possible, but then we are dealing with an inscrutable mystery at whose very threshold we find ourselves and before which we can only open our hearts and spirits for personal communication and communion.

3.1.1 Parallels in Heidegger

It is important to note that Florensky's efforts to revitalize the conceptual tools of thought have their close parallels in other contemporary thinkers, equally impressed by the need for a rejuvenation and revitalization of our conceptual apparatus. One immediately thinks of Martin Heidegger (1889-

[123]PFT, 50.

[124]Ibid. Coming from an Orthodox, this is a somewhat baffling affirmation insofar as Orthodox theology has notably stressed the Monarchy of the Father in respect to the other Divine Persons of the Holy Trinity. Nonetheless, in the personalist perspective of I-Thou-He, Florensky's comment seems fully justified. Each Hypostasis in itself is an I in respect to the Others, which variously can be a Thou or a He.

1976), who is well-known for his attempts to rethink the commonly held assumptions of thought and specifically for his reexamination of the principle of identity as a principle of thinking.

In a lecture given on the occasion of the 500th Anniversary of the University of Freiburg im Breisgau on June 27, 1957, entitled "The Principle of Identity,"[125] Heidegger tries to isolate the core meaning of the principle of identity in terms of the relation of "belonging together," which, he adds, is uniquely obtained in the "event of appropriation" (*das Er-eignis*). Noting in opening his discussion that the "principle of identity is considered the highest principle of thought,"[126] Heidegger expresses his inquietude at merely giving a passive assent to this truth, and stresses that his specific point of interest is "to find out through this principle what identity is."[127]

Defining man as essentially the being who thinks, it becomes apparent to him that man is that being who thinks being, and, thus, that being who is open to Being, and who responds to it in thought.[128] For this reason, man and Being in his view belong together. "A belonging to Being prevails within man, a belonging which listens to Being because it is appropriated to Being."[129] And since man and Being are appropriated to each other, that is, belong to each other, "it becomes clear that Being belongs with thinking to an identity whose active essence stems from that letting belong together which we call the appropriation."[130] Thus, "the essence of identity is," in Heidegger's view, "a property of the event of appropriation."[131]

How has Heidegger, then, changed our understanding of the principle of identity? The answer is clear: by transforming it from being a mere statement about identity to being a

[125]Reprinted in *Identity and Difference* (New York: Harper & Row, 1969), 23-41. The integral German text is given on pp. 83-106.
[126]Ibid., 23.
[127]Ibid.
[128]Ibid., 31.
[129]Ibid.
[130]Ibid., 39.
[131]Ibid. The German text (see p. 103) reads: "Das Wesen der Identität ist ein Eigentum des Er-eignisses."

dynamic consideration of the essential origins of identity.[132] It is in this respect that his undertaking is exactly the same as the one given antecedent elaboration by Florensky, but of which it is doubtful Heidegger could have had any knowledge. Curiously and striking, Heidegger's terminology is virtually the same as Florensky's. When Florensky speaks of "adoption" (*usvoenie*), we are only shades of meaning away from Heidegger's own term, *das Er-eignis,* which he roots in the German word, "*aneignung,*" itself variously translatable as "adoption" (*usvoenie*) and "appropriation" (*prisvoenie*—an obvious cognate of *usvoenie*).

3.1.2 *Parallels in Whitehead*

Further parallels are found in the process thought of Alfred North Whitehead (1861-1947), who devoted his speculative metaphysics to the development of a "philosophy of organism," conceived as a coherent and logical system of general ideas, whose application to the data of experience would faithfully and adequately account for them.[133] Whitehead's overall speculative scheme bears numerous resemblances to Florensky's own philosophical emphases, but, in the present context, we need only indicate where Whitehead's cosmological view seems to be inspired by the same basic insight into the nature of identity that resonates in Florensky's thought.

At the heart of Whitehead's categorical scheme of preliminary notions, which give rise to the philosophy of organism, lie "actual entities," "the final real things of which the world is made up,"[134] or rather the micro-events at the basis of the process, constitutive of reality.[135] Whitehead formu-

---

[132]Ibid., 39f. It is also this new understanding of the meaning of identity that allows for the cultivation of meditative thinking in contrast to the usual calculative thinking, common to men. Cf. Martin Heidegger, *Discourse on Thinking* (New York: Harper & Row, 1969).

[133]Alfred North Whitehead, *Process and Reality* (New York: Free Press, 1978, corrected edition), 3. The first edition of this book, Whitehead's masterwork, appeared in 1929.

[134]Ibid., 18.

[135]Whitehead distinguishes actual entities as either temporal or non-

lates his view on the actual entity in the horizon of identity in his twenty-first category of explanation, which reads:

> An entity is actual, when it has significance for itself. By this it is meant that an actual entity functions in respect to its own determination. Thus an actual entity combines self-identity with self-diversity.[136]

What is of decisive import is that Whitehead, like Florensky before him, seeks to integrate self-identity with self-diversity or otherness. Only in this way does Whitehead believe that we can articulate a truly organic view of the world. In his own words:

> It is fundamental to the metaphysical doctrine of the philosophy of organism, that the notion of an actual entity as the unchanging subject of change is completely abandoned. An actual entity is at once the subject experiencing and the superject of its experiences. It is subject-superject, and neither half of this description can for a moment be lost sight of.[137]

It is Whitehead's consideration of the actual entity as a "subject-superject" that is of direct relevance to our present discussion. The actual entity as an experiencing subject, Whitehead maintains, presides over its own process of becoming, and, as such, is the subject of its own self-revelation. The "to be" of an actual entity is, in other words, nothing less than a potential for becoming. As a superject, on the other hand, the actual entity manifests the fact that it has become its being, that it is that which is self-realized. In Whitehead's own words, an "actual entity is to be conceived both as a subject presiding over its own immediacy of becoming, and a superject which is the atomic creature exercising its function of objective immortality. It has become a 'being;'

temporal. The one, and only one, non-temporal actual entity for Whitehead is God. We prescind from a discussion of this particular problematic concerning the nature of actual entities.
[136]*Process and Reality*, 25.
[137]Ibid., 29.

and it belongs to the nature of every 'being' that it is a potential for every 'becoming.' "[138] In sum, for Whitehead, being
is not something static and immobile, but rather is a dynamic
event in process. To be is to become and to have become.
More in terms of Florensky's consideration of the principle
of identity, we may say that an actual entity or being *is* only
insofar as it is, at once, emergent from its "other" and both
a condition and cause of its "other" that is yet to be.

3.2 *Critical Evaluation of Florensky*

It bears repeating, that what we find here in Florensky is
the makings of a subtle, *heuristic* proof for the existence of
that Absolute Truth, which is God, the Triune God of the
Christian faith. Not denying the hypothetic character of
Florensky's exposition, the points he makes are, nonetheless,
valid antecedent determinations of what a final solution must
envisage in order to overcome the fundamental aporia in
which human thought inextricably finds itself. Our partial
knowing, yielding only incomplete intelligibility, calls out
for complete, unconditional intelligibility, and cannot rest
still until perfect knowing has been achieved. But unless there
is some possible way to fuse immediate self-givenness with
authenticating rationality, no ultimate satisfaction can be
found for this basic cry of man's spirit. Florensky at least
succeeds, it would seem, at laying the groundwork for a *de
facto* fusion.

However, it must be emphasized that a strict deduction of
the Holy Trinity is an evident impossibility. Although Florensky may at times give the impression of trying to deduce
this capital Christian mystery, he himself disavows any real
possibility of doing so.[139] He merely states that attempted
deductions retain a certain value as indicators of the various
dimensions of the mystery. Nevertheless his own attempt at
showing why there should be a triadic structure to the Self-
Proving Subject is, in itself, auspicious of this Holy Mystery,

[138]Ibid., 45. Cf. also p. 222.
[139]PFT, 593.

and favorable to its eventual formalization. Alluding to the Holy Trinity in its various moments, Florensky's remarks are certainly germane, and enjoy a well-founded validity.[140] One of Florensky's critics, Zenkovsky, on the other hand, scores his purported deduction of Triunity and implicitly the Mystery of the Holy Trinity as purely formal, and, therefore, devoid of content.[141] But, on this score, it would seem that Zenkovsky fails to appreciate the real heuristic character and value of Florensky's proffered trial demonstration. Florensky attempts only a quasi-deduction, and merely tries to highlight its probabilistic standing in the face of the human dilemma of truth.

Florensky's speculations concerning the intrinsically necessary trinitarian constitution of the Self-Proving Subject are only a pallid reflection and indeed vainglorious depiction of the real intratrinitarian life of the Three Divine Hypostases, but they do prepare the way for an eventual acceptance in faith and love of the Mystery of the Holy Trinity as the first postulate, as it were, of theoretical reasoning and the ultimate, unquestioned foundation of cognitive certitude. He in no way exaggerates or engages in overwrought poetic embellishment, therefore, when he opens his letter on doubt with a vignette of three interlocking laurel wreaths bearing the inscription, *His ornari aut mori* (Be crowned of these or die).[142] Doubt, in other words, is only removed and truth and certitude

[140]On analogy with the Holy Trinity, Florensky holds that trinitarianess is a general feature of all reality. Cf. PFT, 593-99. He is, however, less successful in explicating this thesis, and gives the initial impression at least, of engaging in unjustifiable theorization. Citing the three dimensionality of space, the three periods of time (past, present, future), the three grammatical persons, and the triple stratification of the human person as body, psyche, and spirit as exemplifications of this doctrine, Florensky seems to be trying to conclude too much. It may be that he has, indeed, made a true *prise de conscience* on this point, but he has not succeeded in convincingly communicating it. It can be granted that his insight may be valid, but it certainly needs further exfoliation for it to enjoy a fuller intelligibility and wider acceptance.

[141]Zenkovsky, *Istoriya*, 2:243 (n. 47); Eng. trans., 883 (n. 2).

[142]PFT, 15. Cf. also Florensky's remarks on PFT, 488. Florensky states (p. 807) that he has taken his vignettes for PFT from the work of Ambodik, *Symbola et Emblemata selecta* (1st ed.). No further information is given by Florensky regarding this book. Three vignettes have been reproduced for this study. Appearing at the beginning of each of its parts, they are rep-

uniquely established in its stead, when the crowns of the Holy Trinity are graciously and fiducially accepted in obedient and loving submission to the eternal designs of God.[143]

resentative of the others and, in our judgment, are the best depictions of the most important junctures in his argumentation.

[143]Vladimir Lossky stresses this aspect of Florensky's thought in his own treatment of the Holy Trinity in his now classic work, *The Mystical Theology of the Eastern Church* (Crestwood, NY: St. Vladimir's Seminary Press, 1976), 65f.

CHAPTER IV

Homoousian Philosophy

Before proceeding to develop his philosophical thesis
about the Self-Proving Subject and the absolute foundation
and criterion of truth in greater detail, Florensky turns his
attention to the more specifically theological side of the
question,[1] hoping to discover new indications for his work
and even, we may say, to receive the suprarational counsel of
faith that his speculations may not veer off the right track.
In order to understand Florensky's methodological move here,
it is worthwhile to draw attention to the fact that Russian
religious thought, as a rule, does not clearly demarcate philosophy from theology, but rather conjoins them in the search
for one common wisdom. In this respect, Russian religious
thought bears a closer resemblance to Augustinian rather than
to Thomistic modes of thought. It is, therefore, not surprising
that Florensky himself would combine both philosophical and
theological approaches as mutually supportive and enriching
in his own religious speculations about his lived experience.
Thus, for example, at the same time that he speaks of triunity
from a more or less strictly philosophical point of view, he
either implicates or directly treats the strictly theological
sphere in the sense that he specifically speculates on the
mystery of the Holy Trinity as such and tries to extend its
scope and bearing to the natural world accessible to human
reason. In fact, one of the most original aspects of his thought
and indeed, according to Nicholas O. Lossky, his chief con-

[1] Cf. Florensky's third letter on triunity, PFT, 51-69.

tribution to a fuller elaboration of a Christian world conception, is his conscious application of the idea of "consubstantiality" as worked out in trinitarian theology to the metaphysics of created being.[2] It is with this conscious application
that Florensky develops his unique conception of Christian
philosophy as *homoousian* philosophy.

As for what he has previously stated about the internal
constitution of Truth as a Self-Proving Subject in triunity,
Florensky is confident that it is true, but readily concedes
whether this can be effectively demonstrated is still another
question.[3] But before proceeding with an examination of this
question, he deems it useful to expound briefly on just what
traditional theology has tried to say about the mystery of the
Holy Trinity and the dogmatic concept of "consubstantiality"
in particular.

1. TOWARDS A THEOLOGICAL UNDERSTANDING OF TRIUNITY

1.1 *Homoousios or Consubstantiality*

It is not necessary to treat the dogmatic development of
the term, "consubstantiality" or *"homoousious"* at length; it
suffices to indicate its basic, dogmatic meaning and import.
The meaning of the term in its present usage[4] was fixed at
the first Council of Nicaea (325), the first ecumenical council, which was convoked in order to respond to the Arian
crisis then ravaging the Christian world and, in particular,
to combat the teaching attributed to Arius (256-336)[5] that
held the Word, the Second Person of the Holy Trinity, was

[2]N. O. Lossky, *History of Russian Philosophy*, 188. We shall return to
this point later (see sec. 3.3, pp. 134-38 below).

[3]PFT, 51.

[4]Prior to Nicaea I, the term *homoousion* had a heterodox meaning. Paul
of Samosata appears to have employed it to indicate the personal identity
between the various persons of the Holy Trinity, thus ascribing to a form
of modalism. He was formally condemned at the Council of Antioch
(268). Cf. Bernard J. F. Lonergan, S.J., *The Way to Nicaea* (London:
Darton, Longman & Todd, 1971), 37.

[5]We prescind from the question of whether Arius himself really subscribed to the heretical teaching bearing his name. The Arian doctrine is

not eternal but created from nothing like the rest of creation, even if prior to the creation of everything else. To counteract this teaching, Athanasius and his followers gave new meaning to the term "consubstantial," interpreting it in the sense of an identity of nature between the Father and the Son. This new teaching was adopted by the Council Fathers at Nicaea, and with this affirmation of the consubstantiality of the Son with the Father in contradistinction to the sole ascription of creaturehood to Him, the Council accordingly underscored the divine nature of the Son of God, which was negated in the Arian understanding of the Word. The most famous, concrete fruit of this council was its Profession of Faith, which expressed the orthodox point of view, and which has become an important, enhancing adjunct of the Divine Liturgy of the Universal Church. The excerpt from this creed relevant to the condemnation of Arianism reads as follows: "We believe . . . in one Lord Jesus Christ, Son of God, the only-begotten, born of the Father, that is, of the substance of the Father, God of God, light of light, true God of true God, born, not made, *of one substance (unius substantiae—homoousion)* with the Father, through whom all things were made"[6] (emphasis ours).

This profession of faith is nothing but a conceptual expression of the lived experience of the Church. As Florensky rightfully notes, the Church experiences the Father, the Son, and the Holy Spirit as a "concrete unity" and as no mere "nominal unity."[7] The term, "consubstantiality" or *"homoousios"* itself captures the thrust of meaning of what constitutes the most fundamental antinomy of all Christian experience, namely, the experience of the *oneness* of God, who, at the same time, is essentially Three Hypostases (Persons). The most typical opening lines of specifically Christian prayer incomparably illustrate this point. Florensky is insistent

unquestionably heterodox, but it is not at all clear whether it was indeed the actual position of Arius on the nature of the Divine Word. On Arius' teaching, see *Way to Nicaea*, 68, 70ff.

[6]Henricus Denzinger, Adolphus Schönmetzer, S.J., *Enchiridion Symbolorum Definitionum et Declarationum de Rebus Fidei et Morum*, 34th ed. (Freiburg im Breisgau: Herder, 1965), 125.

[7]PFT, 53f.

on this point. We pray: " 'In the *name* of the Father, and of the Son, and of the Holy Spirit,' and not 'in the names' of the Three Hypostases."[8] However, this antinomy, if not grasped with the proper balance of emphasis, gives rise to one of two extremes—both heterodox positions. On the one hand, if the unity of the Divine Hypostases is overstressed, there is the evident danger of Sabellianism or Modalism in which no real distinction is held between the Father and the Son and, subsequently, the Holy Spirit. On the other hand, if the distinction of the Three Hypostases is unduly accented, one jeopardizes the unity of the Godhead, and runs the risk of falling into tritheism, or maintaining there are three, not one, gods. Both extremes must be avoided, and the profession of the consubstantiality of the Father and the Son has been deemed the best safeguard in this ever precarious situation. There is numerically only one God, but this God is truly Father, truly Son, and truly Spirit.

1.2   *The Postulate of Mind*

Florensky's investigation for the foundations of truth and the dissolution of scepticism so far has indicated the need for a new justification for the principle of identity. To find this requisite basis, Florensky claims, one must go beyond the confines of reasoning to that domain where reasoning itself finds its roots.[9] This domain, he further notes, must be of the experiential order,[10] or else the formula, "Triunity in Unity and Unity in Trinity," previously seen to be heuristically necessary for the absolute foundation of truth, will remain an empty formalism, and consequently not denote anything for reasoning. Further, the most evident norms of reasoning, the principle of identity and the principle of sufficient reason, themselves demand the self-accountability of any proper point of departure for human   knowing. Since reasoning itself formally requires a Trinity in Unity as its ultimate base, it

[8]PFT, 54f.
[9]PFT, 58.
[10]Ibid.

must establish for itself a *"new* norm"[11] in order to experience this essential "postulate of mind (*razum*)."[12] This norm, according to Florensky, can only be given by the One having authority—a clear reference to the Incarnate Word of God.[13] But to have a vital contact with this norm, reason must renounce its own inherent limitations of reasoning, and freely abandon itself to the victory of faith.[14] Faith is, indeed, in Florensky's view the key to this new vision. Scoring the errant ways of reason, Bishop Feodor justly laments: "It has always sought the incarnation of intuition-discursion in the finite and false, while Christianity has discovered true intuition-discursion in the Triune God, in the bond of knowledge and life, in the living, personal Truth, Jesus Christ."[15]

2. FAITH AND REASON

The domain of faith, which Florensky maintains opens up new vistas for grasping truth and for sustaining our certitudes about reality, does not, however, simply present itself to us, but requires personal effort[16] and an honest admission of our essential finitude and our need for transcendent help in overcoming our personal inadequacies and shortcomings in the

[11]PFT, 59.

[12]Ibid. and also p. 107 where Florensky speaks of the "hypothesis of Triunity."

[13]PFT, 60. Cf. Mt 7:29. On this score we find an additional rebuttal to the charge of Florovsky (*Puti russkogo bogosloviya*, 495) that Florensky overlooks christological considerations in his religious speculations. The fact that the Incarnate Word constitutes, in Florensky's view, the new norm for truth proves he does not relegate Christ to a secondary role in this worldview. He does, however, admit that he has not yet fully developed his christological ideas. Such a development, as we have seen, would necessitate a separate "anthropodicy," a subject matter not presently under his direct consideration. Cf. PFT, 638 (n. 66). Udelov (*Ob o. Pavle Florenskom*, 44f) voices a similar criticism against Florovsky's position in this regard. We have previously brought attention to this point (see p. 44, n. 82, above).

[14]PFT, 60.

[15]Bishop Feodor, "Review," 164f.

[16]In treating the problematic of the knowledge of faith, Florensky does not systematically deal with the dimension of grace and the question of the infusion of faith as a theological virtue in the believer, but he does, nonetheless, seem clearly to implicate the need for grace in his present elaboration.

search for cognitive certitude. Concretely, this means our dis-
avowal of the claims of reason and our moving away "from
the prattle of reason to the obedient listening of faith."[17]

2.1 *The Three Stages of Faith*

This transference of our point of reference from the voice
of reason to the call of faith, however, does not come about
all at once, but only in a gradual process of progressive self-
abandon to the dynamics of faith. The first stage of this
process is, in fact, one of mixed emotions in which we retain
a defiant attitude in the face of our former, haunting dis-
belief. According to Florensky, we may aphoristically express
this sentiment as follows: "*Credo, quia absurdum est.*" (I
believe because it is absurd.)[18] We believe inspite of the
protests of reason; we believe, because we accept the pledge
of something new and higher, which presents itself for our
endorsement. We are willing to make this gamble because
we know we have nothing to lose. If we remain exclusively
within the confines of reason we know there is no final escape
from the despair of sceptical doubt and suspicion towards
all claims of truth.

The second stage of faith is one in which we are secure of
the foundations of faith, and do not hesitate to acclaim it as
the source itself of all higher knowledge and the true foundation which gives discursive reasoning a solid footing on
which to begin its activity. Quoting St. Anselm, Florensky says
at this stage we proclaim: "*Credo ut intelligam.*" (I believe
that I may understand.)[19] That is, we know that without a
reliance on a higher order of intelligibility we can never
transcend the limitations of our reason.

The third stage is the level of "rationalization" of faith
as it were. This rationalization, however, is not to be understood as a process of demythologization in the pejorative
sense of the word, but rather as an attempt to move from a

[17]PFT, 61.
[18]Ibid.
[19]PFT, 62.

blind faith to a more differentiated faith, one fully consonant
with man's reason though beckoning beyond it and truly
evocative of man's real potentialities in life. It is the faith
which responds in hope and love to the *known* God, the God
who is not only believed but also known.[20] It is the faith which
empowers me to exclaim: *"Intelligo ut credam!"* (I understand that I may believe!).[21] At this stage, we truly see that
the borders between faith and knowledge are not at all sharp,
but, on the contrary, are essentially fluid, and that, in a true
sense, each one implies and necessitates the other.[22]

2.2 *The Victory of Faith*

The victory of faith comes at that moment when religious
dogma is held not to be *ab ovo* an absurdity, but is viewed as
a legitimate aspiration of human reason. It is, indeed, at this
juncture that the gnawing doubt of the sceptic begins to be
dispelled, and the possibility of totally overcoming scepticism
is first affirmed. It is also at this point that one is for the
first time confronted with faith's veritable "either-or" challenge, the challenge of either accepting the Triune Christian
God in faith or dying in sceptical madness. Florensky, noting
that no third alternative is in the offing,[23] immediately recasts
this dual alternative in the terms of his previous speculations
about the ultimate foundations of reasoning.[24] In their perspective, he affirms our choice becomes solely one between
the acknowledgment of a necessary, even if postulatory,
metalogical foundation of reasoning in the likes of a Triune,
Self-Proving Subject or the acquiescent admission that the
laws of logic are purely of the accidental order, thus depriving

[20]Ibid.
[21]Ibid.
[22]This point was clearly understood by St. Augustine, who gave it a
beautiful articulation. Expounding on the meaning of Is 7:9 ("If you will
not believe, surely you shall not be established"), he advises: "Intellige,
ut credas—crede, ut intelligas!" (Understand, that you may believe—believe,
that you may understand!) Cf. *Sermo* 43:7-9 in *Patrologia Latina*, ed.
Migne, vol. 38:257-258.
[23]PFT, 63f.
[24]Cf. pp. 100-5 above.

all reason of its properly dispositive character.[25] But even if we opt for the first alternative we still only remain on the hypothetical level. In other words, our problem becomes one of effecting a transition from merely postulatory knowledge *about* Unconditional Truth to a truly experiential knowledge *of* this Truth. To do so, however, one must cross an abyss not bridgeable by human reason alone.[26] How, then, does one span this gap? Florensky responds: by taking Pascal up on his wager and opting in favor of the claims of faith.[27]

2.3 *The Principle of Living Faith*

Only the rationalist can be disappointed by this turn in Florensky's argument. True, Florensky now leaves the properly natural order, and enters into the more specifically supernatural realm, but he does not, however, at all claim to leave the horizon of philosophical understanding. On the contrary, finding himself on terrain where the distinctions between knowledge and faith remain somewhat blurred, and equipped only with his principle of living faith for his cognitive journey, he states that he is only embarking upon a novel type of philosophical journey.[28] And in response to the rationalist, he would only say that as a complainant he merely overstates the claims of reason when he pretends that all possible knowledge must be fashioned according to the strictures of reason. Much remains essentially transcendent to man, and, as such, can never be fully commensurate with human reason. Reason, moreover, is marred by a fatal flaw. Of itself, it is radically incapable of surmounting its inherent limitations and of founding itself as the ultimate norm of all truth. But unless the aporia it finds itself in is not in some way resolved,[29] and is further given some adequate, metalogical justification, the

[25]PFT, 64.
[26]PFT, 65.
[27]PFT, 66, 640ff. Cf. Blaise Pascal, *Pensées* (New York: Penguin Books, 1966), sec. 2, ser. 2, pp. 149-52.
[28]PFT, 67.
[29]Cf. pp. 100-3 above.

only fate which awaits it in the last analysis is extreme scepticism.

On the other hand, our incessant longing to know, our wonder before the workings of the universe, our perplexity before the unsolved riddles of life, all counsel us to remain in alliance with truth and not to opt for the abstention from all judgments of truth. The thematicity of truth pervades our every action, our every thought, indeed, our very existences. Accordingly, its problematic necessarily leads us to questions about ultimate truth, and, in point of fact, arouses within us a longing for intimate contact with that Absolute Truth which is the living source of all being and truth. It is, therefore, only appropriate that we join in with Florensky and together cry out to this Truth: "Lead me Yourself to Yourself!"[30]

But can we, in fact, say that this Truth exists? Florensky says he does not know whether it does, but, upon an introspective consideration of his own needs and aspirations, immediately adds that he cannot possible live without it.[31] Indeed, he notes even when he is doubting he is still in the horizon of Truth and, indeed, within its embrace,[32] since the very existence itself of doubt has for the very condition of its possibility the fact of the problematic of truth and further that of Absolute Truth itself. For this reason, doubt only enjoys a derivative consistency that has no bearing on our existence apart from the question of truth. We are, therefore, clearly justified in our expectations, and can rightfully claim, along with Florensky and the desert father Macarius the Great whom he quotes with full approbation in this regard, that "Truth itself motivates man to search for Truth."[33] And with equal reason, we can share in Florensky's own poignant self-consignment: "My fate, my reason, the very soul of my searching—the need for certitude, I entrust into the hands of Truth itself."[34]

[30]PFT, 67.
[31]Ibid.
[32]PFT, 68.
[33]Ibid.
[34]Ibid.

3. PHILOSOPHICAL CONSIDERATIONS

Florensky's epistemological investigation has brought him to postulate a Triune Self-Proving Subject as the ultimate foundation of truth. It is only with this trinitarian hypothesis, Florensky claims, that we can give an adequate accounting of our experience of truth, that satisfies our mind's need both for full intelligibility and for rational assurance of the validity of its intuitions. Truth, however, is an immediate given of experience, and precisely as an ultimate datum, cannot, as Florensky will later note,[35] be deduced from anything else or be reduced to a lower common denominator. In sum, its existence cannot, strictly speaking, be "proven"; it must simply be accepted as a primary reality.

It follows, Florensky suggests, that the best stand to take in view of the ultimate unprovability of the existence of truth is probabilism, that is, the stance presumptive of its existence, and not scepticism, which ultimately not only presupposes truth for its own particular consistency, but also is, from the practical point of view, continually proven wrong at every turn in the course of daily life, and shown to be no more than a vainglorious cynicism of the mind itself. In other words, from the perspective of probabilistic theory, the most reasonable position to take is one of making an act of faith[36] in the existence of truth and concomitantly in the existence of the heuristically determined Triune Subject of Truth.

Within this particular act of faith, we find the first indications that the object of our search exists,[37] that there is an Absolute Truth at the root of our being and the world around us. Moreover, this act marks the beginnings of our personal communication with this Absolute Truth,[38] which truly becomes the object of our longing and love as well as that of our cognitive inquiry. As Bishop Feodor very profoundly observes in regard to the dynamic orientation of Florensky's

---

[35]PFT, 143.
[36]In this context, the term "act of faith" is used in the broad sense, and not in the strict theological sense of an assent given to a supernatural mystery.
[37]PFT, 70.
[38]PFT, 71.

thought, "the way to the acceptance of truth is faith, while the way to the [experienced] knowledge of truth is love."[39] The insight into the need for a Triune Subject as the unshakeable foundation of all truth thus becomes more than a question for knowledge; it is, above all, the primordial impetus motivating our proffered response in love to this very Principle.

3.1 *The Coordination of Mind and Being*

The mind's drive to know cannot be satisfied with a detached and static intellectual possession of its object of truth, but aims at a total communication with Truth. It desires to partake of the very Being of the Truth, and immerse itself in its very stream of Life. This aspect of participation of man's mind in the very drama of being and life is, in Florensky's view, an inseparable part of man's search for truth. As he observes: "If the mind does not commune with being, then being does not commune with the mind, and, therefore, is a-logical."[40] And if this be the case, it is evident that only scepticism, illusionism, and nihilism can possibly obtain.

There is only one way out of this unsustainable situation, and that is to acknowledge the co-communicatory or co-participatory character of the mind with being, or the activity of knowing with the act of being. Such an avowal is possible because of the essential gnoseological coordination of mind with being. In this coordination, the intentional character of all knowing is manifested. The knowing subject in his act of knowing intends a known object as the content of his knowing. To know is to know *something*. Although Florensky himself does not explicitly use the technical term "intentionality" in his elaboration, he does, however, specifically draw attention to Nicholas Lossky's teaching on gnoseological coordination as the point of departure for his present discussion.[41] Knowledge, in Florensky's view, is a "real *going out*

---

[39]Bishop Feodor, "Review," 169.
[40]PFT, 73.
[41]Ibid. and pp. 644f. Cf. also N. O. Lossky, *Obosnovanie intuitivizma*

from self or,—to say the same, a real *entering into* the known by the knower,—a real union of knower and known."[42] To his mind, this precise understanding of knowledge and the cognitive process is a characteristic mark not only of Russian philosophy in particular but of all Eastern philosophy in general.[43] Of equal importance is the fact that the act of knowledge is viewed not solely in gnoseological terms, that is, as an act exclusively referring to the ideal order, the order of logical truth, but is equally held to be of an ontological nature, that is, concerning the real and the order on ontological truth.[44]

Knowledge, Florensky stresses, is more than just a passive and "lifeless" grasping of an object, but is a vital communication between a knowing subject and known object in which both are diverse personalities, as it were, serving as subject and object for each other. Expressed otherwise, for Florensky, *"essential (sushchestvennoe) knowledge,* understood as an act of the knowing subject, and *essential (sushchestvennaya) truth,* understood as a known real object, are the same thing, and are both real, even if they are distinguished in abstract reasoning."[45]

3.2   The Analogy of Knowledge and Love

At this point, Florensky is in the position to make an important development in his thought by explicating the analogy which obtains between knowledge and love. In the cognitive process one finds a real going-out of the knowing subject from himself and his real entering-into the known object, a process that strictly parallels the act of transcendence found in all true love whereby the one who loves goes out

[Foundations of intuitivism] (Berlin: Obelisk-Verlag, 1924), esp. 75-82. Florensky refers to the 1906 edition of this book by Lossky.

[42]PFT, 73. The idea of "going out," Florensky notes, was especially highlighted by Prince S. N. Trubetskoy in his works, while that of "entering into" has been put into relief by N. O. Lossky, especially in his *Obosnovanie intuitivizma.* Cf. PFT, 644.

[43]Ibid.

[44]Ibid.

[45]PFT, 74.

from himself in order to enter into communion with the one who is loved. Just as there is a real union and sharing of life between lover and beloved, so also is there a real, even if only intentional, union between the knower and the known.[46] In both cases, that is, in the instance of the order of knowledge and in that of the order of love, we witness acts of transcendence through which different dimensions of the real are actuated, thereby serving to constitute the knowing or loving subject. These dimensions are two of the traditional transcendental properties of being, truth and goodness, respectively.[47] In their activation we observe the dynamic functioning of Florensky's revised conception of the principle of identity wherein the living subject becomes one with itself only through its other—whether it be the known object or the loved one.

But, more importantly, we see that in this problematic truth and love always go hand in hand, and especially so, even incomparably so, when it is a question of knowing Absolute Truth. A realized knowledge of Truth, according to Florensky, is a participation in Truth. That is, it is nothing other than a "real entering into the bosom of the Divine Triunity,"[48] which is possible "only through the *transubstantiation* of man, through his divinization."[49] A radical affirmation, indeed—but, it is one given to even simpler expression: "It is in love and only in love that a valid knowledge of Truth can be expressed."[50] To know God is, in other words, to love Him, and, conversely, outside of the ambit of love there is no chance that Truth can reveal itself.

Another conclusion also follows. Our knowledge and love

[46]Robert Johann in *The Meaning of Love* (Glen Rock, NJ: Paulist Press, 1966), on the other hand, appears to deny, or at least downplay, the analogy between knowing and loving, preferring to highlight the difference between the intellect and the will. "While the intellect draws things to and within itself in order to know them," he writes, "the will goes out towards the things themselves" (pp. 20f; cf. p. 83). Nonetheless, the very fact that the mind intends its objects, that is, has a conscious orientation towards them, means that there is essentially a movement of "going-out" in all acts of knowledge.
[47]Cf. p. 68 above.
[48]PFT, 74.
[49]Ibid.
[50]Ibid.

of God are so intimately intertwined with one another that it is impossible to determine which one is the cause and which one is the consequent. As Florensky himself notes, they seem "only to be different sides of the same spiritual fact—the entering of God into me as a philosophizing subject and of me into God as objective Truth."[51]

3.3   Two Philosophies: Homoiousian and Homoousian

At this point we see that knowledge of Truth is no less than a participation in Divine Love, a fact clearly indicating that undergirding this conception of knowledge and truth is a metaphysics of being and love. It is up to Florensky now to develop this point further.

He begins by dividing all philosophical systems into two basic types according to whether the root-concept governing the elaboration of the system maintains the consubstantiality of all created beings or only their mere similarity.[52] A philosophy admitting only similarity or generic likeness Florensky labels, in an appeal to classical trinitarian theological terminology, *homoiousian*. This is the philosophy of rationalism, which is the philosophy of the concept and reasoning. It is merely a philosophy of things, characterized by lifeless inactivity and a static conception of the law of identity. In contrast to this "stale" philosophy of immobility is all Christian or *homoousian* philosophy, which is a philosophy of ideas[53] and

[51]In his *Method in Theology*, Bernard Lonergan, S.J., makes the relevant obervation that we can know God only if He loves us first, thus necessitating the presence of divine grace. The primacy of grace entails therefore, Lonergan notes (pp. 340f), an exception to the otherwise well-founded adage, "nihil amatum nisi praecognitum." Florensky is also of this opinion. He specifically writes (PFT, 110): "The knowledge of Truth, i.e., of the consubstantiality of the Holy Trinity, is accomplished through the grace of the Holy Spirit." Cf. also PFT, 395, for another reaffirmation of this capital theological point.

[52]PFT, 80f. Florensky notably remarks, however, that no pure *homoiousian* or *homoousian* philosophy has ever existed, either in the West or in the East. Zenkovsky (*Istoriya*, 2:416f [Eng. ed., 877]) also scolds Florensky for leaving the impression that all western philosophy is reducible to rationalism, an obvious misrepresentation of the true breadth of western philosophical thought.

[53]That is, in the sense of "concrete idealism" as elaborated above, p. 99.

mind and which, unlike the former philosophy, treats the
personality and creative achievement. It is "spiritual" philosophy founded on a dynamic understanding of the law of
identity.

The cornerstone of Florensky's metaphysics of consubstantiality appears to be his particular understanding of numerical
identity in contradistinction to both generic and specific identity.[54] He pointedly remarks that while numerical identity
indelibly signs the beings of a *homoousian* universe, solely
generic and specific identity are verified among beings or,
more properly, things in a *homoiousian* one. Whereas in a
homoousian universe, the one studied by the philosophy of
consubstantiality, beings are bound together from within,
distinguishing them with true, *internal* unity, indeed, with
numerical identity, in a *homoiousian* universe we can find
only *external* unity,[55] in which external relations alone obtain
among the things or entities comprising it, thus giving rise
solely to a universe of mere similarities.

Though Florensky himself does not specifically instance
this cosmological divergency, the empiricist universe of David
Hume (1711-75) stands out as a perfect example of a
homoiousian description. In Hume's philosophy, all knowledge of the external world is reducible to mere, atomized sense
impressions. He accordingly allows no appeal to *a priori*
metaphysical notions to explain the origin of general ideas
about reality. To account for this knowledge, he claims that
only the principles of association or connection among ideas,
namely, resemblance, contiguity, and causation, can be in-
voked.[56] Indeed, for Hume, these three principles of association constitute the true "cement of the universe."[57] Under-
standably, such a perspective never offers an in-vision of the
entities comprising the world, that is, a grasping of their being
from within, but merely an outward look at them, providing
only for a knowledge of mere similarities at best.

[54]PFT, 78-83, 515-18.
[55]PFT, 78f.
[56]David Hume, *An Enquiry Concerning Human Understanding*, in *The
Empiricists* (Garden City, NY: Doubleday & Co.), sec. 3, 320ff.
[57]Cf. his "Abstract" to *A Treatise of Human Nature*, Bk. 1 (Glasgow,
Wm. Collins Sons & Co., 1962), 353.

Florensky, on the other hand, seeks to penetrate the very core of being with his metaphysics of consubstantiality. Contrary to the Humean description, his *homoousian* world-view considers the universe as an organic whole, not one of whose entities can statically exist apart from all others, but whose constitutive parts are rather all welded together in dynamic, organic interrelationships. From this standpoint, it would appear that Florensky's proffered metaphysical doctrine of consubstantiality is nothing other than an apposite point of departure for developing an explicit metaphysics of participation, in which all reality, including the Absolute Reality, is accounted for by identical, formal principles of being.

A well-articulated metaphysics of participation based on the notion of consubstantiality, however, must commence with a detailed analysis of the manifold applications[58] of this term, an aspect of the problem Florensky does not specifically delve into in his letter, "Light of Truth," where he first introduces his twofold, *homoousian-homoiousian* division to characterize philosophical systems. Moreover, such an analysis of consubstantiality would have to provide for a fully integrated account of his understanding of numerical identity, which, if not properly understood, could appear to be the Achille's heel of his whole suggested system, and, in truth, could subject it to the charge of pantheism. Specifically, how can Florensky reconcile the consubstantiality of the divine Hypostases with the consubstantiality of created species in terms of numerical identity?

In the case of the Persons of the Holy Trinity, we indeed witness a true numerical identity of substance, since there is numerically only one God. But how can we speak of numerical identity in the case of human beings without denying man's unique individuality, let alone speak in terms of a numerical identity, as Florensky seems to do, between God and humanity, which would appear on the surface at least to be an evident affirmation of pantheism? When we speak

[58]Basing himself on Florensky, N. O. Lossky has developed a cosmology dependent upon the distinction between *abstract* and *concrete* consubstantiality. Cf. his *Vospominaniya*, 197f, *History of Russian Philosophy*, 255f, and *Mir kak organicheskoe tseloe* [The world as an organic whole] (Moscow, 1917).

of two creatures as being consubstantial, we typically refer
only to their specific identity, i.e., to the fact that they enjoy
a consubstantiality of species. Thus, "Peter" and "Paul" may
well be two instances of the same species man, but still they
retain their respective, individual substances. Further, even
when we consider humanity's consubstantiality with Christ,
the Second Person of the Holy Trinity, who assumed a human
nature, we restrict ourselves solely to an affirmation of man-
kind's consubstantiality with Christ's human nature and not
with His divinity. Otherwise, we not only render man god-like,
but truly deify him.[59]

How, then, is one to respond to these apparently devastat-
ing objections to the coherency of Florensky's thesis on numerical identity? The most ready key to a possible rejoinder
is found in Florensky's dynamic conception of the principle
of identity. Florensky never applies it to mere things or static
entities as such. In their instance, one may rest contented with
a detached, uninvolved, and blunt affirmation of "A is A."
But the reality of living personalities,[60] if treated exclusively
in the immobile, "egotistical" terms of a mere "A is A," is
necessarily falsified. In its very dynamic organicity, personality is intelligible only in reference to the "other" and ultimately only in dependence on the "Other," who supplies its
true ground and total context of intelligibility. To affirm a
personality's vital, interpersonal existence, "A is A" does not
suffice. One needs to add "if and only if non-A is." In a
personalist universe, accordingly, no "self" *is* in abstraction
from its "other." Therefore, from a truly total standpoint
of personality and the complexus of interpersonal relationships, we may in some sense rightfully say that a "self" is
numerically identical[61] with its "other" and that the "cement"

[59]This remark, however, should not be taken as a criticism of St.
Athanasius' classical insight, "God became man that man might become
god." Indeed, we are attempting a full integration of this doctrine into
Florensky's teaching.

[60]Florensky seems to ascribe "personality" to all created being, making
him therefore an apparent proponent of at least a species of *panpsychism.*
If so, however, it is one uniquely predicated on his particular understanding
of identity.

[61]In this sense, we could also—and possibly more clearly—say that the
self is "one" with its other.

holding them together is none other than love, a pointed criticism of Hume. But, obviously, in other senses the self is not identical to its other. To account for these differences and especially to maintain the critical difference between Creator and creature and, therefore, a viable metaphysics of participation, a doctrine of analogy of being is needed. Analogy, indeed, is the language of participation. That Florensky nowhere appear to consider this aspect of the problematic may well be his chief omission.[62]

But of more specific interest for us here in the present epistemological context, however, are the implications of a *homoousian* world-view for the cognitive experience of Truth itself. Simply put, Florensky seems to maintain that man comes to know Absolute Truth only by partaking of the divine essence in love. This essential participation in the trinitarian life, effected in love, constitutes man's consubstantiality, as it were, with the Triune Godhead, and only through this consubstantiality is the Absolute and Infinite Reality or Integral Unity known.

---

[62]This omission would also explain why Florensky seems to overstress mystical knowledge at the expense of analogical knowledge of God. Cf. François Marxer, "Le problème de la vérité et de la tradition chez Pavel Florensky," *Istina*, 25 (1980): 224.

CHAPTER V

The Antinomy of Truth

Our investigative journey in search of the foundations of truth and certitude has taken several paths and has crossed a few important crossroads. Each crossroad has, in effect, constituted a basic thesis about the nature of truth. Beginning from the experience of truth, we have seen that it presents itself to us in many ways, from divergent points of view, thus clearly evidencing a polyvalent character escaping facile objectification. Formally speaking, however, truth is first encountered and its problematic first thematized in the act of judgment. But judgment as the formal locus of truth is also the place where the problems and doubts concerning truth come to the fore. Doubt is precisely that state of unrest which arises within us when we lack the necessary basis for assenting to the existence of a state of affairs. To remove it, only two means lie before us, either by attempting another immediate look with the hope that a greater acuity of vision and concentration of attention will disclose the missing links holding back our assent, or by discursively reasoning out the difficulties and uncluttering the path to this assent.

But we all too soon become cognizant of the fact that these measures suffice only if we are satisfied with partial knowing of particular truths. If we activate our doubting capacities even more radically, and apply them to call into question the absolute foundations of all truth, we find they are merely stop-gap measures. In the final analysis, neither intuitive insight nor discursive reasoning are very helpful, as the one, immediate insight, seems dogmatic, while the other, the dialectical exercise of reasoning, is never conclusive but proceeds on, at least potentially, to infinity. Does this mean doubt ultimately triumphs? It can do so only if there is no possibility of finding some way to encapsulate the infinitude of discursive differentiation into a truly integral, intuitive unity. Such a condition, however, can be fulfilled, Florensky maintains, in a Self-Proving Subject in Triunity. Thus, he concludes, if we wish to affirm the existence of truth, we must be equally disposed to co-affirm the existence of this Triune Subject as the necessary postulate of all truly grounded knowing.

However, to do even this we must initially make an act of faith in truth's existence, for we are free, after all, to go the way of absolute, systematic scepticism and imprison ourselves within the confines of our solipsistic egos, if we are so determined. But if we opt for truth, we must also let ourselves go the way of self-sacrificing love. The horizon of truth is ultimately only accessible to those who are already in the field of love. The search for Truth is equally a service of love directed toward the One who is Love itself. Truth is for man, the *whole* man, who accordingly must activate not only his intellect, but also his heart and will if he truly desires to open himself up to it.

With this affirmation, Florensky is ready to state his last thesis, namely, that truth is essentially antinomic. This problematic Florensky treats in his sixth letter, entitled simply "Contradiction."[1]

1.   THE KNOWLEDGE OF TRUTH

Florensky opens this letter treating the question of truth as an antinomy with a telling distinction between knowledge *of* Truth and knowledge *about* Truth.[2] Knowledge *of* Truth is perfect knowledge, knowledge in which a total grasp of content, in its full depth and plentitude, is obtained. It is a

[1]PFT, 143-65.
[2]PFT, 143.

knowledge which is at the same time a communion in love with this known Object, which simultaneously gives itself as Truth and Love. However, this knowledge is only imperfectly had in this world of space and time; only in eternity where space and time are transcended can it be fully verified. Our knowledge in this world is always conditioned by space and time and reflects our inherent finitude as beings composed of body and soul. From our standpoint, Florensky affirms, there is always a certain gap between our grasping of the form and content of Truth. But in eternity the two, the form and content of Truth, are identical, and with our *theosis,* that is, with our full participation in the divine, intratrinitarian life, our transfigured bodies can, in the luminosity of the Taboric Light,[3] the Light of Truth, enjoy a perfect, integral vision of this Truth, the Subject of all our longing and joy.

In our temporal world, on the other hand, the absolute unity of form and content given in knowledge *of* Truth is lost, and all that remains is a knowledge *about* Truth, which, as such, is necessarily limited, partial, and conditioned. This knowledge *about* Truth becomes what is simply known as truth. Thus along with Truth we find truth, the contrast of which is in reality nothing other than the contradistinction of God from His creation. And conversely, Florensky adds, the existence of creation is the very reason for affirming the existence of truth, and, at the same time, the reason for the search for the reasons justifying the existence of truth and, ultimately, for the Reason, which is Truth.

2. THE FACT OF TRUTH

Continuing in his argumentation, Florensky draws the conclusion that the "presence of truth is equivalent to the presence of creation."[4] And if this is so, and truth as such entails being and, more concretely, creation, the pivotal ques-

---

[3] An important key to Florensky's solution to the problem of truth is his appeal to the Taboric Light. This explains why Trubetskoy, in "Svet favorskii," most appropriately starts from this point in his illuminating critique of Florensky's thought.

[4] PFT, 143.

tion then changes, and we must now ask: Does creation itself exist?[5] Philosophically speaking, we cannot give an easy answer to this question, since, as Florensky notes, the existence of creation is neither deducible from the *idea* of Truth nor even from the *fact* of the existence of Truth, i.e., God.[6] Arguing thus against the acosmism of Spinoza and pantheism in general, Florensky stresses the fact that we cannot deduce the existence of creation through any reasoning whatsoever, and this being the case, draws still another important conclusion, namely, that in itself the "being of truth is *not deducible,* but can only be *manifested* in experience."[7]

The task of philosophy itself is accordingly determined. Philosophy must simply accept the fact of truth as a given, and only on this basis proceed on to explore, work out, and elucidate all the properties of truth. It can, however, still validly ask about the formal constitution of truth, and then move on to consider the matter or material content of truth, which ultimately means Truth itself. Indeed, for Florensky "truth is always truth about Truth,"[8] and contains, even if only symbolically, something of this Truth. Truth in the created order always bears the monogram of the Divinity, and even if it is only here and now, it points to the eternal. It may show the coloring only of the conditional, but what it depicts is, in truth, the Unconditional.[9] Created entities come and go, are born and die; men argue, people's opinions change from place to place, time to time, and person to person; but truth perdures. It is always and everywhere one and the same; never relative, it is essentially an *"unconditional formula."*[10]

3.   THE ANTINOMY OF TRUTH

3.1   *The Synthetic Judgment*

Since truth is a sign of Truth, and the affirmation of par-

[5]Ibid.
[6]PFT, 144.
[7]Ibid.
[8]PFT, 145.
[9]Ibid.
[10]Ibid.

tial truth a co-affirmation of total, unconditional Truth, a new question arises. "How is it possible," Florensky queries, "that we can construct an *unconditional* formula for Divine Truth from the *conditional* material of the human mind?"[11] In other words, how is it that man in his finitude and conditional existence can make a proper judgment concerning unconditional existence? What type of judgment enables him to acquire this unconditional knowledge? It cannot be given in the analytic judgment because, even if that provides a sure knowledge, it is only a judgment of formal identity which does not materially add to our knowledge. But, then, if the only alternative is the synthetic judgment, that is, the judgment in which the predicate really adds something new to the notion of the subject, what is it that can unconditionally guarantee the truth of the synthesis? Is not the synthetic judgment necessarily conditional, asks Florensky, insofar as it depends on the predicate? Could not another contrary, or even contradictory, synthesis conceivably be effected between the same subject and predicate? And if not at the present time, could it not be so in the future? In sum, what gives it an apodictic, over and above a mere assertory note?

To cite a case in point, Florensky draws our attention to the phenomenon of life.[12] How can we conceptualize in any one formula or judgment the fullness of this datum? Are not all our individual judgments concerning this phenomenon only partial determinations of its true breadth of meaning, conditioned according to the point of view from which they are made? It would thus seem that any particular, rational formulation of life would fully express its truth if and only if it could capture its fullness of signification. It would be fully truthful only once it could somehow contain within itself all the possible determinations of reason concerning it, and thereby overcome all possible objections of reason to it. In this view, truth is, accordingly, formally obtained in "that judgment containing within itself all its countermands."[13] Florensky paradoxically concludes, in other words, that truth,

[11]PFT, 146.
[12]PFT, 146f.
[13]PFT, 147.

at least formally speaking,[14] is simply a "self-contradictory judgment,"[15] that is, at least insofar as any full statement of it inevitably contains multiple affirmations that, in any given instant, seem irreconcilable, or at least mutually exclusive of one another.

3.2   Truth as Antinomic

Is this view on the self-contradictory character of truth coherent? An instinctive response would surely answer in the negative. However, if more than cursory consideration is given to the matter and some critical reflection is devoted to it, we see that Florensky has, in fact, articulated a profound insight concerning the nature of truth. The judgment of truth, by implicitly containing within itself all possible positive determinations and by responding to all potential objections, is truly a plentitude of synthesis, an all-inclusive "togetherness" of content, as it were. By its bewildering coalescence in any one moment of both affirmative and negative elements, that is, by its apparent, forthright self-contradictory character, it is, paradoxically, an essential affirmation in a fashion analogous to the state of affairs obtaining in apophatic theology where denials actually are symptomatic of cryptic affirmations.

Florensky affirms that it is by the confluence of both thesis and antithesis that the synthesis, truth, is reached. This confluence constitutes the antinomy of truth.[16] In other words, for Florensky, truth cannot be expressed except by antinomies. But, then, just what does he understand by the term, anti-

[14]This qualification, which in this particular passage Florensky only implicitly makes, is important. Truth is, formally speaking, a self-contradictory judgment, because, materially speaking, it is a *coincidentia oppositorum*.
[15]PFT, 147.
[16]Ibid. For brief but useful commentaries on this crucial point in Florensky's thought, cf. S. Obolensky, "La sophiologie et la mariologie de Paul Florensky," *Unitas*, 1, no. 3 (1946): 69f, and Paul Evdokimov, *Cristo nel pensiero russo* [Christ in Russian thought] (Rome: Città nuova editrice, 1972), 174. The remarks of Jacques-Albert Cuttat on antinomies in general are also very useful. See his *The Encounter of Religions* (New York: Desclée Co., 1960), 67.

nomy? The notion itself is equivocal. As used in philosophical discourse it may mean either the *apparent* contradiction between demonstrated propositions or the *real* contradiction between apparently demonstrated propositions. Florensky uses the term in the former sense. For him, an antinomy is an opposition whose terms remain incompatible in the logical order, but which find their resolution and, indeed, essential complementarity solely in the metalogical order. The opposition is such that it cannot be disentangled by discursive reasoning, nor is it accessible to intellectual intuition. So, then, how do we account for it? How do we ease its inherent tension so that we can judiciously subscribe to it?

3.3 The Self-Denial of Faith

Florensky's answer to the questions as to the "how" of antinomic assent is immediately forthcoming. It is by the vote of faith[17] and the self-sacrifice and moral effort necessarily implied and entailed therein that one transcends the inherent limitations of reason to affirm the antinomic character of truth, the antinomy of which would otherwise remain an affront to reason. In other words, Florensky affirms, to develop a knowledge of truth on the affirmative basis of antinomies demands the spiritual life in general and works of ascesis.[18] The principles of the natural order, the principles of identity, noncontradiction, and sufficient reason are, in themselves, sufficient to lead us to absolute, unconditional Truth, but they need the spiritual complement of the principle of living faith[19]

[17]At this point we see a certain confusion in Florensky. After designating truth in general as antinomic, when he tries to ground his position further, he seems to go immediately to religious experience and religious faith to find his justification. Thus, one may be left with the erroneous impression that only religious truth is antinomic. Bishop Feodor for one (see "Review," 165), seems to draw this restrictive conclusion. Florensky's doctrine, however, refers to *all* truth. The appeal to "faith" must, for this reason, be an analogous one, depending on the type of truth at stake. Otherwise, Florensky's position leaves us perplexed, and seems hopelessly incoherent. The fundamental, equivocal usage of "faith," characteristic of the Slavophiles, in thus not explicitly overcome by Florensky. Cf. pp. 57, 63, above.

[18]PFT, 147.

[19]Cf. ch. 4, sec. 2.3, pp. 128f above.

to accomplish their specific tasks and arrive at their proper ends, life in Truth.

3.4 The Twofold Character of Florensky's Antinomism

There is one further step to make in order to put the insight concerning the antinomic character of truth into full relief. There is a twofold root to the antinomy of truth. On the formal side, truth is antinomic because of the radical antinomism of human thought itself. The impulse of reason is to search for the unconditional, but its inherent capacities for intuition and discursion, as we have already seen, are limited, and only bring us to the threshold of the unconditional. To arrive at truth we must assiduously concert with reality and, with dialectical advance, progressively grasp its authentic nature. Florensky cites the Platonic philosophical corpus as an example, *par excellence,* of this type of antinomic endeavor. To him, Plato's dialogues are nothing but "dramatized antinomies."[20]

On the other hand, truth, materially speaking, is also antinomic in the sense that it is essentially multifaceted and potentially offers infinite aspects for our knowledge, which, in any given moment, may seem exclusive of one another. The mind, accordingly, can never know it in its fullness nor embrace its total reality. This view is felicitously expressed by the idea, introduced by Nicholas of Cusa and taken over by Florensky, that truth is a *coincidentia oppositorum.*[21]

4. THE ANTINOMIC CHARACTER OF DOGMA

If all particular truth is marked by antinomies, the truth of religion and religious experience must be all the more so. Religion essentially transcends human reason, and precisely for this reason it uses both verbal and nonverbal symbols, both myths and rites, evocative of higher realities and truths, as

[20]PFT, 156.
[21]PFT, 156f.

its language of communication in informing man of his true origins, meaning, and final end. In this sense, as Florensky notes, the mysteries of religion are by nature not given to adequate expression, and rightly remain as "indescribable *experiences* which cannot be expressed in words except through contradictions."[22] Indeed, Florensky declares: "Contradiction! It is the very mystery of the soul—the mystery of prayer and love."[23]

Florensky's deeply felt intuitions concerning the true nature of religious dogma notwithstanding, the requirements of conceptual clarity and terminological rigor demand that he be faulted for his poetic license and propensity for literary flourish. Specifically, we must question whether "contradiction" is the most felicitous choice of words. Florensky often, as in this instance, speaks as if "contradiction," "antinomy," and "coincidence of opposites" are interchangeable terms. Though related, they each denote different things, and should not be confused.[24] In the present context, "antinomy" would have been the better, more properly nuanced choice, even though it connotes the idea of contradiction. Florensky's appeal to "contradiction" may, indeed, more strikingly bring home his point, but it does so only at the price of a certain, conceptual deception and obfuscation.

The dogmas of faith are important in the eyes of Florensky because they stand midway between the one Truth which is in heaven and the multitude of truth found on earth, all "splinters of Truth."[25] Dogma, in the precise delineation of Florensky, is "an ideal limit-boundary where contradiction is annulled."[26] Insofar as reasoning is concerned, it serves as a formal, regulative norm, indeed, as its fundamental categorical imperative. But insofar as the mind or reason itself is concerned, it is a self-proving axiom, given in grace as the "sap of life."[27] Accordingly, dogma is the experienced truth of religious life, accorded to the mind purified by earnest

[22]PFT, 158.
[23]Ibid.
[24]Cf. Trubetskoy, "Svet favorskii," 36, for a similar criticism of Florensky.
[25]Ibid.
[26]PFT, 160. For the discussion which follows, cf. PFT, 160-65.
[27]PFT, 161.

prayer and ascetical practice. As expressive of life, however, it can never receive a perfect conceptual articulation, but must resign itself to the paradox of antinomies to express its plenitude of content. If not assented to in its antinomic wholeness, and if only a partial, unilateral aspect is emphasized, the inevitable consequence is the unfortunate caricature of the whole, exuding the mark of arbitrariness and entailing what is theologically known as heresy. Heresy, Florensky straightforwardly writes, is "a rational onesidedness, affirming itself as *everything*."[28]

The dogmas of faith, as Florensky underscores, are only grasped as true under the impulse of the Holy Spirit, in whom alone we can acquire a fullness of dogmatic understanding.[29] It is the Holy Spirit who grants us the necessary theological insight, which permits us to consider our religious experience in rational terms, that is, in the terms of antinomies, which are no less than the "constitutive elements of religion"[30] itself. Indeed, Florensky bluntly states: "Where there are no antinomies, there there is no faith."[31] Religious experience, dealing as it does with the suprarational and meta-empirical, cannot manifest itself except under the "sign of contradiction" and dogmatic antinomy. It is the experience of the *coincidentia oppositorum*, experience governed according to the principle of faith and finding its best, if not only, conceptual expression in the religious dialectic of dogma. Examples of these dogmas include the affirmation of Three Persons in One Godhead, two natures, the human and the divine, in one Christ, predestination and free will, faith as free response and gift of God, etc.[32]

[28]PFT, 161. Cf. also 690f (n. 241).
[29]PFT, 162.
[30]PFT, 163.
[31]Ibid.
[32]PFT, 164f. A necessary word of caution must be given about the use of antinomies to solve the difficulties of dogmatic experience. There is an attendant danger that they may be employed artificially, and may, therefore, tend to deceive, rather than really edify us. Nicholas Lossky, in our opinion, rightly scolds Florensky precisely on this score in his attempted antinomic resolution of the problems confronting our faith in regard to the last judgment and our fate either to eternal bliss or eternal damnation. Cf. Lossky, *History of Russian Philosophy*, 190, and PFT, 205-59. We shall return to this

The man of rationalistic proclivity, of course, will not be satisfied with the antinomic resolution of the seemingly contradictory multidimensionality and pluriformality of religious experience.[33] If he gives rein to this tendency and accepts reason as his only ultimate norm of truth and allows reasoning to be his sole cognitive tool, he must necessarily dismiss religious experience as, at best, capricious. But having thus lost the only possible source for ultimate truth, the ineluctable consequence for him is an ironic, ultimate distrust, and even cynical despisal, of his own very reason. On the other hand, the man of faith, the man who allows the light of faith to be his surest guide to truth, not only perceives the truth of his religious belief in his lived experience, but he also gains new respect for his own reason, which, in its very antinomic constitution, brings him to the threshold of the Divine, to that Door, the passing through which effects his full entrance into divine life.

5. A WORD IN TRANSITION

Near the outset[34] of his investigative journey in the search of the ultimate foundations of truth and certitude, Florensky notes Pilate's infamous question to Christ: What is truth?[35] Of course, the fact that Truth Himself was before him did not occur to Pilate, who had already resigned himself to despair at ever finding real, incontrovertible truth. Pilate, however, was only a man of his time. And his time was, indeed, one of social disintegration and the loss of meanings and values.

In this respect, possibly pre-revolutionary Russia—and,

point below (cf. pp. 162f). Zenkovsky, *Istoriya*, 2:420 (Eng. ed., 881), for his part says Florensky in general relies too much on the antinomies of thought.

[33]For a contemporary Marxist view of this aspect of Christian thought, cf. M. P. Novikov, "Antinomizm kak apologeticheskii printsip" [Antinomism as an apologetical principle] in *Krizis sovremennoi khristianskoi apologetiki* [The crisis of contemporary Christian apologetics] (Series: Nauchnyj ateizm, no. 12 [1981] (Moscow: Izdatel'stvo "Znanie," 1981), pp. 50-54.

[34]PFT, 23.

[35]Cf. Jn 18:38.

we may add, our own times—have much in common with Pilate's era. For this reason, it is not surprising that a man of intellectual inquietude and spiritual unrest like Florensky should have indefatigably devoted himself to the search of truth and, indeed, Truth itself. He, of course, discovered both the one and the other, or, at least, revived what he always knew—that no truth is really possible without that Truth which is the Lord and Savior Himself.

In the process of his investigation, Florensky gives new meaning to the concept of truth itself. Embracing the message of the Fourth Gospel, which declares Christ is the Truth, Florensky tries to lay bare the philosophical underpinnings of the Christian experience of this "truth which makes us free" (see Jn 8:32). Reason's own exigence of a Self-Proving Subject to be its ultimate foundation and justification in a peerless manner serves to auspicate our initiation into Christian truth and its central Truth who is Christ. It is this Christ who, by His very person, transforms the very meaning of truth for us. No longer can it be mere "doctrine," but is essentially a *person*. The immediate consequence of this radically new view is evident. To know truth one cannot content oneself with intellectual exercise, but must rather immerse oneself into the *life* of truth.

That Florensky claims that man must ultimately entrust himself to Truth in order to establish a vital contact with Truth and enjoy a vision of It, however, does not mean that he lapses into fideism. To the contrary, Florensky fully upholds the claims of natural reason to know objective truth. He would only add that a full experience of truth is possible only to the man who loves. Because we are certain of the truth of our particular knowledges, we can, Florensky insists, rest assured of the existence of an Ultimate Foundation of Truth. But this Truth must be more than just known; it must be loved.

For Florensky, in other words, truth ultimately is not merely the object of "communication," but is also a fruit of *communion*. It is with his proffered metaphysics of consubstantiality and love that he tries to give philosophical articulation to this primordial evangelical insight. He therein indicates that the problem of truth necessarily has for its other side the problem of love. Indeed, the "truth that liberates" is one and the same thing as the power of love of that God who is Hypostatic Love. Florensky's well-chosen epigraph for his *magnum opus,* "knowledge which becomes love," a citation from St. Gregory of Nyssa, beautifully expresses this truth. For Florensky, an indefatigable devotion to truth ultimately manifests itself as a vocation of love.[36] Man inexorably searches for truth, and if he comes close to his coveted goal, it is only through the experience of love and an at least implicit awareness of the God of Love, necessarily implicated in all love. And last, if man wants a fully explicit awareness of this Love, he is necessarily drawn to the Church, his proper mainstay and the place where God deigns to encounter His people.

[36]This affirmation should not lead us to conclude that Florensky would totally *identify* knowledge and love. He makes no statement denying that evil persons can still truly know even though they may have no real interest in truth, and may, indeed, be devoid of love. This is above all the case in the instance of devils, who both know and radically hate at the same time. Cf. Jas 2:19. But it still remains true that a *full* knowledge of Truth is also perfective, and necessarily an experience of love.

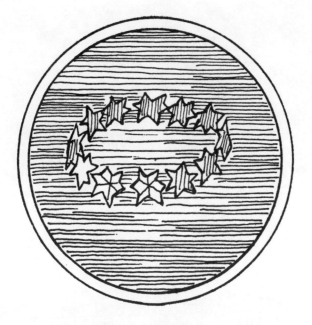

Pignus amoris   (The Pledge of Love)

Part Three

TOWARDS A METAPHYSICS OF LOVE

CHAPTER VI

Man at the Crossroads

The problematic concerning truth and love becomes, for Florensky, none other than the battle for man himself, and more specifically, for his heart. Man is either divided within the intimacy of his heart and then conquered by sin, or is fully integrated within himself and genuinely in harmony with the whole of creation. Philosophically, Florensky expresses this conflict in terms of the drama of self-identity. Man either contents himself with an immobile, empty self-identity of a mere "A is A" or grounds himself in the dynamic self-identity of an "A" which cannot be itself apart from its other. The one occasions the hell of willful self-abandon into solitary confinement; the other the bliss of interpersonal enrichment and mutual sustenance.

1. The Negative Turn: Sin and Gehenna

Florensky begins his account of sin[1] by drawing attention to the familiar morality tale, "Hercules at the Crossroads," in which virtue and vice are personified, and each is seen currying Hercules' favor, and vying for his undivided attention. This fable becomes, Florensky claims, Everyman's true life story, in which he must either follow the road to truth and moral virtue or the downtrodden path of lies and sin.[2]

[1]Cf. his seventh letter, "Sin," PFT, 166-204.
[2]PFT, 166ff.

But the speculative problem that immediately presents itself to Florensky is how this division can exist at all. If God is the Supreme Existent, He Who Is, how is it that there is also sin? One can understand why if God exists, so also do life, virtue, and holiness, all of them being participations in divine life. But the existence of sin and death seems irreconcilable with the existence of a Godhead who is, by definition, both Life itself and the Good. The only plausible conclusion seems to be that even if sin and death *are*, they are not existents. But is this a coherent position? Are we really before an ultimately inexplicable paradox or merely caught in the web of conceptual befuddlement?

1.1 *The Meaphysical Nature of Sin*

To resolve his self-posed dilemma concerning the paradoxical "non-existent reality" of sin, Florensky pursues an ulterior metaphysical reflection on the nature of sin. Florensky opens his discussion[3] of this metaphysical problem placing it in the context of the definition of sin given in 1 Jn 3:4, where we read: "sin is the transgression of the law." Though it may seem, at first, to suggest a purely juridical notion of sin, Florensky stresses that this particular view is a grave misinterpretation of its deepest meaning, since this Johannine definition rather evokes a profoundly ontological understanding of the nature of sin. Indeed, it treats sin in its very essence. "Sin," Florensky writes, "is Lawlessness; it is the perversion of the Law, i.e., of that Order, which is given to creation by the Lord, of that inner Array of the created order, by which it is alive, of that Ordering at the bosom of creation, which is bestowed it by God, of that Wisdom, in which the meaning of the world is found."[4] Florensky adds in an acknowledged, liberal appeal to the Pauline idea that sin is known only through the law (cf. Rom 7:7), that outside of Law sin enjoys only imaginary existence.[5]

[3]PFT, 168.
[4]PFT, 170.
[5]Ibid.

The most apt analogy for conveying this insight Florensky finds in the biological sphere. Sin is a parasite.[6] Like all other evils it exists only insofar as there is a host good to serve as its victim. Just as there is no death if there is no life, and just as there is no darkness if there is no light, so also in the case of sin we find a phenomenon with only a secondary, derivative existence. Sin thrives only on holiness. And once it kills its host, Florensky adds, it can only turn on itself and begin to devour itself. In this manner, he concludes, sin destroys itself.

What this imagery conveys is in fact the same truth put forth in the traditional, Christian understanding of evil as a privation. On the one hand, this teaching does not minimize the tragic reality of evil in life, while on the other it does not attribute an autonomous existence to evil, which would entail its being willed and created by God. Evil has no positive being of its own, but only pretensions to being. It scoffs at being at the same time that it draws its staple sustenance from it.

1.2 Sin and Self-Identity

If Florensky's chosen imagery succeeds in illustrating the parasitic character of evil and of sin in particular, it also intimates another point essential to the understanding of the nature of sin. Sin is a forthright affirmation and proclamation of the "I's" independence from all others and all outside influences. It is a bold and spiteful protest that "I" alone exist and that "I" alone count. This, Florensky affirms,[7] is the essentially egoistic attitude heralded by the stance of empty identity in contrast to that of dynamic identity predicated on interreaction with the other than "I," that is, of a self-identity constituted by the Other, by a Thou. The one is indicative of inorganic independence and absolute autonomy; the other is solicitous for an organic interdependence, and is subject to heteronomy. The former stance, which pretends to exalt

[6]Ibid.
[7]PFT, 177f.

individuality, turns out to be the impetus favoring its self-destruction, while the latter, which at first appears to sacrifice selfhood to otherness, is rather that stance radically serving to strengthen it.

In this vein Florensky pointedly writes: "The self-affirmation of personality in its contraposition to God is the source of dismemberment and decay of personality and the impoverishment of its internal life."[8] The only way to counteract this, he immediately adds, is through love which alone conducts personality back to its primeval unity.[9] Sin, in this perspective, is essentially an experience of the want of love. It is a "moment of disturbance, distintegration, and collapse of the spiritual life"[10] in which the "soul *loses* its substantial unity, *loses* the consciousness of its creative nature, and *is lost* in the chaotic whirlwind of its own states, having ceased being the substance of them."[11] It is such a decay of personality, Florensky interjects, that ultimately leads to insanity.[12] It is a disintegration necessarily implied in any negation of the existence of God. Justifying this position further, Florensky notes that this frightful, existential consequence of the refusal to believe in God has been artistically captured in the works of Lev Tolstoy and Feodor Dostoevsky.[13] As a case in point, one can immediately cite the madness of a Kirillov, a character in *The Possessed* who ends his life in suicide for metaphysical reasons—in order drastically to prove his absolute autonomy from God.

The sole antidote to this type of tragic disintegration of personality, Florensky rejoins, is love. Love is that force which gives internal consistency to personality. It is a force, however, that cannot be self-contained. It bespeaks only an "I"

[8]PFT, 173.
[9]Ibid.
[10]PFT, 174.
[11]Ibid. However, we must also object to Florensky's imputation of personality disintegration to all the subjects of Leonardo da Vinci's portraits. His remarks seem particularly out of place.
[12]In this matter, Florensky also seems extremist in his point of view. Other factors above and beyond moral considerations, for instance, certain pathological disturbances, can also account for the genesis of insanity.
[13]PFT, 173, 696. He specifically draws attention to Tolstoy's *Confession* and Dostoevsky's *The Brothers Karamazov*.

in relation to others and the Other, and which gains its identity solely from them in love. A solitary "I" outside of the orbit of love, on the other hand, having lost its only possible source for internal consistency, cannot but begin to disintegrate. The "I's" refusal to love is indeed, to Florensky's mind, the true, incipient, and progressive cause of a personality's disintegration. It is the true essence of sin. Love, especially love of God, on the other hand, is nothing other than the personality's true moment of integration, vivification, and fortification. It is, in fine, the true "bond of personality."[14]

There is an additional application of this teaching on sin and personality disintegration that Florensky makes in his letter on sin. The "I" with empty identity, the "I" bearing the seal of sin, not only rejects love and denies itself the fruits of love as given in interpersonal communion, but also loses the ultimate truth. As Florensky writes, "sin is that which deprives the possibility of *foundation* and, consequently, of *explanation*, i.e., of intelligibility."[15] This is so because sin, as a prime promoter of the solipsism of the ego, necessarily loosens the ties that the knowing subject has with objective reality independent of his own existence. Sin, accordingly, only serves to disseminate a subjectivistic, hence relativistic, interpretation of truth as something strictly dependent on the knowing subject. Only love can counter this stance. It alone sustains the position that the real foundations of truth and its real sources of intelligibility lie outside the knowing subject. From its standpoint, the knower is an integral part of a greater, objective whole, and is annealed in truth only by objective reality. To foster knowledge of objective truth in this perspective, therefore, means that the personality's bonds with reality must be strengthened. This is one of love's essential tasks. Sin, on the other hand, abhors objective ties and aims only at dissolving the existing ties between the knower and known reality. Thus, it deprives the ego of communion not only with other personalities, but also with truth, which requires an essentially open and searching attitude on the part of the knower for it to disclose itself to him. The primi-

[14]PFT, 173.
[15]PFT, 179.

tive Slavic consciousness, in Florensky's view, was thus inspired by a profound intuition when it conceptually and
linguistically linked the notions "to sin" and "to err"
together.[16] Indeed, in a truly insidious and consequential way,
sin is, *par excellence*, "the principle of unreasonableness, of
incomprehensibility, and of an obtuse and desparate blockage
of intellectual contemplation."[17]

1.3 *The Mystery of Gehenna*

At the heart of evil is a twofold denial. First, dynamic
identity is rejected in favor of static, solipsistic identity.
Second, it also necessarily entails a clear, even if hopeless,
refusal of consubstantiality. If the refusal to love or the disclaiming of dynamic identity is, as we have seen, of the
essence of sin, so also is the repudiation of consubstantiality
in its turn.[18]

Having thus delineated the metaphysical nature of sin,
Florensky sets the stage for a subsequent reflection on the
bearing of sin for man's anthropological structure and his
ultimate fate. At this juncture, he notes the crucial, classical
distinction between the person (*lichnost'*)[19] and its "empirical
character."[20] With this distinction, he hopes to plot out an
acceptable resolution to the momentous antinomy of how the
love of God can sustain, let alone be reconciled with, the
eternal torment of the reprobate in the fires of hell or
Gehenna. Before the baneful prospects of perpetual punish-
ment he shudders, and becomes truly anxious for a more

[16]See ch. 3, sec. 2.5, p. 107 above for previous discussion of this point.
[17]PFT, 179. Cf. also our p. 107 above.
[18]PFT, 213. Elchaninov repeats this idea of Florensky in his *Zapisi*
where he notes that sin is a loss of consubstantiality (p. 103). Cf. also
the analogous remarks of Dumitru Staniloae, *Theology and the Church*
(Crestwood, NY: St. Vladimir's Seminary Press, 1980), 84f.
[19]*Lichnost'* is an equivocal word in Russian just as its equivalents in
other languages frequently are. It can mean both "person" and "personality,"
depending on the circumstances of usage. Their difference in meaning is
notable. The one refers to an ontological notion, the other to a qualitative
one. Florensky's term "empirical character" refers to the latter, qualitative
meaning of *lichnost'*, i.e., to "personality."
[20]PFT, 212.

happy, ultimate end to the life of even the most wretched of sinners.

Florensky's distinction resounds with the truth contained in the traditional, biblical and patristic distinction between the *imago Dei* (*obraz Bozhii*) and the *similitudo Dei* (*podobie Bozhie*). The former indicates the created human being in its ontological dimension of personhood, while the latter points to the human personality as the realization of the *idea* of person, as the actuation of the *imago Dei*. Florensky's distinction is essentially the same, although he gives a variant rendition of the notion "personality" (*similitudo Dei*) with his term "empirical character." He writes:

> The person (*lichnost'*) created by God—and thus, holy and absolutely valuable in its inner core—has a *free creative will*, which manifests itself as a system of acts, i.e., as an empirical *character*. The person (*lichnost'*) in this sense[21] is a character.[22]

The ontological dignity of man as an image of God is founded upon the fact that man possesses freedom of will, that he is a free, creative agent. Endowed with freedom, man has the potency for patterning his own life according to his own designs. He can make himself his own "project." Though a person signed by sin, he can so activate his freedom as to promote the good and foster his own personal development in holiness in collaboration with divine grace. He can thus offer himself back to God as a transfigured vessel of divine life. This, Florensky says, is the meaning of the parable of the talents (see Mt 25:14-30; Lk 19:11-27), when translated into ontological language.[23]

The internal battle waged within each person between virtue and vice constitutes the real drama in life. Man as a person is called upon to choose sides and to opt for an orientation either "of oneself" (*o sebe*) or "for oneself" (*dlya sebya*).[24] The former stance indicates a decision to renew

---

[21]That is, meaning *lichnost'* in the sense of "personality."
[22]PFT, 212.
[23]PFT, 214.
[24]PFT, 212. This choice of orientation is, for Florensky, more radically

and strengthen existing ties with being and its coextensive truth and goodness as grounded in dynamic identity and a consciously lived consubstantiality with the Other. The second option expresses the sentiments of an egoistic self in pursuit of sublime autonomy and impassibility and callous indifference towards other. Not nourished and succored by the Other, it is also uprooted from being. It is a truly substance-less existence,[25] the mere, empty shell of a real life.[26] In sum, the evil self rejects consubstantiality and, like the parasite that kills its host, ironically consumes itself in its own idolatry of self.

Florensky thus draws a distinction between the person himself and his evil, substance-less self,[27] between man himself and his works.[28] Basing himself on it, he subsequently attempts to articulate a defense of what he considers a dogmatically acceptable theory of universal salavation or *apokatastasis*.[29] On Judgment Day, which he calls a day of "universal operation,"[30] a necessary, salvific surgery will be performed on all men in which each person will be separated from his evil self. The person will thus be saved and live on in eternal bliss. The evil self in its turn will be cast into the fires of Gehenna.

This thesis, however, is inadmissable, and in no way overcomes the deficiencies of like theories fashioned by the Origenists and condemned by the Provincial Synod of Constantinople held in 543, whose decisions were approved by Pope Vigilius.[31] Its principal defect lies in its contention that the human person can be divided into two selves, his "real, personal self" and his only "apparent self," the evil self

grounded in the division of man into his selfhood and his evil, substance-less self. Cf. the discussion to follow in the next paragraph.

[25]Ibid.
[26]PFT, 219.
[27]PFT, 212.
[28]PFT, 230. Florensky bases this latter distinction on his reading of 1 Cor 3:10-15, from which he tries to draw support for his thesis on the universal salvation of all men (*apokatastasis*). His exegtical, or rather eisegetical, application of this text, however, is unsustainable.
[29]Cf. esp. PFT, 222, 233f, 237f, 254f.
[30]PFT, 222.
[31]Denzinger-Schönmetzer, *Enchiridion*, 411. Cf. also Cándido Pozo, *Teologia dell'aldilà* [Theology of the hereafter] (Rome: Edizioni Paoline, 1970), 256f.

that is amputated and consigned to eternal torment. But, as Nicholas Lossky has forcibly stressed,[32] this is a metaphysically absurd position which only makes two persons out of one. For the evil self genuinely to experience torment, it would have to be a person in its own right, one conscious of its experiences. F.I. Udelov thus is most certainly correct in his scoring Florensky for trying to dissolve what must remain an inexplicable antinomy—the mystery of the Last Judgment.[33]

Florensky also commits another error. Although he correctly notes that even upon man's original fall into sin, the image of God in man was never completely effaced, a dogmatic point vehemently negated in traditional, orthodox Lutheranism, he mistakenly interprets the Catholic view of man's personal sanctification and justification. He claims that the process of purification as expounded in Catholic teaching concerns only the level of outward appearances, and does not consider man in his inward self. Only Orthodox teaching, in his view, would appear to maintain that man is truly divinized at his very inner core.[34] This is an obvious failure to appreciate the true meaning and import contained in the Catholic dogma concerning "created grace," which is viewed as a necessary, correlative effect of Uncreated Grace, the gift of God Himself in His very energies to man. It renders man an ontologically sanctified being, truly divinized to the core of his being.[35] This teaching, though marked by a shift of emphasis from uncreated to created grace, is nonetheless in full accord with the Orthodox point of view maintained by Florensky, on the engraced as true "partakers of the divine nature" (2 Pet 1:4).

---

[32]*History of Russian Philosophy*, 190.
[33]Udelov, *Ob. o Pavle Florenskom*, 87. He also correctly notes that Florensky, in spite of his efforts to distance himself from Origenism, falls into Origenism in his eighth letter, devoted to the mystery of Gehenna (see p. 89).
[34]PFT, 254.
[35]Cf., e.g., the Tridentine teaching of Denzinger-Schönmetzer, *Enchiridion*, 1528.

2. The Positive Option: The Path of Righteousness

In his analysis of sin, Florensky attempts to isolate the exact, metaphysical nature of sin. He claims that as a negative phenomenon it is marked by a twofold rejection: the negation of dynamic identity and the refusal of consubstantiality. It is a denial, he concludes, that immediately leads to subjectivism and ultimately only to total solipsism. Solipsistic subjectivity fortunately is not man's ineluctable fate. A negative choice against the Other-than-self for the self alone is within man's options, but so is the positive vote for the objective over and against oneself. This latter option is not a denial of self nor a diminishing of self-esteem, but rather an enigmatical receiving of self through the constituting activity of the Other. Such a self is only itself in dynamic interaction with its Other. It is uniquely founded on a relation of dynamic identity, and abhors the vacuum of immobile, empty identity.

2.1 Ascetical Feat

But what can be said of this objective order constitutive of the person in dynamic identity? The objectivity at stake, Florensky simply and directly states, is the "creature made by God."[36] He immediately adds however: "To live and feel along with each creature, not with that creature corrupted by man, but with that which has issued forth from the hands of its Creator; to discern in this creature another, higher nature; to grasp the pure kernel of divine creation through the bark of sin . . . But to say this is just as well to state the need for a restored, i.e. spiritual, personality."[37] In other words, if it is sin that makes us insensate and impassible before created reality, that closes us off from it, then it is only its contrary, virtue, both moral and intellectual, as a true *habitus* acquired through ascetical, moral, and intellectual exploit and struggle, that disposes us to see it and consciously commune with it.

This particular teaching of Florensky on the central im-

[36]PFT, 263.
[37]Ibid.

portance of ascesis in the maintenance and promotion of man's self-identity is intelligible and defensible only on the supposition that between man and reality there is indeed a dynamic, all-embracing unity. In this respect, the heritage of Soloviev's conception of integral knowledge[38] is clearly felt in Florensky. Florensky affirms that with his body man enjoys a "common boundary"[39] with, and indeed is tied in with, the rest of creation. He adds that this "tie is so intimate that the destiny of man and the destiny of all creation are indissoluble."[40]

In this perspective, the heart of man, the center of the unified being that is man, also becomes in some sense the true centering point of the universe, and its purification, which is a necessary condition for communion with God, and which is the usual access to divine love and illumination, likewise becomes the normal channel through which or means by which the love and light of God pass in order to reach the rest of creation and make it shine in splendor. In the words of Florensky, "the light of divine love, diffusing itself, as it were, in the whole person and permeating it, also illuminates the body, which circumscribes the person, from where it proceeds to irradiate the natural order external to the person."[41] It is from this point that Florensky would part in framing the problematic concerning the traditional, Byzantine teaching on the cosmic dimensions of salvation as fully articulated by St. Maximus the Confessor.

Florensky makes one other anthropological reflection in the general context of his discussion that merits attention. It concerns biological homotypy.[42] Homotypy, as Florensky understands it, is the symmetry that obtains between the upper and lower parts of the body, and whose point of focus is the middle part of man. It is an apparent consequence of man's substantial unity as a person. The biological aspects of homotypy—especially as set forth in his appendix on the subject— aside, it is rather his application of it in differentiating the various tendencies in mysticism that is of specific concern.

[38]Cf. pp. 59-62, esp. p. 62 above.
[39]PFT, 271.
[40]PFT, 272.
[41]PFT, 271.
[42]PFT, 266ff, 587-92.

Noting that the natural division of the body pivots around the head, breast, and stomach, which are in turn the symbolic centers of the various dimensions of man's life—the conscious, the emotive, and the nutritive and reproductive—, Florensky then adduces this division as the explanation behind the divergent types of mysticism, which he classifies as mysticism of the head, the breast, and the stomach.[43] According to him, mysticism of the head is especially characteristic of the Hindu religion and its yogic experience, while mysticism of the stomach is typical of orgiastic cults and partly of Catholicism. The truest form of mysticism, ecclesial mysticism, on the other hand, is mysticism of the breast, the characteristic mysticism of Orthodoxy.

Two observations seem, above all, in order. First, Florensky's categorization of the types of mystical experience seems rather artificial and forced. Though this is not the place to pursue a phenomenology of mystical experience, a more convincing division would seem to be one that distinguishes ecstatic, enstatic, and theist mysticism, along the lines of the soul's specific focus of interest, whether it emphasizes movement "out of the self," "into the self" or "towards God."[44] Florensky seems only to have a preconceived schema into which he tries to fit the data of mystical experience in a manner befitting Procrustes.

Second, Florensky's characterization of Catholic mysticism is especially gratuitous. Indeed, it earned him the swift and stern rebuke of Nicholas Berdyaev, who held St. Francis of Assisi in very special esteem.[45]

2.2 The Postulate of Science

A true feeling for nature, Florensky affirms, can only be born in adherents of consubstantiality.[46] It is an attitude of humility on the part of the creature before its Creator and the whole created order. It is an attitudinal stance in which,

[43]PFT, 267, 273.
[44]Cf. Mariasusai Dhavamony, *Phenomenology of Religion* (Rome: Università Gregoriana Editrice, 1973), 268-87, esp. 284ff.
[45]"Stilizovannoe pravoslavie," 115.
[46]PFT, 288.

Florensky further notes, we can find the two feelings or ideas that undergird the possibility of the rise of science, the first being the unified regularity of creation, the second, its authentic reality.[47]

Theologically speaking, Florensky says these two postulates of science in their turn presuppose two foundational, yet antinomical, dogmas. Creation's unified regularity is predicated upon a belief in the Providence of one Godhead, not many, while its basic, independent reality supports a credence in the dogma of creation. If Divine Providence wills an orderly universe, its actual creation by God must, nonetheless, allow for the creature's free and independent existence. Taken together, these two dogmas synthetically express nothing more than the dogma of divine love for creation. It is solely in the Godhead who is Love, in His divine idea of it, that each creature has its truest foundations. For Florensky, in fine, it is uniquely the dogma of Triunity, i.e., of a Triune Godhead of Love, that founds the possibility not only of philosophy but also of all science.[48] He further writes: "God loves His creature and agonizes for it, agonizes with its sin. God extends His hands to His creature, entreats it, calls it, waits for the return of the prodigal son to Himself."[49]

If all of God's directives and actions towards His creatures are guided by love, the response of the creature must also be one formed only by love. It is, as we have seen, the proper task of ascesis to guarantee such a pure response in love. But it also has a superabundant effect in the soul of the ascetic, since it opens the eyes of his mind to true intelligibilities and to the true objectivity of the created order. The very ascetical discipline and exercise that brought him to love his Creator as his unconditional root in being also brings him to a new and heightened awareness of all of creation. It is this new cognizance that raises a new question for him, that of his next letter, the question about Sophia.[50]

[47]PFT, 278.
[48]PFT, 278f.
[49]PFT, 289f. Whitehead also is incisive on this point. In *Process and Reality* (p. 351), he writes: "God is the great companion—the fellow sufferer who understands."
[50] PFT, 318.

CHAPTER VII

Sophiology: An Exigence of Human Thought and Experience

Having examined the question of the bridge giving the creature access to its Unconditional Root, Florensky concludes his ninth letter, stating that there is an equal need to elaborate upon the nature of the creature, or creation, itself.[1] If ascesis serves as the connective between the creature and his Creator, it is still no less, Florensky adds, his vinculum with the rest of creation. Ascetical practice helps the creature overcome its egoism and empty identity, and in this fashion enables it truly to center its life in the objective, created order, which enjoys an importance in itself as an independent creation of the same Godhead.

All of creation, all creatures and created realities, no matter what their place in the hierarchy of being, are expressions of the Wisdom of God. They are willed actualizations of His Divine Wisdom. To understand the meaning of creation and individual creatures in themselves, therefore, means no less than to probe the secrets of Divine Wisdom. Of course, this probing must needs be only inadequate and merely approaching a full *prise de conscience,* since the object of scrutiny, in fine, is none other than the essence, or rather super-essence, of God Himself, whose very nature, nay, supernature, is Wisdom and Love.

Florensky gives us a unique insight into his views on

[1]PFT, 318.

Divine Wisdom, the Holy Sophia, on a more popular level in the course of eulogizing his friend, Feodor Dmitrievich Samarin (†1916), who had, in a letter dated June 29, 1912, heartily thanked him for making the Divine Office to Holy Sophia, the Divine Wisdom, available in printed format,[2] and thereby confirming him in his own conviction that the idea of Holy Sophia was not the mere invention of philosophical contemplation, but rather the fruit of living religious consciousness.[3] Commentating on this letter of five years previous, Florensky observes that the idea of Holy Sophia, indeed, "determines Russian religious consciousness in its very sources, and in it is precisely the deepest foundation of its originality."[4] He even goes so far as to state elsewhere, in one of his own letters to Samarin, that "Russia" and "Russian" without Sophia are contradictions in terms.[5] In the same connection, he further remarks that to his mind all contemporary philosophical and theological problems both flow from and return to the problem of Sophia.[6] No one has managed better than Zenkovsky to capture the essence of these latter sentiments of Florensky. In his *History of Russian Philosophy*, he most properly describes sophiology as "an organic synthesis of cosmology, anthropology, and theology."[7]

As an all-embracing problematic, however, sophiology has always seemed an intimidating topic, and has lent itself to facile criticism. Indeed, the word itself has easily conjured up thoughts of the bizzare, and has readily excited fears of

[2]TM, 1, no. 2 (1912): 1-23.
[3]Pavel Florensky, "Pamyati Feodora Dmitrievicha Samarina" [To the memory of Feodor Dmitrievich Samarin] (Sergiev Posad, 1917), 14. Also published in TM 1, no. 4 (1917): 464-77. Cf. also "Perepiska F. D. Samarina i P. A. Florenskogo" (The correspondence of F. D. Samarin and P. A. Florensky), *Vestnik*, 125 (1978): 251-71, in particular, p. 256.
[4]"Pamyati," 14, and "Perepiska," 257.
[5]Cf. his letter to Samarin dated August 1, 1912; "Perepiska," 259.
[6]Cf. Florensky's remarks quoted in "Perepiska," 255. In the present context, we are primarily concerned with the philosophic problematic associated with sophiology. A full sophiological treatise, on the other hand, would have to include a discussion of a host of other theological issues, both exegetical and speculative, not treated here. In particular, detailed exegeses of those passages in Sacred Scripture where the divine attribute of Wisdom is personified (e.g., Prov 1:20-33, 8:1-36, 9:1-6; Sir 24:1-22) would have to be pursued.
[7]*Istoriya*, 2:411 (Eng. ed., 871).

Gnosticism and ill-defined theosophy. Sophiologists themselves have surely been partly to blame. Their penchant for unusual and daring vocabulary and for broad characterizations of their material certainly has not always favored the understanding of others. Florensky's aestheticism and unconventional manner of presentation of his ideas have also been handicaps that have effectively alienated many a potentially sympathetic reader.[8] Unfortunately, the real contributions Florensky has had to offer have been overlooked due to these premature estrangements. Our task is thus clear: to enter into Florensky's thought and to attempt an equilibrious exposition of his sophiological views.

1. THE EXPERIENTIAL BEGINNINGS OF
SOPHIOLOGICAL SPECULATION

1.1 *Florensky's Chosen Point of Departure*

Florensky opens his tenth letter on Holy Sophia with an observation and reflection on the beauty of a personality steeped in spirituality. It radiates a twofold spendor, being at once both objectively and subjectively beautiful.[9] The holy person, the saintly personality, is objectively beautiful insofar as it is the object or focus of the admiration and contemplation of others who come into contact with it. It is subjectively beautiful because it possesses a purified heart that opens it up to expanded horizons, thereby enabling it to have a more privileged and commanding vision of reality. Thus, the saint, beautiful twice over, is a very special object for our contemplation. By contemplating the life and deeds of a saint, our contact with the primordial beauty of original creation is restored indeed. Further, in this act of contemplation, we genuinely and profoundly enjoy an experience of ecclesiality (*tserkovnost'*). As Florensky writes: "Ecclesiality is the beauty

[8]Cf. e.g., S. Tyszkiewicz, S.J., "Réflexions du théologian russe moderniste Paul Florensky sur l'Eglise," *Gregorianum*, 15 (1934): 255-61, whose critical judgment would be shared, at least in part, by Orthodox like Florovsky.
[9]PFT, 321.

of a new life in Absolute Beauty, in the Holy Spirit."[10] It is this experience that gives rise, at once, to a reflection and a question: "How are we to understand this holy and beautiful moment of the creature? What is its objective nature? What is it metaphysically?"[11]

1.2 *The Logos of Creation*

To embark upon an answer to these questions, Florensky repeats the fundamental idea conveyed in his previous letter on creation, namely, that it is preeminently the ascetic who enjoys a perception of the eternal roots of creation as embedded in God.[12] It is he who, in contemplating the eternal value of creation, in deciphering its internal necessity, is uniquely adept at perceiving the *raison d'être* of a creature, the *logos* of its objective being. The creature's logos accordingly is only secondary, insofar as it is derived from a primary reason in the Absolute Mind, and basks in the Light of Truth. Thus, Florensky affirms, "the reason of a thing is, from the point of view of the creature, that act by means of which the creature relinquishes itself, goes out from itself, and by means of which it finds its affirmation in God."[13] Otherwise expressed, "the reason of a thing, from the creature's point of view, is love for God, whence its vision of God and its particular idea of him—a *relative idea of the Absolute.*"[14] The divine counterpart to the reason of the creature, on the other hand, is an "*absolute idea of the relative,* the idea of God of a particular thing."[15] It is, in other words, "that act by which God, in an ineffable self-effacement of His infinity and absoluteness, together with the divine content of His divine thought, *deigns* to think about the finite and limited, to carry the scanty, semi-being of the creature into the fullness of the being of Trinitarian intimacy, and to confer it an autonomous

[10]Ibid.
[11]Ibid.
[12]PFT, 323.
[13]Ibid.
[14]Ibid.
[15]Ibid.

existence and self-determination, i.e., as if to establish the creature on the same level as Himself."[16] Or, more concisely yet, Florensky writes: "from the point of view of God, the logos of the creature is the self-emptying love of God for the creature."[17]

Thus, to discover the logos of creation we must, it would seem Florensky is saying, contemplate the horizon of love, an expanse which includes the moving humility of divine love superabounding in creation, as well as the dauntless audacity of creatural love which dares to alter the order of the Hypostases of the Holy Trinity in relation to itself, introducing itself as Florensky interjects, a "love-idea-monad" or "fourth hypostatic element,"[18] that at once is vouchsafed by the Holy Trinity and evocative of the Godhead's free correlation in love with creation.[19] Florensky pointedly explains himself: "Remaining in Himself almighty, God relates to His creation as if He were not almighty: He does not *coerce* the creature, but *convinces;* He does not *compel,* but *entreats.*"[20] In the West, this idea has probably been best captured by Alfred North Whitehead, who with poignant similarity declares: "God's role is not the combat of productive force with productive force, of destructive force with destructive force; it lies in the patient operation of the overpowering rationality of his conceptual harmonization . . . he is the poet of the world, with tender patience leading it by his vision of truth, beauty, and goodness."[21] Florensky does not (nor would it seem does Whitehead) wish to subtract anything from the Godhead. God retains His full majesty; He is still absolutely One in His Three Hypostases. But it is only that in His free willing to create, God truly humbles Himself, and makes Himself "Other" in relation to the creature,[22] thereby effectively relativizing His own aseity in some real, if only derivative, sense.

[16]Ibid.
[17]Ibid.
[18]Ibid.
[19]PFT, 324.
[20]Ibid.
[21]*Process and Reality,* 346. We prescind from a specific treatment of Whitehead's views on creation, which he appears to deny in the fuller context of this passage, but which lie beyond the scope of this study.
[22]PFT, 324.

In this way, the act of creation can rightfully, according to Florensky, be viewed as a kind of *kenosis,* itself evocative of the work of redemption as the agency of a new creation.

1.3 *The Monad for Florensky*

Before addressing the problematic of divine correlativity further, other salient points in Florensky's exposition should be elaborated upon first. Florensky abjures any gnostic intent, and says that his speculations should not be understood as being inspired by Gnosticism. His words, he says, are merely "wretched schemata for what is experienced in the soul."[23] The "love-idea-monad" or simply "monad" of which he speaks is not meant to be some sort of metaphysical essence derived *a priori* by detached, logical determination, but is rather an *a posteriori* given of lived experience. It is embraced only by the humility of unfeigned receptivity, and is not a by-product of prideful, speculative construction. A monad, as Florensky describes it, is a "certain real unity."[24] It is such because it is an entity excluding other entities or monads from itself. But, Florensky is prompt to add, it should not be taken to be isolated or closed off from other monads.[25] It enjoys a true, elemental unity with all monads, which taken collectively all form one, structural whole, internally and organically linked together,[26] giving rise, as it were, to a "uni-multiple being."[27] "All," Florensky cryptically notes, "is uni-substantial, and all is pluri-hypostatic."[28] This is, in essence, his cosmic experience of consubstantiality. The essential unity of the cosmos, however, is not one of mere, coincidental fact; it is one realized by an eternal act. Florensky remarks that

[23]Ibid. Cf. also p. 73 above.

[24]Ibid. So described, it resembles Whitehead's "actual entity."

[25]In this respect, Florensky's position is in strict opposition to the monadology of Leibniz, in which each monad is "closed off" from all others.

[26]PFT, 325. Here we find another parallel with Whitehead, whose "nexus" is a set of actual entities. Cf. *Process and Reality,* esp. pp. 22 and 24.

[27]PFT, 325.

[28]Ibid.

this unity is "a mobile equilibrium of hypostases similar to the variable equilibrium of energy ascertained in the constant exchange of energy among ray-emitting bodies—it is an *immobile motion and mobile rest.*"[29] But what precisely is this eternal act or energy-conserving, poli-hypostatic equilibrium? Florensky responds simply: It is Divine Love. "The Love of God flowing through this Being," Florensky writes in regard to the whole of creation, "is the creative act by which it receives first, life; secondly, unity; and thirdly, being."[30] True being for Florensky thus shows the mark and input of love. It is "a substantial relation to the other and a movement from self, which both gives unity and derives from the unity of being."[31] It is thus love that explains the dynamics of the universe. In the words of Florensky:

> Love eternally "empties" each monad, and eternally "glorifies" it. It draws the monad out of itself, and establishes it in and for itself. Love eternally takes away in order eternally to give; it eternally mortifies in order eternally to vivify. Unity in love is that which extracts each monad from the state of pure potentiality, i.e. of spiritual sleep, spiritual emptiness, and formless, chaotic existence, and that, in this manner, confers reality, actuality, life and vivacity to the monad. The purely subjective, isolated, and blind "I" of the monad, empties itself for the "Thou" of the other monad, and through this "Thou," the "I" becomes purely objective, i.e., justified. Perceived by a third monad as justifying itself through a second one, the "I" of the first monad finds itself justified in the "He" of the third, i.e., it completes the process of self-justification, and becomes "for itself" (*dlya sebya*), acquiring at the same time its own "of itself" (*o sebe*), since the justified "I" is an objectively perceived "for another" (*dlya drugogo*) of this "of itself" (*o sebe*).

[29]Ibid. Nowadays we would use the term "radioactive" instead of the compound "ray-emitting."
[30]PFT, 325f.
[31]PFT, 326.

> From a naked and empty self-identity—"I!"—the monad, becomes an act full of content in which the "I" is synthetically linked to the "I" (I = I), that is, it becomes an organ of the one Being.[32]

Appealing to Acts 17:28, which claims that only in God do we live, move, and have our being, Florensky sums up his position affirming that "each monad exists only insofar as it allows Divine Love into itself."[33] The great being of creation itself is, in turn, nothing but a realized Love of its Creator, and when viewed in its primeval, incorrupt beauty as a union of love with its Creator, it is simply Sophia, the realized Wisdom of God.[34]

2. HOLY SOPHIA

Florensky finds in Holy Sophia the living link between God and His creation. From this standpoint the problem of Sophia simply poses the ontological problem of the relations obtaining between the Creator and the creature. This is the key problem underlying all sophiological reflection. As a living link between the divine and the terrestrial, Holy Sophia partakes of the two, and accordingly must be considered in both its divine and terrestrial aspects.[35] As divine, Holy Sophia is of the very essence of the Godhead. It is God's creative love. As terrestrial, Holy Sophia is rather the realized love of God in His divine energies, His manifested, creatural wisdom. Holy Sophia is, therefore, neither fully divine nor fully creatural, but something both absolutely transcendent to the world, yet still immanent to it. In the succinct words of one contemporary Russian theologian, Archbishop Pitirim

[32]PFT, 325.
[33]PFT, 326.
[34]Ibid.
[35]Serge Obolensky, in his schematic synopsis of Florensky's sophiology ("La sophiologie et la mariologie de Paul Florensky"), bases himself upon the distinction between uncreated and created Sophia in relation to both creation and divinization. Our elaboration, however, will be more genetic, and will thus try to follow Florensky more closely according to his own exposition.

(Nechaev) of Volokolamsk, " 'Sophia' is something that
exists and has real being, being neither God nor the world."[36]

2.1 *The Great Root of the Total Creature*

Since Holy Sophia is an all-embracing reality, no one
concept can capture its essence and describe its nature fully.
Florensky must, therefore, resort to various figures to try to
elucidate his sophiological insights. One of his most basic
intuitions is that Holy Sophia lies at the basis of, or more
profoundly, is the transcendental unity of all created being.[37]
As such, it serves as the mystical basis of the cosmos and the
substratum that integrates the whole created order into an
absolute unity of the real. Florensky's own imagery used to
depict this function of Holy Sophia is most apropos. "Sophia,"
he writes, "is the Great Root of the total creature . . . by
means of which the creature penetrates into the intimacy of
Trinitarian life and through which it obtains eternal life from
the one Source of Life."[38] It is the creative love of God which
constitutes the essence of each creature, and owing to which
all of creation partakes of the God of Love. If the creature
is denied the sap of this Source, its true font of life and being,
then only death can await it.

---

[36]Archbishop Pitirim of Volokolamsk, "Osnovnye problemy sovremennogo
bogoslovskogo issledovaniya v ikh razvitii s kontsa XIX veka" (Fundamental problems of contemporary theological investigation in their development from the end of the 19th century), TS, 5 (1970): 222. Sophia, nonetheless, is in some other sense both "of the Godhead" and "of the world."

[37]On this and other points, cf. our previous study, "La sophiologia di
Pavel Florenskij e la sua attualità oggi" (The sophiology of Pavel Florensky
and its relevance today), *Unitas*, It. ed., 37, no. 4 (1982): 250-66. We
must, however, disclaim one editorial revision. In speaking Of the speculative
schemes of sophiology and process philosophy, we label them as *panentheistic*
theories, and not as pantheistic ones as improperly understood by the
editors. We do, however, acknowledge that Thomists generally reduce panentheism to pantheism, even though we do not. See pp. 263, 265 of our
study.

[38]PFT, 326.

2.2 The Guardian Angel of Creation

Continuing in this line of viewing Holy Sophia as the substratum of the world's unity, Florensky appeals to another image to help bring out this fundamental oneness. In its relation to creation, Florensky calls Holy Sophia at once the "guardian angel of the creature"[39] and the "ideal personality of the world."[40] As the guardian angel of creation, it protects creation from without and maintains its external configuration. This is the sense of the vignette depicting a cherub, which Florensky uses to introduce his sophiological speculations. It bears the inscription: *Omnia conjungo.* (I join all things.) As creation's ideal personality, it also guarantees its essential, internal consistency, providing it a common, animating principle or cosmic soul as it were. Without it, in other words, only chaos obtains.

In this perspective also, Florensky affirms, we find an important key for understanding the creation of the world by God. To him, Sophia is the "constitutive content of the God-Mind, his 'psychical content,' eternally created by the Father through the Son, and crowned in the Holy Spirit."[41] In this way, Florensky allows that "God thinks by means of *things*,"[42] adding that nothing can exist, not even in the spiritual world, apart from being thought and known by God.[43] Sophia is thus, at once, not only the constitutive, "physical" content of the God-Mind, but is also the constitutive logos of the creature, its true *raison d'être* as determined by Absolute Reason itself.[44]

2.3 The Eternal Spouse of the Word of God

Developing his views on the act of creation further, Florensky proceeds to say that Holy Sophia cannot be thought

[39]Ibid.
[40]Ibid.
[41]Ibid.
[42]Ibid.
[43]PFT, 327.
[44]PFT, 326.

of in abstraction from the Word of God, the Logos, and is, indeed, His eternal Spouse,[45] from whom it receives its creative power and is diffused throughout the created order. Florensky immediately places this discussion within the context of the classical problem of the One and the many, affirming that Holy Sophia is One in God and many in creation.[46] He thus construes his sophiology as nothing but a restatement and elaboration of philosophy's first and perennial problem, only giving it a specifically Byzantine key. Concretely applied to man, Sophia not only secures his ideal personality as his guardian angel, but also serves as the "manifestation of the eternal dignity of the person and as the image of God in man,"[47] that "sparkle"[48] of the divinity found in the multitude of men.

2.4 The Ideal Moment of Created Being

In conjunction with his consideration of the theological corpus of St. Athanasius the Great,[49] to whom he attributes the inspiration for his present work and in whose writings he finds the doctrinal leitmotivs—"the consubstantiality of the Trinity, the divinization of the flesh, the need for asceticism, the expectation of the Spirit-Consoler, and the admission of a precosmic, imperishable meaning for the creature"[50]—for his own speculations, Florensky details his views on Holy Sophia as the "ideal moment of creatural being,"[51] claiming this patristic giant as his authority. Sophia in this sense is creatural Wisdom bearing the imprint of divine, creative Wisdom and also lying in its shadow, to use, as Florensky does, the imagery of Athanasius.[52]

Florensky, continuing in the line of Athanasius, stresses

[45]PFT, 329.
[46]Ibid.
[47]Ibid.
[48]Ibid.
[49]PFT, 343-49. Florensky chiefly refers to Athanasius' work, *Against the Arians.*
[50]PFT, 348.
[51]PFT, 344.
[52]PFT, 348.

that creatural Wisdom "is not to be limited to a sole, psychological or gnoseological process of the interior life of the creature, but is, above all, the *metaphysical* nature of creatural being."[53] "Wisdom in the creature," he adds, "is not only activity, but it is also substance; it has a substantial, massive, concrete character."[54] But this same creatural Sophia, which is realized in time in the experiential world, nonetheless, enjoys a preexistence in the Logos or True Wisdom,[55] in which it is a "precosmic, hypostatic concentration of divine prototypes."[56] Florensky, with Athanasius before him, quotes St. Paul's letter to the Ephesians as corroborative of this doctrine:

> Blessed be the God and Father of our Lord Jesus Christ, who has blessed us in Christ with every spiritual blessing in the heavenly places, even as He chose us in Him before the foundation of the world, that we should be holy and blameless before Him. (Eph 1:3-4)

Sophia in its divine dimension, however, is not identical to the Logos or Second Person of the Holy Trinity, but, as Florensky has already noted,[57] is only a "fourth hypostatic element" in the Holy Trinity. As he writes in expanding upon this point:

> Sophia participates in the life of the Trihypostatic Godhead; it enters into the bosom of the Trinity; and it partakes of Divine Love. But, being a *fourth,* created, that is, non-consubstantial Person, it does not "*constitute*" Divine Unity, nor "*is*" Love, but only *enters* into the communion Love, and *is allowed* to

[53]PFT, 346.
[54]Ibid.
[55]Cf. ibid. for this important distinction between "True Wisdom" or the Logos and "creatural Wisdom" or Sophia. This distinction, however, does not account for Divine Sophia, which is not to be identified with the Logos or Second Person of the Holy Trinity, but which is rather only a "fourth hypostatic element" of the Holy Trinity. Cf. PFT, 349, for a discussion of this point as well as our discussion in the paragraph to follow.
[56]PFT, 348.
[57]PFT, 323.

enter into this communion by the ineffable, unfathomable, unthinkable humility of God.[58]

As only a participation in the Tri-hypostatic Life of God,
reflecting various essential elements of the Holy Trinity,
Sophia is only analogously personal, and rather serves only
to exemplify and explain the different moments in the creative activity of the Holy Trinity. Florensky elaborates:

> From the point of view of the Hypostasis of the
> *Father*, Sophia is the ideal *substance*, the foundation
> of the creature, the power or force of its being. If we
> turn to the Hypostasis of the Word, then Sophia is the
> *reason* of the creature, its meaning, truth (*istina*) or
> justice (*pravda*). And lastly, from the point of view of
> the Hypostasis of the *Spirit*, we find in Sophia the
> *spirituality* of the creature, its holiness, purity, and
> immaculateness, i.e., its beauty. This triune idea of
> *foundation-reason-holiness*, in splitting up in our rea-
> son, presents itself to the sinful intellect in the three,
> mutually exclusive aspects of *foundation*, *reason*, and
> *holiness*. In point of fact, what does the foundation
> of the creature have in common with its reason or
> with its holiness? For the corrupted intellect, i.e., for
> reason, these ideas are by no means conjoinable into
> a unitary image: according to the law of identity, they
> are impervious to one another.[59]

Thus articulated, Sophia seems to be nothing more than an
all-embracing transcendental, one encompassing the other

[58]PFT, 349.

[59]Ibid. That Florensky sees a threefold moment in the act of creation
should not be taken to mean that he would deny the dogma, as expressed by
the Catholic Church at the Fourth Lateran Council (1215) and the Council
of Florence (1442) (see Denzinger-Schönmetzer, *Enchiridion*, 804, 1331),
that the Holy Trinity acts as One in creation. His teaching only more
profoundly articulates the biblical and patristic principle that the Father
creates through the Son in the Spirit. For him, therefore, there is only one
common creative act, but it is one bearing the threefold mark of the Holy
Trinity. When, therefore, a determinate operation is appropriated by the
human mind to each Hypostasis, this operation must not be viewed as a
separate principle as such, but only as a particular moment of one creative act.

transcendentals of unity, truth, goodness, and beauty. It is, in
fine, the one total property of creation, at the same time that
it is the one cosmic principle which can explicitly convey the
richness of meaning in the biblical and patristic principle that
the Father creates through the Son in the Spirit.

2.5   Other Determinations

Having characterized Holy Sophia as One in God and
many in creation, Florensky not surprisingly adduces other
determinations for Sophia besides those of the transcendental
order. If Sophia is, as Florensky has affirmed, the Great Root
of creation, it is only to be expected that it sprouts up and
gives rise to many dependent branches. These additional
differentiations are compactly treated together, and, to use
another image, flow one right after another in concentric
circles. As Florensky notes, in addition to its relation to the
divine economy, Sophia "has a whole series of new aspects,
fractionizing the one *idea* of it into a multitude of dogmatic
concepts."[60] The first of these for Florensky is Sophia understood as the "germ and center of the redeemed creature—the
Body of the Lord, Jesus Christ, i.e., the created nature assumed
by the Divine Word."[61] By conjoining ourselves to the Body
of Christ and participating in His life, we are engraced with
the fruits of the Holy Spirit, and, accordingly, endowed with
Sophia understood as the "pre-existent, purified Being of
the creature in Christ or the *Church in its celestial aspect*."[62]
Next, Sophia also includes the "*Church in its terrestrial aspect,*
i.e., that totality of persons, who have already embarked upon
the ascetical path of restoration, and who have already entered
into the Body of Christ with their empirical aspect."[63] But
since this life in Christ and in the Spirit which realizes Sophia
in the creature is itself the work of the Spirit, Florensky re-

[60]PFT, 350.
[61]Ibid.
[62]Ibid. It would seem that Florensky should have said "pure" and not
"purified" in this context. Purification rather implies the element of time
and not preexistence.
[63]Ibid.

marks that, in truth, "Sophia is the *Spirit* insofar as it has divinized the creature."[64] "In this sense," Florensky adds, "Sophia is *virginity*,"[65] since it is the chief manifestation of the Spirit within us. And if Sophia is virginity, then the exemplar-bearer of virginity herself, Mary, the maiden full of grace, is incomparably Sophia.[66]

Florensky offers us a concinnous epilogue to his reflections on the dynamic multiplicity of Sophia:

> If Sophia is the total Creature, then humanity, which is the soul and conscience of the Creature, is Sophia *par excellence*. If Sophia is all humanity, then the Church, which is the soul and conscience of humanity, is Sophia *par excellence*. If Sophia is the Church, then the Church of saints, which is the soul and conscience of the Church, is Sophia *par excellence*. If Sophia is the Church of saints, then the Mediatrix and Patroness of the creature before the Word of God, who judges the world and cleaves it in two, the Mother of God, the "purification of the world," is, once again, Sophia *par excellence*. But, the true sign of Mary, full of grace, is her virginity, the beauty of her soul, and this Virginity is, properly speaking, Sophia.[67]

2.6   Mary and Sophia

Florensky especially ponders over the sophianic mystery, that is Mary, the God-bearer.[68] Most beautifully and elegantly, he calls her the one "true ornament of human being."[69] Sophia realizes itself in the cosmic beauty of all creation, but does so especially, indeed, incomparably so, in the Virgin Mother

[64]Ibid.
[65]Ibid.
[66]Ibid.
[67]PFT, 350f.
[68]For a valuable synopsis of Russian sophianic mariology, see Bernard Schultze, S.J., "La mariologie sophianique russe" in Hubert du Manoir, S.J., ed., *Maria. Etudes sur la Sainte Vierge* (Paris: Beauchesne, 1961), 6: 213-39. Pages 223-29 are devoted to Florensky's mariological views.
[69]PFT, 351.

of God. Her chaste heart radiates spiritual beauty and can only inspire us in its sophianic splendor.

For Florensky, she is variously the "model of virginal purity,"[70] the heart of the Church just as the Lord is its head,"[71] creatural beauty personified,"[72] the "bearer of Sophia,"[73] and both the "bearer and focal point of celestial purity—the ever-Virgin Theotokos."[74] Further, Mary serves at once as the "focus of ecclesial life"[75] and the "center of creatural life."[76] Indeed, she has "*cosmic* power."[77] "She is," Florensky exults, " 'the sanctification of all terrestrial and heavenly elements,' 'the benediction of all the seasons.' "[78] She is, in sum, the " '*Queen of all.*' "[79] Not without reason, therefore, Byzantine Christians extol Mary in one of their liturgical hymns with the words, cited by Florensky:[80]

> In You, O Woman Full of Grace, the angelic choirs and the human race—*all creation*—rejoices. O Sanctified Temple, Mystical Paradise and Glory of virgins . . . In You, O Woman Full of Grace, all creation rejoices. All praise be to You!

She is, indeed, as another hymn proclaims, also quoted by

[70]PFT, 354.
[71]PFT, 355.
[72]Ibid.
[73]PFT, 356, 358.
[74]PFT, 358. This is the truth, Florensky says (p. 765 [n. 639]), that Catholics express—he adds "crudely and rationalistically"—in the dogma of the Immaculate Conception. For Catholics, Mary was conceived without the taint of original sin, being, by divine election, *ever*-sinless and *ever*-pure. Florensky's understanding of this dogma, at least in this specific context, seems inexact. Cf. Obolensky, "La sophiologie," 36f, on this point. It should be noted that Soloviev clearly upholds this dogma in his sophianic mariology. Cf. Soloviev, *Sobranie*, 11:183f, 352, 382, 397. Bulgakov, on the other hand, rejects it in its present formulation. Cf. *Kupina neopalimaya* [The burning bush] (Paris: YMCA Press, 1927), 77-109.
[75]PFT, 359.
[76]Ibid.
[77]Ibid.
[78]Ibid.
[79]Ibid.
[80]PFT, 356. The hymn is sung during the Divine Liturgy of St. Basil the Great.

Florensky: "More honorable than the Cherubim and beyond compare more glorious than the Seraphim."[81]

3. ICONS OF HOLY SOPHIA

Explicit and extended, sophiological speculation may not have been the general preoccupation of Byzantine thinkers throughout the ages. A conscious attempt to work out a full, philosophic-theological synthesis in a sophiological key may, indeed, only be verified in the corpus of Sergius Bulgakov, whose sophiological views proved so controversial that he earned, even if not fully merited, ecclesiastical censure for them. But, Florensky, who was Bulgakov's mentor in sophiology, would certainly not agree that sophiological reflection is foreign to Byzantine thought. As we have already seen, he not only considered this topic indigenous to Russian thought in particular, but also saw it as an intrinsic part of patristic thought, especially in St. Athanasius the Great. Thus, it is important to distinguish explicit synthesis from primordial intuition. The former may not have flowered much until Bulgakov, but the latter, as Florensky seeks to demonstrate, is inalienable to Byzantine consciousness. Before pursuing our philosophic investigation further, therefore, it behooves us briefly to consider, along with Florensky, some of the iconographic, liturgical, and ecclesiological elements, which are intelligible only in the context of a sophianic vision, and which, further, provide the essential matrix for explicit, sophiological speculation.

Florensky commences his discussion of iconography and Holy Sophia,[82] noting the different variants of icons dedicated

---

[81]PFT, 358. The hymn is from the Divine Liturgy of St. John Chrysostom.

[82]It must, however, be stressed that Florensky only offers a plausible explanation of the meaning of the basic kinds of icons to Holy Sophia. For other treatments of sophianic icons, cf. Prince Evgeny Trubetskoy, *Umozrenie v kraskakh* [Contemplation in colors] (Paris: YMCA Press, 1965; Eng. trans. by Gertrude Vakar, *Icons: Theology in Color* [Crestwood, NY: St. Vladimir's Seminary Press, 1973]), passim; and Paul Evdokimov, *La teologia della bellezza* [Theology of beauty] (Rome: Edizioni Paoline, 1971), 393-402. Cf. also, A. Nikol'skii, "Ikona sv. Sofii, Premudrosti Bozhiei" (The icon of Holy Sophia, the Wisdom of God), *Rodnaya starina* (Native

to Holy Sophia and concluding that "already this demonstrates that in sophianic iconography there was a genuine religious *creativity,* coming from the soul of the people, and was not a mere, external borrowing of iconographic forms."[83] For schematic purposes, he reduces the types of icons dedicated to Holy Sophia to three principal ones: the angelic, ecclesiological, and mariological, which in turn he classifies according to the city in which their best examples are found, namely, Novgorod, Yaroslavl, and Kiev, respectively.[84]

3.1   *The Novgorodian Type*

The most venerable and remarkable variety of icon to Holy Sophia, Florensky notes, is that typified by the patronal icon of the Church of Holy Sophia in Novgorod.[85] The church itself dates from 1045-52, and it is more than likely that the icon is of the same period. Although not all of the details of this icon are of immediate interest, attention should be called to certain of its aspects. The central figure in the composition

land), no. 5-6 (1928): 17f, and G. V. Florovsky, *O pochitanii Sofii, Premudrosti Bozhiei, v Vizantii i na Rusi* [On veneration of Sophia, the Wisdom of God, in Byzantium and in Rus'], *Trudy V-go sezda russkikh akademicheskikh organizatsii za granitsei,* Chast' I [Studies of the 5th congress of Russian academic organization abroad, part 1] (1932), 485-500. From this literature it becomes apparent that it is most difficult, if not impossible, to assign definite interpretations to these icons. This is especially true in regard to the meaning of the angel in the Novgorodian type of sophianic icon, which has been variously held to be the personification of the divine attribute of Wisdom (Florensky), the Logos or Son of God (Nikol'skii and Florovsky), and the Holy Spirit (Evdokimov).
[83]PFT, 370.
[84]PFT, 371. Attention should be called to the study of Aloiz Litva, S.J., "La 'Sophia' dans la creation" ("Sophia" in creation), *Orientalia Christiana Periodica,* 16 (1950): 39-74, in which he criticizes Bulgakov and Florensky for their interpretation of icons according to *a priori,* philosophical, and not historical, perspectives in order to justify their sophiological views (p. 42). Similarly, Zenkovsky (*Istoriya,* 2:428) remarks that Florensky cannot appeal to these icons to prove his pan-unity theory. These objections, however, are not entirely well-taken. Florensky does not attempt any sort "proof" here, but only appeals to these icons to substantiate some of his remarks on Holy Sophia. Furthermore, although the existence of the icons may not prove his theory, they also do not disprove it. More significantly, they indicate a certain *Weltanschauung.*
[85]PFT, 371.

is an angel seated on a throne (itself resting on seven columns) and dressed in the apparel characteristic of Byzantine, and later Russian, civil and ecclesiastical rulers. It is also both wearing and holding the usual insignia of imperial office. The head of the angel bears a crown and is surrounded by a golden nimbus, while its hands, face, and wings are fiery in color. At the angel's right hand stands the Mother of God, holding a greenish-colored disk with the Christ Child on it. To the angel's left, one finds St. John the Baptist. Both his and the Holy Virgin's nimbuses are greenish-blue. Finally, above the image of Sophia, the All-Merciful Savior is depicted.

Forgoing mention of other details for the moment, it is now possible to venture a basic, even if not exhaustive, interpretation of this icon.[86] The angel, of course, is Holy Sophia. Its wings reveal it is of the heavenly world, and their fiery color its fullness of spirituality. Its imperial vesture and badges of office point to the measure of its influence in the rule of the universe. Its cosmic power over the heavens is specifically indicated by the turquoise-hued, star-filled, concentric circles encompassing the image of Sophia. Sky-blue, in this fashion, Florensky affirms, is primordially the natural symbol of Sophia, and only through it, derivatively, does it apply to the Theotokos as the bearer of Sophia.

One last point in Florensky's interpretation bears mention. The icon maintains a definite hierarchy. Christ is given the preeminent position of dignity at top center. Holy Sophia is in the exact center, under Christ, and is thus inferior to Him, even if centrally important for creation. The human race is then represented by the Virgin Mary and John the Baptist, in that order.[87] The colors of the nimbuses also indicate this ranking. Christ and Holy Sophia have golden haloes, while the Virgin Mary's and the Baptist's are greenish-blue.

But, we must inquire, what is the meaning of the identification of Holy Sophia with the angel? Florensky specifically gives his interpretation at the end of his discussion of icons of Holy Sophia. Considering his account of Sophia as the

[86]PFT, 374ff.
[87]Florensky, however, omits to place the Baptist in this hierarchy. Cf. PFT, 375f.

guardian angel of all creation, his forthcoming answer, however, is not difficult to divine. The angel personifies the abstract, divine attribute of Wisdom.[88]

3.2 The Yaroslavian Variant

The second type of icon to Holy Sophia is, according to Florensky, characteristic of the sixteenth and eighteenth centuries. He particularly highlights one fresco in the Church of St. John Chrysostom in Yaroslavl.[89] In this fresco we see a Crucifixion scene. Christ on the Cross is framed within the context of the eucharistic. The cross is positioned on an altar under a baldachin supported by six columns. The cross itself serves as a seventh column. The inscription written in the top-center of the composition, which reads *"Premudrost' sozda sebe khram* (Wisdom has built her temple), clearly alludes to Prov 9:1-2: "Wisdom has built her house, she has set up her seven columns; she has dressed her meat, mixed her wine, yes, she has spread her table." The ecclesiological import of Divine Wisdom is thus being clearly underscored. The Church as the privileged locus of Holy Sophia is particularly and profoundly brought out by the two inscriptions on each of the six columns plus the cross, one referring to a sacramental mystery, the other to an ecumenical council, both basic, constitutive factors and essential moments in the life of the Church. There are various other features throughout the composition, both inscriptions and depictions, which equally refer to the ecclesiological realization of Holy Sophia. One of these inscriptions pointedly reads: "The foundation of the Divine Church of the Old and New Testaments is the blood of martyrs, the preaching of the apostles, the blood of prophets, apostolic teaching, Christ, the rock of faith, upon which stone I shall build my Church." Of the ten groups of saints depicted in heavenly clouds, we find the following: hermits, male martyrs, female martyrs, the venerable, the just headed by Joachim and Anna, confessors, bishops, kings and

[88]PFT, 383.
[89]PFT, 376ff.

princes, prophets with John the Baptist as the head, and the apostles with St. Paul in the lead. Under these heavenly choirs, we see six groups of ordinary people with the inscription, "Rally all peoples." The general sense of the icon is thus clear; it refers to the Church in its totality.

But for Florensky one problem remains unsolved: With whom precisely is Holy Sophia identified in this icon, given that it is Sophia, who "has built her temple?" Since God the Father,[90] the Holy Spirit, the Crucified Christ, plus the Mother of God are all prominently represented, an exact determination, Florensky concludes, is difficult to make, although he himself, it would seem, favors an identification of the Holy Sophia in this composition with the Crucified Lord and Savior.

3.3 *The Kievan Sophia*

The last remaining general type of icon to Holy Sophia considered by Florensky is the marian, Kievan type, which most interestingly, Florensky immediately adds, bears many close analogies with the Yaroslavian type. Specifically, this type of icon is also inspired by Prov 9:1-2; its elements (columns, personages, etc.) continue the imagery of "seven," and the inscription from Proverbs is also found. Its major difference is that Holy Sophia is unmistakably linked with the Theotokos,[91] who is the focus of the icon.

The most notable example of the marian type, according to Florensky, is the patronal icon on the iconostasis in the Cathedral of Holy Sophia in Kiev, which dates from the eighteenth century, but whose antecedents go back to the sixteenth century. Its central figure, the Mother of God bears numerous Latin influences (head uncovered, the crown being held above her head by two angels, the Latin cross in her hand, etc.), but, more outstandingly, is its allusion to the woman clothed in the sun of the Apocalypse (see Rev 12). She is standing on a half moon, and trampling upon a seven-

---

[90]Florensky cautiously notes this figure could be Christ. Cf. PFT, 378.
[91]PFT, 379.
[92]PFT, 381.

headed serpent. Being thus both a crowned queen and the woman clothed in the sun of the Apocalypse, she has, at once,—"by sincretistic conjunction"[92]—rule over both the earthly and heavenly Churches.

A further connection, Florensky notes, is made between the Theotokos and the Church in the Kievan cathedral. The singularly striking and most important artistic creation in it is the massive Virgin "orantes" in mosaic on the apse, which dates from the eleventh century. Although one cannot but help think of the Mother of God in beholding this mosaic, Florensky hastens to suggest that since the Christ Child is missing from the composition, what we actually witness is the Virgin Mother as a type of the Church.[93] In other words, this iconographic marvel links Holy Sophia to both the Theotokos and the Church.

4. THE DIVINE OFFICE TO HOLY SOPHIA

Considering the time-honored principle, *lex orandi lex credendi,* it is highly significant that there exists a special Divine Office to Sophia, the Wisdom of God in Old Church Slavonic (which has frequently gone unnoticed). As editor of the *Theological Messenger,* Florensky published a manuscript copy of this service, which he had unearthed at the parish church in Moscow near Lubyansky Square under the patronage of Holy Sophia, and which he wished to make more widely known.[94] From rubrical indications, we learn that it was composed for annual celebration in the Church of Holy Sophia in Novgorod on August 15, the Feast of the Dormition of the Mother of God.[95] Textual analysis shows that for the most part the office contains the standard propers and readings for the vespers and matins for the Feast of the Dormition, with the exception of a few clausal changes, a new troparion

[93]PFT, 382.
[94]TM, 1, no. 2 (1912): 1-23. Cf. also PFT, 388f, 778f.
[95]The patronal feast for the Cathedral of Holy Sophia in Kiev, on the other hand, is the Nativity of the Mother of God (September 8).

and kontakion,[96] and one major addition, a special canon for matins in honor of Sophia, the Wisdom of God.

The service dates from the seventeenth century, and the rubrical preliminary for the canon indicates that its author can be acrostically identified from the troparia of its eighth and ninth odes.[97] He was Prince Simeon Shakhovskoy, a Moscovite lay theologian, who was so moved by the Novgorodian Icon to Sophia that he decided to compose a service in its honor. This service lacks the poetic excess sometimes characteristic of Byzantine hymnology and is notable for its ascription of a multiplicity of meanings to Holy Sophia,[98] variously identified as the Mother of God,[99] the Word of God,[100] and a creative power.[101]

[96]Both a "troparion" and a "kontakion" are species of Byzantine liturgical hymns.

[97]While Florensky himself does not note who the author was, Th. Spassky has done so in his *Russkoe liturgicheskoe tvorchestvo* [Russian liturgical works] (Paris: YMCA Press, 1951), 254-73. He also lists its author in his presentation of his French translation of this particular Divine Office in *Irénikon*, 30 (1957): 164-88.

[98]Cf. the observations of Spassky, *Russkoe liturgicheskoe tvorchestvo*, 268f, and of Florensky, PFT, 389.

[99]—Let us gather, O Orthodox peoples, and contemplate the miraculous icon of the Wisdom of God, of His Mother most pure, for she radiates light in her most venerable temple, and gladdens the hearts of those who approach with faith and behold this most pure icon with reverence and fear... (Kontakion)

—Confirm my mind and thought for the good, O God the Father Almighty, for I dare sing in praise of the all-immaculate Virgin, the Protectress of the world; her virginal soul You have called Your Divine Church, and for the sake of the Incarnation of Your World, You have named her also Sophia, Wisdom of God... (Ikos)

—How more venerable is the ensouled Tabernacle, built not by Bezalel [see Ex 31:2], but ordered by God Himself and called Sophia, in which God the Word Himself has lived... (Ode 8, 3rd troparion)

—The spiritual vine is the temple of Sophia, the Wisdom of God, that is to say, the womb of the most holy Mother of God... (Ode 8, 4th troparion)

—The Only-Begotten Son and Word of God has built Himself a temple in the most fair bosom of the Virgin Mary for the sake of our salvation, and has given her, the soul of virgins, the name Sophia, Wisdom of God... (Ode 9, 3rd troparion)

[100]—We search with all our hearts the Wisdom of God, incarnate of the most pure Virgin... (Ode 1, 3rd troparion)

[101]—The Wisdom of God is soundly loved. It is the Counsel of Mystery for all men, and nothing under the heavens resembles it. Let us cherish it like the apple of our eyes, and it will grant us rest on Judgment Day. (Ode 4, 2nd troparion)

5. Developments in the Theology of Holy Sophia

The manifold significations of icons in honor of Holy Sophia are also reflected in developments in the theological consciousness of Sophia. Florensky sees three fundamental, developmental stages in the theological understanding of Divine Wisdom.[102] The oldest of these is characteristic of the Greeks and their speculative thought. It is clearly christological in character, and treats Divine Wisdom as virtually identical with the Son, the Word of God. That Justinian's basilica to Holy Sophia was dedicated to the Incarnate Word of God would, to Florensky's mind, corroborate this claim.[103]

The second stage in theological development is that of the early Slavs, and was greatly molded by an acute, ascetical sensibility, which concentrated on the moral dimensions of Divine Wisdom. Accordingly, it focused on the Mother of God as the most pure vessel of divine grace, and not surprisingly, its sophiological views were prevalently mariological in emphasis, a fact borne out, as we have seen, in the numerous Churches of Holy Sophia dedicated to the Mother of God, judging from their feast days and patronal icons.

The final stage, the one more or less characteristic of the contemporary era, is notable, Florensky says, for its interest in the cosmological dimension of Divine Wisdom. The crying concern of our day is to find the unity of all creation in God through the mystical Church. The ecclesiological dimensions of this problem, themselves implied by this aspiration and, furthermore, intrinsic to any final resolution of it, are thereby also underscored.

These three aspects of sophiological consciousness, though formally distinguishable, need, however, as Florensky stresses, to be synthesized into a genuine unity of vision and inspiration. The christological emphasis given in the "soar of theological contemplation," the mariological coloring to the moral

---

[102]PFT, 389-92.
[103]PFT, 384. Cf. also Sergius Bulgakov, *Wisdom of God*, 185f. The common feast day in honor of Divine Wisdom in the Greek perspective is that of Mid-Pentecost. The Gospel reading for the day is Jn 7:14-30, which relates Jesus' teaching in the temple.

"feat of internal purity," and the ecclesiological extract founding the "joy of universal unity" respectively constitute, to Florensky's mind, the essential, indelible moments of the "triple life of faith, hope, and love."[104] This trinitarian life is the real meaning of sophianic life, that is, that life grounded in a vision and lived understanding of Holy Sophia, the Wisdom of God.

6. SOPHIOLOGICAL SPECULATION: PARAMETERS FOR DISCUSSION

To respond to all the questions raised by Florensky's epistolary meditation on Holy Sophia requires both considerable circumspection and speculative initiative. His text is extremely densely written and, at times, his thoughts seem rather cryptic to say the least. This is not all that surprising, however, considering the recondite nature of his problematic. There are few problems more foundational and yet more difficult to shed light uopn than the relation of God to the world, or rather their interrelationship. Florensky himself offers us a plethora of indications for exploring this interrelationship and for mapping out its basic contours. But his presentation still leaves many avenues untraversed, and, accordingly, gives rise to many more questions than it actually answers. Many of philosophy's most vexing problems seem somehow to enter into the problematic, thus rendering his sophiological enterprise a veritable Pandora's box of difficulties.

The two charges most commonly leveled against sophiological speculation are, of course, Gnosticism and pantheism. From the general lines of our exposition as given up to now, however, it can readily be seen that the former accusation is not really relevant. The common feature of all Gnostic theories is the postulation of some *intermediary being* between God and creation. For Florensky, on the other hand, Holy Sophia is no such independently existing intermediary. As divine, it is only the "precosmic, hypostatic concentration of

---

[104]PFT, 391.

divine prototypes,"[105] and as creatural, it is simply creation itself, it being coextensive and coterminous with all created being and thus a true transcendental in the Scholastic sense of the term. In this perspective, accordingly, Florensky's sophiological teaching in no wise contradicts the Christian doctrine of *creatio ex nihilo*.

Leaving the charge of Gnosticism thus to the side, the chief specter haunting sophiology is pantheism. Florensky for his part, of course, spurns pantheism, but his formal disclaimer notwithstanding, the possibility that he may be materially guilty of the imputation has yet to be discounted. Just as there are good indications that Florensky should be fully exonerated from the charge of pantheism, there are also counterindications which must be taken into consideration before any final verdict can be delivered.

6.1   *Positions Anterior and Posterior to Florensky*

To facilitate a speedy and equitable judgment concerning this matter, certain factors or parameters must be borne in mind. The first of these is that no matter whatever other thinkers of the sophiological school may have subscribed to, Florensky was still an independent thinker. The errors and shortcomings of both those before and after Florensky should not therefore be generalized, and automatically imputed to him by his mere association with them. Soloviev and Bulgakov especially come to mind. Soloviev's teaching on Holy Sophia and pan-unity, in particular, seems marked by a pronounced, pantheistic moment.[106] This deficiency, however, did not escape the attention of Florensky, who rather offers a discerning, if not extended, criticism of Soloviev's views.[107] Florensky specifically faults Soloviev for a certain rationalism, clearly reminiscent of Spinoza,[108] in which his foundational

---

[105]PFT, 348.

[106]Cf. the study of V. Zenkovsky, "Ideya vseedinstva v filosofii Vladimira Solv'eva" (The idea of pan-unity in the philosophy of Vladimir Soloviev), *Pravoslavnaya mysl'* [Orthodox thought], 10 (1955): 45-59.

[107]Cf. esp. PFT, 775 (n. 701).

[108]Zenkovsky also notes Spinoza's influence on Soloviev as well as the latter's fascination with him. See "Ideya vseedinstva," 50.

principle and point of departure is not the notion of living Hypostasis, but that of substance, of which the hypostasis is only a manifestation. Such a conception of substance, Florensky claims, can only be understood impersonally, and thus only as a "thing." This position, according to Florensky, essentially disposes Soloviev to Sabellianism, Spinozism, and Schellingism,[109] positions from which he specifically disassociates himself.

It is above all important not to overaccentuate the similarities between Florensky's and Bulgakov's sophiological conceptions, not because they are not real and striking, but because the one is only germinal, while the other alone has fully flowered. Whereas Florensky merely sketches the rough features of sophiology, Bulgakov provides a full picture. One therefore should not read Florensky anachronistically on the basis of Bulgakov, whose system, simply because it is much more developed, offers many more possible pitfalls and troublesome spots for the serious observer. In this respect, the ecclesiastical censures that were leveled against Bulgakov's system should not, even if they were fully valid in themselves—a fact open to serious question—be interpreted as necessarily condemnations of Florensky. Besides the repudiation of Bulgakov's strict views on Holy Sophia, it is the christological and soteriological positions which he tries to draw from his sophiological tenets that, above all, come under sustained attack in these censures. Florensky may have been one of Bulgakov's chief mentors in sophiology, but this does not mean that he would have necessarily subscribed either to Bulgakov's developed, sophiological positions or to his other controversial views in theology.[110] The limits of this study, however, do not allow us fully to enter into a discussion of the sophiological controversies of the 1930's,[111] which

[109]PFT, 775 (n. 701).

[110]Florensky himself was never able to devote much time to christological and soteriological pursuits. His vain attempt to resuscitate the doctrine of *apokatastasis* has already been subjected to thorough criticism by us (see pp. 162f above).

[111]For some of the relevant material, cf. the two decrees of Metropolitan Sergius (Stragorodskii) of Moscow dated September 7 and December 27, 1935, both issued in brochure format under the heading *Ukaz Moskovskoi Patriarkhii preosvyashchennomu Mitropolitu Litovskomu i Vilenskomu*

primarily centered around Bulgakov's theological corpus, and which also in great part concerned matters expounded only after Florensky's own stated views. This later debate, however, is relevant in a couple of respects, namely, insofar as the critical opposition to the doctrine of Holy Sophia says that it renders a quarternity out of the Holy Trinity,[112] thus destroying the Christian conception of God, and further intimates that all speculation concerning it is per se pantheistic.

6.2   The Danger of Pantheism

It is true that Florensky sometimes refers to Holy Sophia

Elevferiyu [Decree of the Moscow Patriarchate to the Most Reverend Metropolitan Eleutherius of Vilna and Lithuania], the memorandum of Bulgakov to Metropolitan Evlogy of Paris, entitled *Dokladnaya zapiska Mitropolitu Evlogiyu po povodu opredeleniya arkhiereiskogo sobora v Karlovtsakh otnositel'no ucheniya o Sofii Premudrosti Bozhiei* [Memorandum to Metropolitan Evlogy in regard to the determination of the Synod of Bishops in Karlovci concerning the teaching about Sophia, the Wisdom of God] (Paris: YMCA Press, 1936), and the discussions in C. Lialine, "Le débat sophiologique," *Irénikon*, 13 (1936): 168-205, and in V. Lossky, *Spor o Sofii* [The dispute about Sophia] (Paris, 1936). Both the Moscow Patriarchate and the Synod of Russian Orthodox Bishops headquartered in Karlovci, Yugoslavia, censured Bulgakov's writings, while Metropolitan Evlogy of Paris came to Bulgakov's defense.

Attention must also be called to Archbishop Seraphim Sobolev's lengthy and highly polemical study, *Novoe uchenie o Sofii Premudrosti Bozhiei* [The new teaching about Sophia, the Wisdom of God] (Sophia, 1935) in which he subjects both Bulgakov's and Florensky's sophiological views to stern rebuke. Unfortunately, due to a lack of philosophical acumen, he only manages radically to misconstrue their thought. His root error consists in his failure to grasp Holy Sophia as an all-embracing transcendental. Accordingly, he lacks the proper conceptual tool for understanding the true manifold of meanings and applications of Sophia. It is this oversight which prevents him from seeing how Florensky can free himself from bondage to both Gnosticism and pantheism. It is beyond the scope of our present synthesis to enter into a detailed, point-by-point discussion with Sobolev, especially in regard to his other criticisms of Florensky, e.g., the latter's appeal to Athanasius for support of his views and his particular interpretation of sophiological icons.

[112]This aberration is not something new with the doctrine of Holy Sophia. Already in 1147 at the Council of Rheims a similar condemnation was issued against the theories of Gilbert de la Porrée, who was faulted with having made God's nature a fourth term in the Godhead, giving it an equal standing with the Three Divine Hypostases. Cf. Denzinger-Schönmetzer, *Enchiridion*, 745.

as a Fourth Person,[113] but he never intends it to be a hypostasis in the full sense of the word on a par with the Three Divine Hypostases, Father, Son, and Holy Spirit. For him, it is rather a "fourth hypostatic element"[114] that communicates Intra-trinitarian Life "by divine condescension"[115] to the creature, enabling it to participate in this Life and proportionately share its being. Sophia, Florensky writes, "partakes of Divine Love. But, being a *fourth*, created, that is, non-consubstantial Person, it does not *'constitute'* Divine Unity, nor *'is'* Love, but only enters into the communion of Love . . ."[116]

Furthermore, Florensky says he never interprets Divine Sophia in Soloviev's apparent terms as the "Substance of the Holy Trinity,"[117] which to him smacks of pantheism, whereby creatural Sophia, as obtained in the world, would be nothing other than an emanation or mode of the Divine Substance. In his own perspective on creation as realized Divine Wisdom, on the other hand, Florensky goes only so far as to consider Holy Sophia as the "ideal personality of the world"[118] or the ideal moment of creatural being."[119]

The critical question, however, is whether Florensky himself really fully manages to escape the clutches of pantheism. Formally speaking, he opts for a creationist doctrine, which accentuates God's free activity as the sole cause of creation. But when he appeals to Holy Sophia as the principle of cor-relativity between the Creator-Hypostases of the Holy Trinity and creation, it must be asked whether he does not thereby lapse into pantheistic categories. The crucial passage in his argument reads as follows:

> By an indescribable act(—in which the ineffable humility of Divine Love and the incomprehensible audacity of creatural love touch one another and mutu-

[113]PFT, 349.
[114]PFT, 323. Cf. p. 180 above.
[115]PFT, 349.
[116]Ibid. Cf. p. 180 above.
[117]Cf. PFT, 775 (n. 701) and also pp. 194f above. Florensky explicitly rejects the theory of emanation on PFT, 288.
[118]PFT, 326.
[119]PFT, 344.

ally collaborate—), this love-idea-monad, this *fourth* hypostatic element enters into the life of the Divine Trinity, which is above order (—as the number "3" has no order—), and calls out a distinction in the order —κατὰ τάξιν—of the Hypostases of the Most Holy Trinity in relation to itself. The Most Holy Trinity *deigns* this correlation of itself with its creature and the consequent determination of itself by the creature, and thereby "exhausts" or "empties" itself of absolute attributes. Remaining in Himself almighty, God relates to His creation as if He were not almighty: He does not *coerce* the creature, but *convinces;* He does not *compel,* but *entreats.*[120]

From this passage, we can see how in Florensky's view Holy Sophia as a fourth hypostatic element functions as the point of connection or bridge between the Holy Trinity as Creator and the creature. It is, in effect, a correlating medium for an all-embracing unity between them. But precisely at this point critics of the sophiological enterprise begin their attack. In a word, for them, the question of establishing an ontological bridge between God and the world is a false problem.[121] Nicholas Lossky makes this objection specifically in reference to Bulgakov's sophiological system,[122] but he could have readily stated it in reference to Florensky's own thought on this point. Lossky insists that God cannot be subjected to the terms of any relation, not even correlation, because such a procedure would limit Him, and reduce Him to the level of created being. God, Lossky continues, is above the logical order of being, and therefore it is improper to call Him the Absolute. Instead, He is the "super-Absolute" of the metalogical order. "The super-being of God and the being of the world," Lossky writes, "are so different from one another,

[120]PFT, 323f, Part of this passage was cited above on p. 173.

[121]Cf., e.g., V. Lossky, *Spor o Sofii,* 20f, 23.

[122]*History of Russian Philosophy,* 228ff, and esp. his *Uchenie o. Sergiya Bulgakova o vseedinstve i o Bozhestvennoi Sofii* [The teaching of Fr. Sergius Bulgakov about pan-unity and about Divine Sophia] (South Canaan, PA: St. Tikhon's Press, n.d.), 6, 10f.

that no relation of limitation can exist between them."[123]
Between God and the creature only an abyss exists, and the
best we can do is to affirm the existence of the Creator "together with"[124] the creature. Moreover, Lossky stresses, whenever we attempt to make any positive affirmation about God
on the order of "God is Life," "God is Wisdom," etc., we
must always bear in mind that He remains incommensurable
with human reason, and that He is really supra-Vital, super-
Wise, etc., as the Pseudo-Dionysius taught centuries ago.

Lossky's critical line is also sustained by Georges Florovsky in his own implied critique of sophiological and pan-
unity theories about creation. Speaking of the idea of creation
in Christian philosophy, he says that some ultimate duality
in existence between "God *and* the Creature"[125] is always
implied. "This *and*," he adds, "is an 'and' of *absolute freedom*."[126] Further, he specifically rejects the idea that we can
treat this duality in terms of the correlates, Absolute and relative, Infinite and finite.[127] The reason seems clear. Correlation
implies essential complementarity of terms, and thus if
appealed to in the instance of the God-creature duality, the
two would become interdependent, and not only would the
creature be transformed into an autonomous principle along
with God, but also the infinite distance between them would
be canceled.

What can Florensky say in his own defense? Although he
does not substantially say much more beyond what has already
been quoted, the bits and pieces one finds suffice for the
formulation of a coherent, even if not exhaustive and defini-

[123]*Uchenie o Bulgakova,* 6.
[124]These exact words Lossky uses in his *History of Russian Philosophy,*
312, specifically in reference to the speculations of Karsavin, another member
of the pan-unity school. Charles Hartshorne draws attention to these words,
"together with," in his extended study, "Total Unity in Russian Metaphysics:
Some Reactions to Zenkovsky's and Lossky's Histories," first printed in the
Review of Metaphysics, 7 (1954) and subsequently reissued in his *The
Logic of Perfection* (La Salle, IL: Open Court Publishing, 1973), 263-79.
See esp. p. 267. We shall shortly be returning to this point, as it has a
bearing on our whole problematic.
[125]"The Idea of Creation in Christian Philosophy," *The Eastern Churches
Quarterly,* 8 (1949), supplementary issue, p. 55.
[126]Ibid.
[127]Ibid.

tive, response. The observations of Charles Hartshorne, an important exponent of the process philosophy of Alfred North Whitehead in America, concerning the Russian pan-unity school in particular are germane to the present discussion.[128] Although his knowledge of this school is by and large only through secondary sources, not being himself versed in Russian, this has in no way impeded him from making penetrating observations. Since his philosophical matrix, panentheism in general and Whitehead's philosophy of organism in particular, shares numerous points of concern with the Russian religious metaphysical tradition, he is in a unique position to offer rather novel, and fully relevant, comments of no small importance.

Most importantly, he successfully isolates the critical juncture where the proponents and critics of pan-unity part ways over their respective theories. The sophiologists and metaphysicians of pan-unity insist on the need for an Absolute, which somehow includes the creature in order to secure the very absoluteness of the Absolute. If the creature were totally separate from and out of the range of the Absolute, the Absolute would be essentially limited by it, and thus would not be absolute any longer. For Florensky, it is Holy Sophia which provides that all-embracing unity in which somehow all is contained in, or better yet, founded upon and belongs to that Absolute, who is God. This is essentially the pan-en-theistic content of Florensky's sophiology.[129]

The critic, however, disclaiming any possibility of framing the problem in these terms, can only read pantheism in this endeavor. The absoluteness of God, according to him, cannot be sufficiently safeguarded by correlating all else with it within some all-embracing unity. In truth, his procedure serves only to evacuate God of His absolute transcendence, as it fails to observe the canons of apophatic theology properly, and merely flounders in its too unilateral, cataphatic approach to God, erring by its undue preoccupation with articulating the

---

[128]Cf. n. 124, p. 199 above.

[129]Florensky's formal position, it must be stressed, is not pantheism. He never considers the world as identical with God nor as a part of His divine substance. Cf. again our comments in n. 37 on p. 177 above.

full scope and depth of the Creator-creature relationship at the cost of a fundamental rationalization of a basic mystery. This mystery is none less than the inscrutability of God, who has willed that creation be. According to Lossky, the faithful safeguarding of this mystery enjoins us only to assent to the existence of God the Creator "together with" the creature.

Here Hartshorne enters in with his objection. Lossky, he claims, misses the chief point in the whole discussion. It is precisely the aspect of "together with" that demands explanation. "This togetherness," Hartshorne writes, "must be something, a real property of creation, or of God, or a third something on its own."[180] Whatever one's choice, it must figure among these. But if it is one of the first two, then it would seem that either the world embraces God as one of its constituents or that God merely contains the world as one of His own, both options evidencing a monist and pantheistic outlook. If, on the other hand, the selection to be favored is the third one, then there would seem to be some entity greater than God—a manifest impossibility. But if there is not some one element which can comprise the two poles, divine and creatural, including them within itself, we only find ourselves in a *regressus in infinitum* in the search for that "togetherness" explaining the total *complexus* of the "all" and being in itself a quality inclusive of the *complexus* and itself. It is the precise task of the doctrine of Holy Sophia, both as Divine and creatural Wisdom to take this dilemma by its horns, and it is in this sense, as Hartshorne notes, that it is in some way inevitable for speculative reason.[181]

Critics of pan-unity also point to another difficulty implicit in it. The insistence on correlativity within an all-embracing unity would seem to obviate the need for creation. The terms, Absolute-relative, Infinite-finite, even Cause-effect, necessarily imply one another, and therefore lie beyond the realm of freedom, and supply us only with a conceptual framework in which the idea of creation is simply an unintelligible notion.

[180]Hartshorne, *Logic of Perfection*, 267.

[181]In our previously cited study, "La sofiologia di Pavel Florenskij," we refer to this "inevitability" of the sophiological enterprise. Editorial revision (cf. p. 263), however, rendered this as "incomprehensibility."

And if one attempts to speak of creation in the context of pan-unity, its meaning seems ineluctably evacuated of its true content. God no longer creates *according to* His idea in true freedom, but only *out of* His idea[132] with the flow of inner necessity. Only emanation seems to obtain, and not the radical actuation of the Divine Will as demanded by the Christian dogmatic understanding of creation.

Florensky, however, would rejoin that he fully respects the reality of divine freedom, and that creation for him is only the superabundant fruit of God's unimpugned freedom and diffusive love. Indeed, he explicitly says that it is the Holy Trinity itself that deigns its own correlation with the creature and its consequent determination by the same.[133] But, then, what would he reply to the objection, the traditional one in Christian philosophy, that God cannot be subjected to a relation of determination with the creature, but, at most, to a relation of reason, in which the creature alone is affected by the knowledge and love of God, but not God Himself,[134] there being the question of only a nonreciprocal relation of the creature to a perfect God?[135] How would he respond to the customary objections of a more perennial strain of Christian thought that if the determinative relation between God and the creature were a predicamental one, then God would acquire a new accidental relation and perfection from the creature or, more seriously, if it were a transcendental one, then God would be dependent upon the creature, at least as the very condition of the creature's being, and thus become Himself a radically contingent being? Though these questions may never have been put to Florensky in these exact terms, they do, nonetheless, express the valid

---

[132]Florovsky, "The Idea of Creation," 64.

[133]PFT, 324.

[134]Traditional philosophy would say that the most we can affirm of God is that we are known and loved by Him. We are therefore not speaking of a positive knowledge or love that would enrich God as such.

[135]In these paragraphs we make use of the poignant remarks of Walter E. Stokes, S.J., concerning the analogous dispute over this issue between Thomism and process philosophy as found in his article, "Is God Really Related to this World?" *The Proceedings of the American Catholic Philosophical Association* for the year 1965, pp. 145-51.

and deeply set worries of those anxious about the protection
of the absoluteness and infinity of the Godhead.

The faithful follower of Florensky could begin by underscoring the personalist perspective of *homoousian* philosophy,
in which 'the cosmos is characterized by dynamic, organic interrelationships. The primary category in this world view is that
of *person*—not the person understood in a static manner with
empty self-identity, but rather the person as constituted by
dynamic identity. For the disciple of Florensky, the person
is truly himself only in relation to his other. It is this other,
the "non-I" that gives the person to himself, that lets him
receive his own identity.

The impersonal universe of *homoiousian* philosophy, on
the other hand, has no room for such dynamic interrelationships, since it remains confined within the conceptual framework of unchangeable nature and substance, which does not
admit of that level of insight in which entities would be perceived as mutually constituting. In essence, the *homoiousian*
universe is Greek in heritage, at least insofar as it is the heir
of its philosophical notion of unchangeable nature,[136] and is
thus markedly foreign to the personal world of Christianity,
in which self-sacrificing love with all its inherent hopes and
attendant risks and vulnerabilities, and not necessary nature,
is the dominant force and real motivational wellspring of
activity.

If God is a person, then, Florensky would submit, He
cannot be subtracted from the same aspirations and gambles
common to all persons, even created persons. What else
could have elicited his moving affirmation that God does not
oblige but persuades; that He does not constrain but sup-
plicates?[137] Florensky, however, would vigorously deny that
with this stance he thereby divests God of His full majesty
or that he in any way undermines His absolute aseity. God,

---

[136]Hume's universe, as we have seen, is also *homoiousian*, but for different reasons. For Hume, the very notion of unchanging nature or substance is unintelligible. But he rejected it for more gravely erroneous reasons.
For him, real, internal interrelations among dynamic substances (or subsistent relations) are also unintelligible. He allows only for external relations or similarity based on customary conjunction.

[137]PFT, 324.

as revelation informs us and trinitarian theology elaborates
for us, is Three Persons in Relation. Expressed in more
philosophical terms, the thought conveyed is that the Godhead is structurally relational. From within, God is constituted
by Subsistent Relations, by the Father, Son, and Holy Spirit in
Intratrinitarian Relation animated by reciprocal Love. From
without, this relational dynamism of the Godhead super-
abounds in creation. God in His freedom decides to offer
Himself in relation to His creature. This process of self-
relation, however, does not change God's immutable nature
nor does it imply an enrichment in God's perfection is to be
gained from the creature. Rather, it is only a mysterious,
freely willed actuation of His essential perfection as a person
in self-relation.

Having *de facto* become a Creator, God correlates Himself to His creature, and thereby establishes the sophianic
quality of created being. The creature for his part becomes
cognizant of his sophianic worth once he realizes that he is,
in essence, a logos uttered by the Logos. This *prise de conscience* does not, however, come immediately to the creature,
but rather materializes only upon the realization of his
dynamic identity as a substantial relation, that is, a relational
being founded upon and constituted by others and ultimately
the Other and, therefore, only upon his explicit co-affirmation
of his own creaturehood along with the Infinite and Necessary
Being, which is the radical ground and source of his finitude
and contingency. This personal consciousness of one's sophia
as correlate of a Divine Sophia is the experiential point of
departure, *sine qua non,* for any proof of the existence of
God to convince. Without such an experience of the presence
of God in the created world no argument, however traditional,
could possibly be appealed to in order to conclude to the existence of a transcendent God.

But, it is important to add, the sophianic vision of reality
cannot remain exclusively within the framework of correlation. A further differentiation is needed, if God's Absolute
Transcendence is not to be compromised. The terms of correlation may serve to explicate the mystery of God's immanence in the world, considering that the essence of the per-

sonalist meaning of creation is that God chooses to make a gift of Himself to the world and even to depend, as it were, on it. But the fact that God does not by His nature need to create this or any other world should not be overlooked. God is not just relational to the creature in His Divine Energies, but also remains absolutely and infinitely Subsistent and Unfathomable in His Essence. In this sense, God is Totally Other than the creature, and decidedly beyond the terms of any correlation.

What can we, therefore, conclude from this discussion? The answer seems clear: Florensky's category of correlativity needs further qualification, if we are fully to explicate the real relations obtaining between God and the creature. The needed corrective also suggests itself. In true antinomical fashion, we may advance the category of "asymmetrical correlativity" as the best framework in which to secure not only God's aseity, but also to account faithfully for His relationality *ad alium*.[138] In particular, it falls to the aspect of asymmetry to ensure a faithful expression of the Christian dogmatic conception of *creatio ex nihilo*, while that of correlativity helps explain God's providential conservation of the world once created.

6.3 *The Analogy of Holy Sophia*

As already indicated, one of the chief reasons for the apprehensiveness about sophiological and pan-unity theories has been the fear that some form of pantheism is inevitable. This suspicion is not without its justification. The language of correlativity, which is typically encountered in these theories, is not sufficiently put under critical examination by the thinkers of these schools,[139] who seem not fully aware of

[138]Our solution is thus a variant of that proffered by Stokes himself. See "Is God Really Related to this World?" 151. The addition of this aspect of asymmetry also represents a development in thought respective to our previous treatment of correlativity in "La sofiologia di Pavel Florenskij," 257f, 261.

[139]Besides Florensky, we especially think of Soloviev, Bulgakov, Karsavin, and Frank. Florensky and Bulgakov have decidedly theological interests, while Karsavin and Frank remain more strictly on the philosophical plane.

the real, attendant dangers in this type of speaking. Specifically, the language of correlativity seems to eliminate the infinite distance between God and the creature by making the two mutually interdependent terms of a correlation. How can God really be transcendent to the creature in such a framework? Indeed, does He not therein become contingent upon the creature?

To safeguard the Absolute Transcendence of God and still to make His real presence in the world genuinely felt, recourse must be made to the analogy of being. But it is precisely a theory of analogy that is lacking in Florensky, a fact which is all the more surprising since in his reflections he repeatedly draws from the matrix of analogy without, however, ever really singling it out for explicit consideration. For example, he straightforwardly asserts in one place that Holy Sophia is One in God and many in creation.[140] He then immediately proceeds to indicate the true manifold of applications and meanings it bears in the created order. What results is a veritable multiplicity of entities, both similar and dissimilar among themselves, partaking of Sophia in different degrees or proportions. The various features of this manifold, however, are nothing other than the ontological presuppositions of analogy,[141] the existence of which is itself merely deduced from the evident, irrefutable fact that there is a unity in diversity among beings, which concomitantly signals them with likeness in difference. It is the specific function of analogy to explicate this antinomy or apparent paradox of likeness in difference among beings.

The problematic of analogy is also encountered, but again not explicitly thematized, in Florensky's noteworthy passage[142] in which he considers Holy Sophia, at once, as the cosmic principle explaining how the Father creates in the Son through the Holy Spirit and as a transcendental in line with the traditional transcendental properties of being—unity, truth, goodness, and beauty. In terms of the Father, as we

[140]PFT, 329.

[141]Battista Mondin, S.X., *The Principle of Analogy in Protestant and Catholic Theology*, 2nd ed. (The Hague: Martinus Nijhoff, 1968), 62-76.

[142]PFT, 349, and our p. 181 above, esp. n. 59.

have seen, Sophia is the ideal substance or foundation of creation; in those of the Son, it is the reason or logos of creation; while lastly, in those of the Holy Spirit, it is the holiness or beauty of creation. This sophianic triad of foundation-reason-holiness found within the Holy Trinity is carried over into the created order, manifesting itself, proportionately, i.e., analogously, as the unity, truth, and spiritual beauty[143] of each creature. It is in these transcendental properties, Florensky appears to be saying, that every creature, each in its own way, bears the impress of the Holy Trinity.

But what needs to be understood is that the very mechanism of speech at work in this type of affirmation is nothing other than analogy, which can be simply defined as that mode of predication, standing midway between univocity and equivocation, in which something is known by proportion to or by imperfect likeness with something else. Its importance lies in the fact that it can explicate the common notes of entities, while still respecting their particular individualities. This feature of analogy takes on crucial importance in theological discourse in which the referents are God Himself and the creature. It is in analogy that we find the needed tool which allows us to speak coherently of God, yet in a way that does not reduce His Divine Reality to our own finite, creatural level.

Objections to the language of correlativity have arisen precisely as a protest against treating God on a univocal plane with man. To speak of man as the correlative effect of a Divine Creator is erroneous for exactly this reason. This mode of speaking may convey the idea of God's immanence to the world, but it also seems to promote the identification of God with the world. On the other hand, if there is not some common measure for speaking of the one and the other, God will be so removed from man not only to obviate the need for religious and theological discourse itself, but, indeed, to render the very notion of it incoherent. If God is Totally Other and in no way in the world, He may as well not be.

It was the great merit of St. Thomas Aquinas to have grasped the paramount importance of this problematic for

[143]Florensky conjoins goodness and beauty into one transcendental.

religious discourse, and it is in his proffered solution that we find the needed complement which can save sophiological speculation from lapsing into pantheism. Leaving the vast problematic of analogy for the most part to the side, we need draw attention only to the specifically metaphysical[144] analogies of intrinsic attribution[145] and proper proportionality and only insofar as they directly enter into the solution of the immediate problem at hand.[146]

In the analogy of intrinsic attribution, a common element is intrinsically attributed to both the primary and secondary analogates based on a relation of efficient causality. In our specific context, we may say that Sophia belongs properly and intrinsically not only to God, but also to man. There is, accordingly, a similarity between Divine Sophia and creatural Sophia, even if the latter is only an infinitely pale reflection of the former. This the analogy of intrinsic attribution says explicitly. It also implicitly states that the relation of creatural Sophia to man is only an infinitely imperfect imitation of the relation of Divine Sophia to God. The specific function of the analogy of proper proportionality is to make this similarity of relations explicit.[147]

There are, of course, Thomists, who follow the line of Cajetan and refuse to recognize the analogy of intrinsic attribution, and who, in consequence, would not accept this analysis. But we appeal to this specific type of Thomistic analysis, subscribed to by Mondin and others, because the

[144]The non-metaphysical analogies are those of extrinsic attribution in which the analogated perfection belongs properly to only one of the analogates, but is attributed by the mind to another by a relation of either material, exemplary or final causality, and of improper proportionality, which is a simple case of metaphorical language.

[145]Cajetan and the Cajetanists do not recognize this kind of analogy for reasons explained below, and only make a trichotomous division of analogy: the analogy of inequality (which is really only a special case of univocity or generic predication), the analogy of attribution (which would be our analogy of extrinsic attribution), and the analogy of proper proportionality (which for them is the only metaphysical analogy). For a fuller discussion of Cajetan's classification, see Mondin, *Principle of Analogy*, 35-51, 69.

[146]For a more complete treatment of this problem, see *Principle of Analogy*, esp. 67-74, 85-102.

[147]In this discussion, we base ourselves closely on Mondin, *Principle of Analogy*, 70.

suspicions against it are analogous to those shown towards the language of correlation used in sophiological theories. The objection of the Cajetanist would be that the analogy of intrinsic attribution does not succeed where the language of correlation fails, as it too seems eventually to fall into univocation. Specifically, they would question whether the recourse made to the principle of efficient causality in the analogy of intrinsic attribution really sheds substantially new light on the problem. Since its possibility rests solely on the validity of the principle of likeness between the cause and effect (*omne agens agit simile sibi*), they would pointedly ask whether that would not render God the Creator in some sense finite, temporal, and imperfect in this type of analogous relationship, if the created effect is only finite, temporal, and imperfect.[148] For them, therefore, only the analogy of proper proportionality can be resorted to in speaking of the relationship between God and the creature.

Although it is impossible fully to respond to all the issues at stake here, solutions have been worked out by Thomists themselves. The most crucial, single issue to be addressed is how the Creator may be present in His creature a way that, at once, allows a likeness between the creature and Himself and yet does not subtract from His divinity. The gist of the suggested solutions centers around the excellence of divine causality in which the analogous perfection is predicated *essentially* of the primary analogate, in this case, God, and of the secondary analogate, that is, the created effect, only by *participation*.[149] By linking the finite creature in this way to his Divine Creator, it is hoped that God's immanence to the world is given a faithful and adequate expression, one which, at the same time, does not detract from His transcendence.

If Florensky himself had explicitly treated the question of analogy, he would have found the needed tool for complementing his notion of correlativity which accounts for God's immanence to the world but seems to jeopardize His

[148]Cf. Mondin's discussion, *Principle of Analogy*, 67.
[149]Ibid., 101.

transcendence.[150] A fully conscious awareness of analogy's importance in discourse would have also helped him in his methodological search for a criterion of truth, as we have already seen in chapter two of this work,[151] and would have enabled him to have more fully appreciated the central role analogical knowledge of God has to play in religious discourse apart from either a strict or vague mystical knowledge of Him.[152]

The critics of sophiological and pan-unity theories also could learn from this discussion. Indeed, we might even say that the sophiological controversies of the 1930's, which shook Russian Orthodox circles, could have been mollified had the insights of Catholic Thomists regarding analogy been brought more clearly into the picture. These critics were rightfully concerned about the dangers of pantheism, which seems almost inherent to sophiological speculation, but their articulated counter positions did little to shed much light on the real issue at hand.

If we take Nicholas Lossky's critique of Bulgakov as a case in point, we find that his analysis is chiefly marred by its insufficient hermeneutic of analogy. Having criticized Bulgakov for submitting God to the terms of a relation with the creature, Lossky proceeds:

> It is asked: How is it possible to combine negative theology with positive theology, in which God is thought of as a Person, as Mind, Love, etc., and even, on the basis of Revelation, as Three Persons? The answer to this question is as follows: If the One God

[150]The lack of a clear understanding of analogy is also probably one of the chief defects of Whitehead's system. Whitehead's concern is for a God who is not above general metaphysical principles, but is rather their chief exemplification. For this reason, he thinks that all reality must be on a univocal plane. Speaking of God and other actual entities which make up the world, Whitehead writes: "But, though there are gradations of importance, and diversities of function, yet in the principles which actuality exemplifies all are *on the same level*" (emphasis ours). *Process and Reality*, 18. Cf. his remarks in *Religion in the Making* (New York: World Publishing, 1954), 69, 87.

[151]Cf. pp. 67-69 above.

[152] Cf. our comments p. 138 above, esp. n. 62.

exists in Three Persons, this means that the word "person" is applied to God only by analogy—not by logical analogy according to which two analogous objects have an *identical* aspect, but rather by *metalogical* analogy, because there is not any kind of identical aspect between God and the world. The Super-Being of God and the being of the world are separated from one another by an ontological abyss. When we speak about God as a Person, Mind, Love, we have in mind something Supra-Personal, Supra-Rational, etc., which has in Itself that value, which we cherish in personhood, in mind, but to such a superlative degree, that it is incommensurable with our personhood, our mind, etc. In other words, even in positive theology, we, strictly speaking, remain on the terrain of negative theology. Positive theology is not anthropomorphism in the teaching about God.[153]

Lossky correctly grasps the need to conjoin negative and positive theology. Negative theology is needed to ensure God's transcendence, while positive theology points to God's immanence to the world through the element of similarity. But his error lies in his inadequate division of analogy into logical and metalogical analogy. Lossky's understanding of metalogical analogy fairly well covers the analogy of proper proportionality. However, he does not seem sufficiently cognizant of its ineptitude to express God's immanence to the world. His logical analogy, on the other hand, alludes to the analogy of intrinsic attribution, but fails completely to consider any relation of efficient causality, which is essential to a proper understanding of intrinsic attribution. He is, therefore, not capable of arriving at that level of insight which would allow him fully to appreciate God's creative and conservative presence in the world, the lived experience of which inspires sophiological reflection.

---

[153]*Uchenie o. Sergiya Bulgakova,* 10f.

6.4 The Role of Love

There is one last constant to bear in mind in any consideration of Florensky's sophiology, namely, that both its
point of departure and point of arrival concern an experience
of love. In the sophianic vision, God's infinite love is grasped
to be the true, creative cause of the ordered beauty of the
cosmos. The creature, however, is able to understand this
causal mystery and then fully participate in creation's own
beauty, only if he has been internally purified by the cathartic
fires of love. Love is, indeed, the spark that initiates creation,
and also the energy force that sustains it. It is also, at once,
the key and the hallmark to Florensky's metaphysics of consubstantiality in which all reality, both divine and creatural,
is bound together by dynamic interrelationships of love.

This stance may serve to explain why Florensky seems to
affirm panpsychism, insofar as all created beings or monads
seem to be endowed with "personality" as the necessary condition of their entering into the type of dynamic interrelationships required by his metaphysics of consubstantiality.[154] But
panpsychism may not be integral to his doctrine, if subper-
sonal realities are merely considered by remote analogies with
personal beings. At any rate, the more essential point is that
even impersonal creation can only be properly accounted for
if done in a nonstatic way, that is, by grounding it in its
"other" according to the principle of sufficient reason.

Lastly, it is love which ultimately secures Florensky's
sophiology from the reproach of pantheism. Florensky says
that God freely deigns to correlate Himself with the creature,[155] and thereby place Himself in dynamic interrelationship
with it, even hazarding a real, fiducial "dependence" on it.
A convinced pantheist could only abhor such an affirmation.
For him, only the famous but ghastly words of Spinoza hold:
Deus proprie loquendo neminem amat (Stricly speaking,

---

[154]Cf. p. 137 (n. 60) above. Curiously, Whitehead explicitly subscribes
to panpsychism.
[155]PFT, 324.

God does not love anyone).[156] Whatever its defects, Florensky's sophiological world-view is certainly preferable to the
one heralded by a ruthlessly consistent pantheism. It not only
gives an organic accounting of the cosmos, but it also permits
a credible explanation of man's highest calling—the life of
prayer—and God's tender and all-merciful response to it.

[156]Benedict de Spinoza, *The Ethics*, pt. 5, prop. 17, corollary, in *The
Rationalists* (Garden City, NY: Doubleday & Co., 1960), 391. In the full
quote, Spinoza adds "or hate anyone."

CHAPTER VIII

The Metaphysical Roots
of Friendship

At the end of his epistolary meditation on Holy Sophia, Florensky connects three grand ideas: Sophia, Truth, and Friendship.[1] Sophia is defined as the *true* Creature and the Creature in *Truth*. However, Florensky adds, to know Sophia truly, one must experience Truth and abide in its presence. But how is this particular subsistence possible? What maintains it? Only friendship can, Florensky responds, defining it alternately as the "mysterious birth of the Thou" or "that milieu in which the revelation of Truth is begun."[2]

Friendship, in its turn, is a mode of love. So it ultimately falls to love to condition the possibility of the knowledge of both truth and Truth. Love, in the words of Florensky, is "that spiritual activity in which and by means of which the knowledge of the Pillar of Truth is given."[3] Not every sort of love, however, will do. It must be the "love of *grace*"[4] that both gives the initial spur to search for truth and then provides the sustaining force for a life in Truth. This engraced love is the love of friendship, and it is the friend who serves as the pledge that this grace will neither disappoint nor fail us. In him we find both the "source of hope for victory and the symbol of the future."[5] It is in him that we have the

[1]PFT, 391f.
[2]PFT, 392.
[3]PFT, 395.
[4]Ibid.
[5]PFT, 396.

first, inaugural experience of that life to be had ultimately in its fullness only in communion with Truth, since it is he alone who initially lets us ground our dynamic self-identity, and thereby live our consubstantiality with him. And not only with him but with all humanity, with the whole of creation, and even with the Lord of creation Himself.

In his pages devoted to the theme of friendship, Florensky's probing, philosophic genius comes to the fore. It is also in them that we see that many of his own intuitions concerning being and love truly anteceded the very same ones given wider distribution in Russian émigré circles by Simeon Frank and throughout the contemporary western world in general by Martin Buber and Gabriel Marcel.

1. THE POLYVALENCY OF LOVE

True to his accustomed method, Florensky begins his reflections with a brief, etymological inquiry[6] into some of the root meanings of love concentrating almost exclusively on the Greek language, noted for its rich vocabulary for expressing this particular woof in the fabric of life.

1.1 *Four Dimensions of Love*

The Greek language has four words for love, each expressing a different modality of love and marked with its own particular bent. These terms are *eros, philia, storge,* and *agape.* The first, *eros* expresses the love of passion, and is characteristically marked by an intensity of feeling directed towards its intentional object. *Philia,* on the other hand, is attenuated in its feeling, although it is still disposed to genuine, cordial relationships with persons, thus making it the characteristic love called friendship. It also carries, according to Florensky, the sense of the kiss as a natural, external expression of a felt, interior closeness. To Florensky's mind, it also lacks any tinge of moralism. The next love is *storge,*

6Cf. PFT, 396-400, for the discussion to follow.

the love of deep affection and attachment. It is neither passionate, nor does it incline towards intimacy, but rather expresses a profoundly peaceful and constant sentiment in the bosom of the one who loves. It characteristically reveals itself in parental, filial, and marital love and in the patriotic love of country. Lastly, there is *agape*, the love better known as charity. It is a rational love, so to speak, that is capable of valuation and respect. It concentrates on the objective appraisal of the one loved. Its attendant sentiment, for this reason, is neither passionate, glowing, nor tender. In addition, since this love implies valuation, it must also imply the notion of comparison and, more fundamentally, that of the freedom of the will, which is capable of choice and the direction of its focus.

These four loves, however, do not stand in isolation from one another, but are rather specified by determinate interrelationships. Both *agape* and *philia*, for instance, concern the person, but in different ways. *Agape* is signed by morality, and chiefly considers the properties or qualities of personhood and the person. *Philia*, on the other hand, does not, at least immediately, come under the formality of morality. It rather attends to the establishment of objective bonds and close ties with a particular person. *Philia* and *eros* are also interrelated. Florensky notes that though they may be close as to their "matter," they certainly differ as to "form."[7] The former aims at close contact and interior intimacy, while the latter has sensual intentions, and may even carry pathological overtones. Lastly, *storge* stands in relative opposition to the other three loves, it being basically a "generic" feeling and the others specifically "personal" ones.[8] *Storge*, Florensky suggests, rather arises out of man's inherent nature, and, accordingly, is not dependent upon a special individual.

1.2 *Distillations for Friendship*

Florensky's particular focus of interest at this juncture is, however, with *philia* or friendship. He appeals to the Greek

[7]PFT, 399.
[8]PFT, 400.

language to find both immediate insights and clues to guide his further reflections, although he does not expect that his etymological query, as such, will quench his intellectual thirst. Indeed, he specifically notes that upon examination none of the four classical Greek determinations for love quite designates the species of friendship he is treating in his present and next to last letter.[9] The phenomenon of friendship he is trying to elucidate is, he says, somewhat of an admixture of *philia, eros,* and *agape,* through *philia* captures its sense best of all.[10]

Philia has four specific marks which he thinks are worth highlighting. It is, first of all, notable for its immediateness and its direct foundation on personal contact. It does not limit itself to a detached evaluation of a person's qualities, but rather seeks to penetrate into his very selfhood. *Philia,* moreover, is nonrational in character. But this does not mean that it is therefore impulsive or passionate; it rather remains peaceful and heart-felt. Its final mark—and most essential motif—thus presents itself, namely, closeness on a truly personal level.

Florensky continues his discussion of friendship by especially focusing in on *philia* and *agape.* Though the particulars of his further determinations are not essential to his subsequent, philosophical point, in a sense they pave the way for his more specifically philosophical reflection. After considering some of the synonyms for *philia* in ancient Greek, he concentrates his attention on Sacred Scripture and its vocabulary for love.[11] Noting that *eros* is almost excluded from the Old Testament, and is not even admitted into the New Testament, and further observing in passing that *philia,* for its part, is spiritualized in the New Testament, it being used to express Christian relationships of love among those desirous of communion on a personal level, Florensky remarks how *agape* is the preferred word of the New Testament for love.

[9]"Friendship" is the title of his eleventh letter. Cf. PFT, 393-463.
[10]PFT, 400. He adds that possibly the word, *philophrosúne,* is the closest Greek word in meaning. It translates as "affectionateness," "benevolence," and "amiability."
[11]PFT, 402-6.

He then proceeds to isolate the four aspects of *agape* thematized in the New Testament. First, he notes it is always used in the context of free will and personal decision for the object of love (cf. Mt 5:44; Heb 1:9). Secondly, and in a closely related sense, it is used in passages which treat instances of both positive and negative election, that is, in cases of opting for or against someone or a state of affairs (cf. Mt 6:24; Lk 9:35). Next, it is employed in pericopes narrating episodes of willful, and not merely spontaneous, compassion (cf. Lk 7:5; 1 Thes 1:4).[12] And lastly, *agape* is used to describe the historic ties of brotherhood among Christians. Florensky then concludes his consideration of *agape* observing that the term is conspicuously foreign to extra-biblical, secular language. This is not all that surprising, Florensky intimates, insofar as it truly expresses or points to *sacrificial* love, which properly bears divine and absolute characteristics, and not human and conditional ones.

There is one last point worth noting.[13] Love, as the various Greek words for it convey, has both a personal and a social side to it. The "personal" loves are *eros* and *philia,* while the "social" ones are *storge* and *agape.* Significantly, the ancient pagans and the first Christians can be distinguished according to their personal and social attitudes towards love. In the heathen world, *eros* and *storge* best capture, Florensky says, the personal and social dimensions of love respectively. For a Christian society, on the other hand, only *philia* and *agape* can faithfully depict the personal and social experiences of love, and only they, Florensky adds, can provide the necessary leaven and salt for a stable and fervid Christian existence.[14] *Agape* itself, according to Florensky, is based on *philia.*[15] The experience of love given in friendship, i.e., in any one friend, serves as the impulse for our love of all men.

---

[12]Sometimes the passages Florensky cites, however, do not lend themselves to easy classification. We might wish to question some of Florensky's choices, but this aspect of the problem is not crucial to his overall problematic.

[13]Cf. PFT, 410. One still may want to question the full accuracy of Florensky's accounting of pagan society.

[14]PFT, 413.

2. A Philosophy of Duality

These etymological and exegetical data need to be synthesized, however, if the real genius of the Christian world-view
is to be truly appreciated. Florensky's specific aim is to provide such a synthesis. He begins by briefly exploring the theme
of friendship in both the Old and New Testaments,[16] and
what he discovers throughout is a new antinomy—that of
friendship, the antinomy of the "*person-dyad*."[17] Christianity
is not only to be distinguished for its communitarian and
"philiarchtic" relationships in its overall hirerachical and
ecclesial structure, but, more radically, even down to its
smallest unit. In Christianity, the most fundamental unit,
Florensky stresses, is not the individual man understood as an
atomic unit, but is rather the pair of friends, which is to be
considered the basic molecule.[18] Man alone by himself cannot
exist in the Christian framework. Only man as essentially
constituted by his other can accord with Christianity. The
Christian world-view, accordingly, makes dynamic identity its
hallmark.

Florensky's exegetical support which he adduces for his
position may not be fully acceptable according to strict, scientific principles, of course, but he definitely makes a relevant
observation. Our Lord's custom, he notes, was to send the
apostles out "two by two" (Mk 6:7; Lk 10:1) in order to
pursue His mission of evangelization. Was this mere coincidence? Florensky thinks not. Personal apostolates are necessarily collaborative efforts, and this basic truth was, Florensky
claims, being implicitly brought out by our Lord in His
selection and pairing of the apostles,[19] whether as brothers as
in the case of Andrew and Peter, the sons of John; or James
and John, the sons of Zebedee; or as friends as in the instance
of Philip and Nathanael Bartholomew; or Matthew Levi and
Thomas the Twin; or as colleagues as for example Timothy
and Paul; or Luke and Silas.

[15]PFT, 412.
[16]PFT, 413-28.
[17]PFT, 419.
[18]Ibid.
[19]PFT, 426f.

Not only do we need a close collaborator or friend for us to fulfill our personal missions in life, but we need one to facilitate, even render possible, our understanding of heavenly truth. Florensky movingly writes: "The mystical unity of *two* is the condition of knowledge and thus of the manifestation of the Spirit of Truth, which provides this knowledge."[20] This is the true depth of import borne in that commonplace, but often uncultivated, reality known as friendship. It should thus be approached in reverent gratitude, and never be treated lightly nor be interpreted nominalistically nor from the mere point of view of plain actions and sentiments, but rather from a realistic, metaphysical point of view as that reality making the soul's inner unity fully possible.[21] Indeed, Florensky observes it is in a friend that one finds one's true *alter ego,* the one who truly allows one, at once, to break out of one's self-contained selfhood and truly to find oneself as constituted by the other, the friend, and thus as a truly unified self.[22]

The bond of friendship, Florensky repeats, is properly metaphysical in nature, and thus must be viewed not only psychologically and ethically, but, more importantly, ontologically and mystically.[23] How is friendship, therefore, to be defined in this dual, ontological-mystical perspective? Florensky replies that it is the "contemplation of oneself through the friend in God."[24] Otherwise expressed, it is the "knowledge of oneself through the eyes of another, but before the face of a third, namely the Third."[25] But this knowledge is nothing other than the knowledge of love. Florensky, therefore, asserts that only in one's love of another does one come to treasure one's own innate value as a person. Further, this love is not possible outside the Love of God. Both lover and beloved exist only insofar as they are beloved creatures of the one God who is Love. The mutually constituted bond between friends thus not only interiorly links them to one another,

[20]PFT, 430.
[21]PFT, 431.
[22]PFT, 433.
[23]PFT, 438.
[24]Ibid.
[25]PFT, 439.

but also, at a hidden, deeper level, strengthens their primordial bonds with the all-embracing Godhead. The friend is like a mirror. It is only in the perception of his other that a man becomes conscious of himself as a "co-existent" along with this other. One's own identity and selfhood, Florensky claims, are properly received only in an act of *assimilation* or *appropriation* of the other than oneself, of the Thou.[26] He writes: "In being reflected in a friend, the 'I' recognizes its *alter ego* in his 'I.' "[27] The antinomy of friendship thus arises. "A friend," Florensky elaborates, "is not only an 'I,' but *an other* 'I,' *another* for 'I.' "[28] "The friend is this 'I,' which is not-'I': the friend is *contradiction*, and in its very concept an antinomy is devolved."[29]

These profoundly meaningful insights into the nature of friendship may not sound particularly new to the ears of a westerner who is well-versed in the thought of the Hasidic Jewish philosopher, Martin Buber, who also captured the full import of the I-Thou antinomy, and gave it a masterful elaboration. Although he did so independently of Florensky, his classic work, *I and Thou* was only written after him.[30] Buber, however, gives striking, limpid expression to some of Florensky's ideas. Noting how the "other," the Thou, is constitutive of the "I," Buber writes: "If *Thou* is said, the *I* of the combination *I-Thou* is said along with it."[31] Elsewhere, he remarks:

> I become through my relation to the Thou; as I become *I*, I say Thou.
> All real living is meeting.[32]

---

[26]Cf. PFT, 48, and our discussion on p. 109 above.

[27]PFT, 439.

[28]Ibid.

[29]Ibid. Once again, Florensky uses the word "contradiction" in a very wide sense.

[30]*Ich und Du*, the German original, first appeared in 1923. English translation, *I and Thou*, 2d ed. (New York: Charles Scribner's Sons, 1958).

[31]*I and Thou*, 3.

[32]Ibid., 11.

More bluntly, he simply says: "A subject deprived of its object is deprived of its reality."[33]

Buber also grasped the critical difference between empty and dynamic identity, even if he did not employ Florensky's exact vocabulary. This particular *prise de conscience* is evident in his contrast of the "free" and "self-willed" man. In his own words:

> The free man is he who wills without arbitrary self-will. He believes in reality, that is, he believes in the real solidarity of the real twofold entity *I* and *Thou*. He believes in destiny . . .
>
> The self-willed man does not believe and does not meet. He does not know solidarity of connexion, but only the feverish world outside and his feverish desire to use it.[34]

Implicit in these words is an affirmation of the realization of personal identity through the act of appropriation. Buber shortly makes this idea fully explicit. He remarks:

> Individuality neither shares in nor obtains any reality. It differentiates itself from the other, and seeks through experiencing and using to appropriate as much of it as it can. This is *its* dynamic, self-differentiation and appropriation, each exercised on the *It* within the unreal.[35]

Buber assuredly would also agree with Florensky's further development of this insight in regard to dynamic identity. The dynamic identity of man which is obtained in the act of adoption and assimilation of the other is especially verified between friends as a true *"exchange* of beings,"[36] in which each is complemented by the other. Is this real sharing of one's very *being* with the beloved not the metaphysically latent meaning behind the beautiful, and possibly universal,

[33]Ibid., 90.
[34]Ibid., 60f.
[35]Ibid., 64.
[36]PFT, 440.

expression, "being in love"?[37] The lover, that is, lives in the being of his beloved, and becomes, as it were, his "property."[38] Florensky, however, does not mean that the loved one thereby becomes a mere "thing" for arbitrary use or selfish enjoyment, but only that lovers belong to one another because they commune with one another and complement one another. On this score, Florensky says he is only following in the venerable line of Plato,[39] who uses the concept of property[40] to convey the idea of mutual belonging and the image of the androgynous man or hermaphrodite[41] to express the essential feature of complementarity in love. Both Plato's concept and imagery, Florensky adds, merely offer an abbreviated, alternative restatement of his own antinomy of "I" and "not-I."[42]

Florensky becomes even more emphatic, however, and outright submits that "friendship is an essential condition of life."[43] Without it man can neither know himself nor develop himself, since it falls to the "other" to serve, at once, as the occasion for man's self-knowledge and as the motivation for man's self-development. Friendship, thus, is not solely the means for self-knowledge; it is, in turn, the opportunity for self-improvement and, more consequentially, for self-donation in love and service of the other. It is the Thou who renders me present to myself, and thus makes my self-knowledge a possibility and a reality. It is also the Thou who can occasion my act of love, my act in which I actively render my being back to him.[44] My transparency to myself, i.e., my full self-possession, is comprised of two moments: my self-knowledge and my self-donation in love, both of which require the "other," the Thou. Florensky is thus most poignant when he remarks that "this transparency of the 'I' to its very

[37]Frederick D. Wilhelmsen, *The Metaphysics of Love* (New York: Sheed & Ward, 1962), 21.

[38]PFT, 440.

[39]Ibid.

[40]*Lysis* 221E-222A.

[41]*Symposium* 189D-193D.

[42]PFT, 440.

[43]PFT, 441.

[44]Cf. the profound insights on this point in Johann, *Meaning of Love*, 76f.

self is achieved only in the *lived*, reciprocal activity of persons who love."[45]

Florensky's discovery is that of intersubjectivity or the fact of friendship as a radical *a priori*. He unequivocally expresses this insight: "The ideal of friendship is not *innate* to man, but is rather *a priori* for him—it is a constitutve element of his nature."[46] Friendship is not merely something inborn to man that unconsciously flowers in him by a law of nature as he grows and matures, but is a true, objective bond between persons which only arises upon the "I' "s grasping of a Thou. More significantly, the "I" itself knows no real "selfhood" until it perceives the "other-hood" of the Thou. They are, in other words, perceptually co-given. This insight is developed by Simeon Frank in a beautiful and profound way in his masterwork, *The Unfathomable*, where he speaks of the essential correlativity of the "I" and "Thou."[47]

For Florensky also, the correlativity of the "I" and "Thou" is a primary datum in the *homoousian* universe, itself irreducibly founded upon the dynamic identity of its constitutive entities whereby no one of them is its own sufficient explanation. Each entity in such a universe, in other words, essentially needs its "other" for its justification. That is, the "non-A" is the very condition of the possibility of "A." There is no "I" without a "Thou," and no "Thou" without an "I." They are, in sum, correlatives.

The dynamic identity which is a general feature of all reality above all obtains in the personal sphere. For Florensky, it is among personal beings that we especially witness how being is a dynamic and not a static concept. To be means to be *with*. To exist means to participate. The fact of participation is thus an *a priori* of experience, immediately given to us.

The egocentric man, however, enclosed within himself, does not partake of the plenitude of being, and remains essentially isolated in his own world, which in turn must be unfounded and hence meaningless. The generous, selfless man

[45]PFT, 441.
[46]PFT, 443.
[47]*Nepostizhimoe* (Munich: Wilhelm Fink Verlag, 1971), 154-60. The original was published in Paris in 1939.

alone participates in the fullness of being, and finds a justified existence and objective meaning in the world. He is the friendly man, the man constituted by the friend, the one who begins his speculations about reality, starting not from his *a priori* selfhood in a rationalist, Cartesian fashion, but from the *a priori* fact of his communion with others. This is the meaning of Florensky's "methodological we" as the proper point of departure for metaphysics.[48] In the West, no one has grasped this insight more lucidly than Gabriel Marcel, who makes precisely the same critique of rationalist thought, and who, interestingly enough, adopts the same point of departure for his own metaphysical reflections. A radical anti-Cartesian, Marcel emphatically describes his own approach to being as "a metaphysic of *we are* as opposed to a metaphysic of *I think*."[49] For Florensky as well as for Marcel, the fact of being entails the communion of all being within Being. Friendship is only one manifestation of this more foundational reality and truth.

If friendship is a primary datum of reality, it must also be a first-order task in life. Seeming however to back away from his own position on the *a priori* character of the bond of friendship as constitutive of persons, Florensky writes: "This reciprocal penetration of personalities, however, is a *task,* and not an original *given* of friendship."[50] Florensky does not hereby contradict himself. Friendship remains constitutive of persons, but the intersubjectivity and compenetration of personalities implied therein is never a mere blunt facticity. It rather demands personal commitment, without which persons remain solely contiguous to one another and deprived of all internal links among themselves. For these links to be cemented, fidelity becomes the call of the day and the *sine qua non* not only of friendship but of personal existence itself as well.[51] The person radically needs his other. The very Russian verb for "to kiss," "*tselovat'*," which literally means "to make whole," Florensky notes, testifies to this

[48]"Razum i dialektika," 97. Cf. our pp. 71f above.
[49]*The Mystery of Being* (Chicago: Regnery, 1960), 2:10.
[50]PFT, 447.
[51]PFT, 447f. "Creative fidelity," of course, is also a frequently encountered theme in the philosophical and theatrical works of Gabriel Marcel.

need,[52] and, he adds, the tears shed by lovers in the course of the trials and tribulations which seem to be necessary accompaniments of all attempts at establishing and deepening meaningful relationships provide nothing less than the true "cement of friendship."[53] As for the virtue of fidelity itself, it becomes the true sap of life.

3. JEALOUSY, THE PLEDGE OF LOVE

Having highlighted the indispensable role of fidelity in the fostering and maintenance of friendship, Florensky still has to pronounce his final word on love. Oddly, this privileged, last word belongs to jealousy. But does not he thereby end on a discordant note? Florensky thinks not. In fact, he says that there is an important issue he has yet to resolve. Friendship may be an essential condition to life, and may be the single most important constitutive element of personality, but in its mere generality it has still to explain that friendship is also necessarily particular. It is not "friends-in-general" that constitutes us, but the friend, a friend. Why, then, do we love one friend and not another? Why do we sacrifice ourselves in some instances and not in others? To answer these questions another principle or "force" must be given account. This particular principle is jealousy.[54]

Florensky remarks that there are two essential moments to love.[55] First, there is the centrifugal moment in which the self breaks the chains of its bondage and transcends itself by uniting itself with its other. At this stage, the self admits that it is not its own being and that it must seek its fulfillment and justification outside of itself. The dynamism of this moment is *towards* the real, and culminates in the affirmation of the "non-A" as its essential correlate. But there remains the fact that the drive of love is not towards just anyone; it

[52]PFT, 442.
[53]PFT, 445.
[54]Florensky formulates this difficulty at the end of his eleventh letter (cf. PFT, 462f). His response is given in the twelfth and last letter, "Jealousy" (PFT, 464-82).
[55]PFT, 462.

is always directed at some particular individual, and manifests a desire of union and life exclusively with him. Although Florensky does not specifically consider the psychological aspects at stake in the affective process, like the need for a basic affinity between the lover and the beloved and for points of common interest between them, he does signal the importance of the subsequent attraction between the two. In this instance, the particular force under examination is centripetal, and its role is to complement or delimit the range of the centrifugal force and center it on determinate individuals. This centering force, Florensky says, is jealousy. It is an intrinsic moment to love, because it allows for the *concretization* of love in life, and ensures its constancy. As such, it holds sway in all areas of life—in friendship, in marriage, in parochial and monastic communities, in dioceses, etc.

But, largely due to its negative connotations of resentful distrust and envy, this term evokes suspicions. Although no one seems to question the notable importance jealousy has in praxis, Florensky complains that from the point of view of theory, it has never received its real due as a philosophic category.[56] And when, as in Spinoza, treatment has been afforded it, it is generally misconstrued. Spinoza's own definition of jealousy as hatred towards the loved object and envy towards any rival, Florensky suggests, epitomizes these misconstruals.[57]

Florensky gives an excellent summary of Spinoza's reasoning, which leads him to this unilaterally negative stance towards jealousy.[58] All love tends toward perfect reciprocity. Any disparagement of or attack on this relationship is experienced as self-disparagement and a painful attack on oneself. Moreover, Florensky adds, perfect love is "omnivorous,"[59] since we desire to possess the object of our love totally and not share it with anyone. But when the one we love prefers someone else to ourselves, our own relationship with this person is threatened, and great anxiety befalls us. As a

[56]PFT, 464.

[57]PFT, 466. Cf. *The Ethics*, pt. 3, prop. 35 and following note. Florensky mistakenly says this definition is found in pt. 1. Cf. PFT, 790 (n. 815).

[58]PFT, 466f. Cf. *The Ethics*, pt. 3, prop. 33-38.

[59]PFT, 466.

countermove, we begin to hate the source of our unhappiness
—the very one we love—and to envy the one who is the bene-
ficiary of the loved one's attentions. Thus, our love manifests
itself as jealousy, and becomes something "which simultaneously hates and envies."[60]
In Spinoza's favor, Florensky notes how he perceives an
intelligible link between jealousy and love, and subsequently
tries to elucidate this tie between them in contrast to popular
sentiment, which often tends to hold that jealousy is simply
inimical to love and in no way pertaining to its very nature.
Spinoza, on the other hand, maintains not only is jealousy
not inimical to love, but is also its "faithful shadow,"[61] appearing whenever love is either put into question or is betrayed.
In such circumstances, Spinoza says that love is necessarily
transformed into jealousy, which is the immediate by-product
of love under threat. He does not, of course, affirm that love
is jealousy, nor does he uphold the view that whenever love
is present jealousy necessarily enters into the picture. It does
so only once the lover realizes his object cannot be totally his.
Then love manifests itself as jealousy.

But it is precisely at this point that Florensky thinks he
can isolate Spinoza's error. Spinoza, he claims, confuses love
with desire, and consequently cannot distinguish jealousy
from greed. The root of this confusion is the absence of the
category of person in Spinoza's system.[62] All persons are
subsequently reified, and attraction toward them is treated
on the same level as attraction towards objects.[63] But persons
can never be possessed in the way that objects can be. Persons,
to remain persons, must retain their respective independences.

[60]PFT, 467.
[61]PFT, 468.
[62]Ibid.
[63]Johann, *Meaning of Love*, 72f, makes an important insight in this
matter, which is most useful for understanding the true dynamics of
Florensky's thought. Johann notes that man has a double insufficiency. As
a *nature* or *taleity*, he is in need of new accidental determinants to perfect
his deficiencies in nature. Nature is complemented by the object of desire.
As a person, man's deficiency is his metaphysical isolation, which can be
complemented only by a person, another *ipseity*. The object of direct love
concerns the communion of persons. While in desire we see a relation of
potency to act, in love we witness a relation of act to act.

Consequently, the communion between them can never entail
the annihilation of one or both of the personalities. On the
contrary, the relation of reciprocity means anything but self-
absorption; it signifies only mutual compenetration and enrichment. True love, accordingly, is not "omnivorous" in any
sense of the word. But if it is so viewed on the analogy of
desire for objects—even if they genuinely add to our existences—love can only be reduced to greed ultimately.[64] In this
perspective also, it can only favor egoism and the selfish
identity, which cuts one off from vital contact with others
and interdependence on them.

Authentic love, on the other hand, Florensky maintains,
can only foster dynamic identity as gained from organic ties
of interdependence. Jealousy, in this perspective, is nothing
other than zeal for love and dynamic identity,[65] and accordingly belongs to love's very nature as its safeguard and
patron. Unfortunately, Florensky laments, jealousy's creden-
tials to love often have been challenged owing to a false
identification of the virtue of jealousy itself with some of its
unfortunate and misguided manifestations.[66] But, Florensky
asks, is it reasonable to mock and despise justice simply because coldness of heart sometimes characterizes those who
mete it out? If justice maintains its positive value even in
such circumstances, why cannot jealousy? Jealousy, indeed,
Florensky insists, has its positive side. It is that side repeatedly
spoken of in the Bible when the God of Israel is referred to
as a *jealous* God.

It is the positive side of jealousy that is of the essence of
love. Florensky asserts that it is, at once, the foundation and
background of love.[67] As an essential moment of love, jeal-

[64]Significantly, Florensky (PFT, 469) says that the "correlate of greed
is hatred with envy."

[65]Florensky (PFT, 478f) makes a brief etymology of the Russian word
revnost'. It primarily means "jealousy," but can, in certain instances, signify
"zeal." The more usual word for zeal in Russian, however, is *rvenie*. Josef
Pieper in his *About Love* (Chicago: Franciscan Herald Press, 1974) distinguishes "jealousy of" from "jealousy for" (pp. 52f). The latter corresponds to "zeal," while the former to the negative meaning of jealousy
as "covetousness" or "greediness."

[66]PFT, 469.

[67]PFT, 470.

ousy shares in love's free election of one person out of many to be the recipient of this love, and essentially participates in its exclusive character. Accordingly, it does all in its power to ensure the union of persons which is intrinsic to all love. As a necessary consequence, it also must be solicitous of the welfare of the loved one. This watchfulness is jealousy's second essential element.

From the point of view of identity, there is thus, according to Florensky, a critical difference between jealousy and greed. Numerical identity, understood in the sense of the self's radical constitution by the other, is an exigence of jealousy, while only generic identity is demanded by desire.[68] Desire bespeaks only the insufficiency of man's being as a *nature* in need of corporal and psychical sustenance and accidental perfection.[69] It concerns him alone in his static isolation from others. Jealousy, on the other hand, addresses the human being's needs as a *person,* that is, as a being pining to overcome its metaphysical isolation and genuinely in need of both human and divine fellowship. Jealousy, furthermore, attends to this fellowship once established. Its basic attitude toward the Thou is a vigilant one that, on the one hand, tends to the Thou's specific needs, and, on the other, tries to prevent its falling into impassibility whenever this danger may be present.[70] In sum, jealousy is anything but egoistic; it is rather the true pledge of love.

Jealousy, Florensky repeats, is no mere psychological or ethical concept. Its true nature is of the ontological order[71] as expressive of man's need for dynamic identity. It is, however, no less a virtue in God. Sacred Scripture, Florensky insists, eschews all anthropomorphisms when it speaks of God as jealous for His chosen ones. It rather reveals that God's love for His creatures is, above all else, a solicitous one that not only edifies but also reproves and seeks to amend man's ways. In an analogous fashion, it is also reflected in man, who also needs jealousy as a "force that realizes good

[68]PFT, 471f.
[69]Cf. n. 63, p. 229 above.
[70]PFT, 472ff.
[71]PFT, 481.

intentions."[72] It is the force that keeps him on the straight and narrow path, revivifies his fallen spirits, repristines his faded loves, and, in sum, enables him to persevere to his coveted goal, the Pillar and Foundation of Truth.[73]

[72]Ibid.
[73]PFT, 482.

Conclusion

When Florensky described his understanding of philosophical inquiry in terms of a nature walk,[1] he found a most apt metaphor for conveying the spirit of his particular style of philosophy. *The Pillar and Foundation of Truth* is a superb manifestation of his philosophic talent at work. It evidences not only the open-ended character of his speculative temper, but also the profundity of its actual achievement. It is, of course, possible that at the beginning of this work there was no inkling of what would finally be obtained at the end. But this should not be taken to mean that the work itself lacked any inner unity. Whenever one embarks upon any investigative journey, one can never be sure of what, if anything, lies ahead. Real discovery may await the searcher, but then no guarantees can be made either as to the course of the investigation or as to its final results.

In Florensky's instance, what began as an epistemological inquiry into the ultimate criterion of truth ended up as a metaphysical reflection on the nature of love. What were the chief markers along the way? It may be remembered that Florensky noted that two conditions must be fulfilled for any state of facts to convince. A state of facts must be immediately given and yet be grounded in its very givenness at the same time. It must enjoy, in other words, the note of grounded immediateness, and thus be accessible to "rational intuition," which itself is only a resultant fruit of the collaborative activity of two principles, the principle of identity and the principle of sufficient reason, the one accounting for the "what-ness" of the state of facts, the other for its "why." Further, for ultimate truth to obtain, ultimate synthesis must

[1]*Pervye shagi filosofii*, 3. Cf. our p. 52 above.

also be given. That degree of synthesis, Florensky posits
however, is verifiable only in a Self-Proving Subject that is,
at once, One and Three. Why? Because even such a Subject
of Truth must have its grounded-ness in its Other. This entails, Florensky submits, the need for eternal, triadic relations within the Self-Proving Subject of Truth whereby the
One is constituted by its Other *in conspectu* of a Third. If
such a Trinity of Relations is not possible, Florensky suggests,
no truth at all is ultimately possible.

The dynamic identity constitutive of the Triune Subject
of Truth, however, Florensky maintains, is not a feature
unique to the Godhead, but is analogously reflected in all
created being, whose truth is also always founded in relation
to its other. "A" is "A" only because it is grounded in "non-
A." The principle of dynamic identity, which is Florensky's
central philosophical discovery, serves thus at the same time
as the cornerstone of his personalist, *homoousian* philosophy,
the consubstantiality of all creatures being only a consequence of the fact of dynamic identity. Creation itself is thus
a cosmos, a unified, organic whole expressive of Sophia, the
Wisdom of God. As such, it is also indicative of Divine Love
of which it is only a superabundant effect. If creation, moreover, is nothing other than creatural Sophia, it is no less a
supreme actualization of the love of God, indeed, a sublime
manifestation of Love. Florensky affirms that there is truth
because there is Truth; he immediately adds, however, that
there can be Truth only if there is Love. Love is thus the
very condition of the possibility of Truth.

Because God is Love, he is also Truth. Analogously, only
when love obtains among men does truth have importance.
For this love to be solidified, however, man must freely activate his dynamic identity, and conscientiously live his consubstantiality with others. This is the central message of
Florensky's metaphysics of love. It is, of course, only an
incipient metaphysics, but it is well founded. Dynamic identity and consubstantiality are its sure points, which offer a
secure base for future, speculative developments.

Florensky comes off well in this study in contrast to the
negative judgments meted out to him by some of his own

contemporaries. Nonetheless, we have tried not to lionize him. There is, after all, dross as well as gold in him and his thought. But it is the latter that especially speaks to us today. In Florensky, we truly meet an enigmatic—and anguished— personality, but one who dared to maintain his own individuality and remain faithful to his deepest convictions and calling in life, even when the tide of history went against him. Indeed, he remained dauntless before his ultimate fate.

When Florensky once described martyrdom as "blood bespeaking truth,"[2] little did he know that he too would be summoned to be an ultimate witness to Truth. It is that Truth that will vindicate him in time. It is also in his message of Truth that we find the truly universal and therefore ecumenical import of his thought. The Orthodox Florensky experienced and struggled with the same anxieties and aspirations for man as many of this century's profoundest thinkers in the West. It is, indeed, in their deepest—and common— longings and searches, that we come across not only the same impasses, but also the same, headway-making insights into the nature of truth and reality. More importantly, we meet the same, zealous commitment to truth and unified humanity; in sum, we find a similar, unstinted dedication to the cause of a well-founded consubstantiality of all men in truth and love.

[2]FTH, 163.

Bibliography

I. PRIMARY SOURCES*

1. Books and Book Length Studies by Pavel Florensky

Ekkleziologicheskie materialy (Ecclesiological materials), *Bogoslov-skie trudy* (Theological studies; hereafter listed as TS), 12 (1974): 73-183.

Ikonostas (Iconostasis), TS, 9 (1972): 80-148. For abridged versions: "Ikona," *Vestnik russkogo zapadno-evropeiskogo patriar-shego ekzarkhata* (The messenger of the Russian western European patriarchal exarchate), 65 (1969): 39-64; "On the Icon," *Eastern Churches Review,* 8 (1976): 11-37. It. trans. (integral), *Le porte regali* (The royal doors) Milan: Adelphi, 1977.

Iz bogoslovskogo naslediya svyashchennika Pavla Florenskogo (From the theological heritage of the priest Pavel Florensky), TS, 17 (1977): 85-248.

O dukhovnoi istine (Of spiritual truth). Moscow, 1913.

Pervye shagi filosofii (First steps of philosophy). Sergiev Posad, 1917.

Smysl idealizma (The meaning of idealism). Sergiev Posad, 1915.

Stolp i utverzhdenie istiny (The pillar and foundation of truth), *Voprosy religii* (Questions of religion), 2 (1908): 223-384. This is an earlier version of the more famous and much expanded 1914 edition.

Stolp i utverzhdenie istiny—opyt pravoslavnoi feoditsei v dvenadtsati pismakh (The pillar and foundation of truth—an essay in Orthodox theodicy in twelve letters). Moscow, 1914. It. trans., *La colonna e il fondamento della verità.* Milan: Rusconi Editore, 1974. Fr. trans., *La colonne et le fondement de la vérité.* Lausanne,

*This bibliography lists only those works actually consulted in writing this book. For a complete bibliography of Florensky's works published in Russia/Soviet Union (but *not* including those published in the West), see Andronik (Trubachev), Hierodeacon, "K 100-letiyu so dnya rozhdeniya svyashchennika Pavla Florenskogo. Ukazatel' pechatnykh trudov" (The centenary of the birth of the priest Pavel Florensky. Index of published works), TS, 23 (1982): 264-309.

Suisse: Les Editeurs l'Age d'Homme, 1975. A limited (99 copy) edition was published in Berlin by "Rossica" in 1929.

2. Articles and Pamphlets by Pavel Florensky

Antonii romana i Antonii predaniya (Anthony of the novel and Anthony of tradition). Sergiev Posad, 1970. An extract from *Bogoslovskii vestnik* (Theological messenger, hereafter listed as TM), 1, no. 1 (1907): 119-59.

"Biograficheskie svedeniya" (Biographical information), *Vestnik russkogo khristianskogo dvizheniya* (The messenger of the Russian Christian movement, hereafter listed as *Vestnik*), 135 (1981): 54-59. Up until the 112 (1974) issue, the word *studencheskogo* (student) was also contained in the title of this journal. The full former title was *Vestnik russkogo khristianskogo studencheskogo dvizheniya*.

(with I. N. Elchaninov), *Dannyya k zhizneopisaniyu arkhimandrita Serapiona (Mashkina)*, (Data for a biography of Archimandrite Serapion [Mashkin]). Sergiev Posad, 1917. Reprint from TM, 1, nos. 2-3 (1917): 317-54.

"Druzhba" (Friendship), TM, 1, nos. 1-3 (1911): 151-82, 467-94.

"Dukh i plot'" (Spirit and flesh), *Zhurnal Moskovskoi Patriarkhii* (The journal of the Moscow Patriarchate, hereafter listed as JMP), no. 4 (1969): 72-77. This article is only an extract from the ninth letter ("The Creature") of *The Pillar and Foundation of Truth*. Editorial indications say it was contained in the collection, *Na zaprosy dukha* (For the demands of the spirit). Moscow, 1914, pp. 179-90.

"Ekskurs o revnosti" (Excursus on jealousy), TM, 1, no. 3 (1911): 494-507.

(Trans.) "Immanuil Kant. Fizicheskaya monadologiya" (Immanuel Kant: the physical monadology), TM, 3 (1905): 95-127.

"In Pace. (Akafist)" (In peace [akathist]), *Khristianin*, 1, no. 4 (1907): 862-64.

"Itogi" (Summations), *Vestnik* 111 (1974): 56-65.

"Khristianstvo i kul'tura" (Christianity and culture), JMP, no. 4 (1983): 52-57. Preface by Hierodeacon Andronik.

"Kosmologicheskie antinomii I. Kanta" (The cosmological antinomies of I. Kant), TM, 1, no. 4 (1909): 596-625.

"Kostromskaya storona" (Kostromskoy region), *Khristianin*, 1, no. 4 (1907): 862-64.

"K pochesti vyshnyago zvaniya" (To the honor of a higher calling), *Voprosy religii*, 1 (1906): 143-73.

"Lektsiya i Lectio" (Lecture and *lectio*), TM, 1, no. 4 (1910): 614-20.

"Makrokosm i mikrokosm" (Macrocosm and microcosm), TS, 24 (1983): 230-41.

"Molennye ikony prepodobnogo Sergiya" (Prayer icons of the venerable Sergius), JMP, no. 9 (1969): 80-90.

Nachal'nik zhizni (The author of life). Sergiev Posad, 1907. A reprint from *Khristianin*, 1, no. 4 (1907): 705-9.

"Naplastvovanie egeiskoi kultury" (The stratification of Aegean culture), TM, 2, no. 6 (1913): 346-83.

" 'Ne voskhishchenie nepshcheva' " ("He thought it not robbery"), TM, 2, nos. 7-8 (1915): 512-62. Separate booklet: Sergiev Posad, 1915.

"Novaya kniga po russkoi grammatike" (A new book about Russian grammar), TM, 2. no. 5 (1909): 138-45.

"O Bloke" (On Blok), *Vestnik*, 114 (1974): 169-92.

"Obshchechelovecheskie korni idealizma" (The universally human roots of idealism), TM, 1, no. 2-3 (1909): 284-97, 409-23.

"O nadgrobnom slove o. Alekseya Mecheva" (On the funeral sermon of Fr. Aleksei Mechev) in N. A. Struve, ed., *Otets Aleksei Mechev* (Father Aleksei Mechev). Paris: YMCA Press, 1970.

"O simvolakh bezkonechnosti" (On symbols of infinity), *Novyi put'* (The new way), no. 9 (1904): 173-235.

"O sueverii" (On superstition), *Novyi put'*, no. 8 (1903): 91-121.

"O tipakh vozrastaniya" (On types of growth), TM, 2, no. 7-8 (1906): 530-68.

"Otstoyat' Optinu . . ." (Save Optina . . .), *Vestnik*, 135 (1981): 94-96. A letter of Florensky to N. P. Kiselev.

"Pamyati Feodora Dmitrievicha Samarina" (To the memory of Feodor Dmitrievich Samarin). Sergiev Posad, 1917. Also in TM, 1, no. 4 (1917): 464-77.

"Pamyati Vladimira Frantsevicha" (To the memory of Vladimir Frantsevich [Ern]), *Vestnik*, 138 (1983): 99-104.

"Perepiska F. D. Samarina i P. A. Florenskogo" (Correspondence of F. D. Samarin and P. A. Florensky). *Vestnik*, 125 (1978): 251-71.

"Pis'ma P. A. Florenskogo k B. N. Bugaevu (A. Belomu)" (Letters of P. A. Florensky to B. N. Bugaev [A. Belyi]), *Vestnik*, 114 (1974): 149-68.

"Prashchury lyubomudriya" (Forebears of philosophy), TM 1, no. 4 (1910): 621-44.

Preface to "Plach Bogomateri" (The weeping of the Theotokos; the canon for the compline of Great Friday). *Khristianin*, 1, no. 3 (1907): 601-6. The canon plus prayers are on pp. 607-14.

"Predely gnoseologii (The limits of gnoseology), TM, 1, no. 1 (1913): 147-74.

"Pristan' i bul'var" (Quay and boulevard), *Prometei* 9 (1972): 138-48.

"Propovedi" (Sermons), TS 23 (1982): 310-20. The following

sermons are found: "Nachal'nik zhizni" (The author of life),
310ff; "Zemnoi put' Bogomateri" (The earthly path of the
Theotokos), 312-16; "Radost' na veki" (Joy unto ages), 317-20.
Radost' na veki (Joy unto ages). Sergiev Posad, 1907. A reprint
from *Khristianin*, 1, no. 2 (1907): 248-57.
"Razum i dialektika" (Mind and dialectics), TM, 3, no. 9 (1914):
86-98.
Review article of V. V. Zavitnevich, *Aleksei Stepanovich Khomyakov*
(vols. I [Bks. I-II] -II), TM 2, no. 7-8 (1916): 516-81.
Review of Jules Tannerie, *Kurs teoreticheskoi i prakticheskoi arifme-
tiki* (A course of theoretical and practical arithmetic), TM, 3,
no. 12 (1913): 864-72.
Review of N. M. Solov'ev, " 'Nauchnyi' ateizm" ("Scientific" athe-
ism), TM, 2, no. 6 (1915): 374-76.
(Ed.) "Sluzhba Sofii Premudrosti Bozhii" (Service to Sophia, the
Wisdom of God), TM, 1, no. 2 (1912): 1-23. Fr. trans. (with
preliminary note by Th. Spassky), *Irénikon*, 30 (1957): 164-88.
"Sofiya" (Sophia), TM, 2, nos. 5, 7-8 (1911): 135-61, 582-613.
"Spiritizm kak antikhristianstvo" (Spiritualism as anti-Christianity),
Novyi put', no. 3 (1904): 149-67.
"Svideteli" (Witnesses), *Vestnik* 135 (1981): 71-93.
Voprosy religioznogo samopoznaniya (Questions of religious self-
knowledge), Sergiev Posad, 1907. A reprint from *Khristianin*, 1,
no. 1 (1907): 205-10; 1, no. 3 (1907): 635-53.
"Vospominaniya detstva" (Reminiscences of childhood), *Vestnik* 99
(1971): 49-84; 100 (1971): 230-54; 106 (1972): 183-200.

II. SECONDARY SOURCES

1. *Books and Articles on Florensky*

Accarini, Giuliana, "La ricerca di una nuova via spirituale in 'Colonna
e fondamento della verita' di Pavel Florenski" (The search of a
new spiritual way in "Pillar and Foundation of Truth" of Pavel
Florensky), *Rivista di Filosofia neo-Scolastica*, 67 (1975): 726-37.
_____, *Pavel Florenskij e la filosofia dell' unitotalità* (Pavel
Florensky and the philosophy of uni-totality), unpublished dissertation. Milan: Universita' Cattolica del Sacro Cuore, 1974-75.
Andronik (Trubachev), Hierodeacon, "K 100-letiyu so dnya rozhdeniya svyashchennika Pavla Florenskogo. Ukazatel' pechatnykh
trudov" (The centenary of the birth of the priest Pavel Florensky. Index of published works), TS, 23 (1982): 264-309.
_____, "Osnovnye cherty lichnosti, zhizn' i tvorchestvo svyash-
chennika Pavla Florenskogo" (Fundamental features of the
personality, life, and creative achievement of the priest Pavel
Florensky), JMP, no. 4 (1982): 12-19. Eng. trans., "The Per-

sonality, Life and Work of Father Pavel Florensky," JMP, Eng.
ed., no. 5 (1982): 18-29.

Baron, Roger, "Intuition bergsonienne et intuition sophianique," *Les études philosophiques,* 18 (1963): 439-42.

Berdyaev, Nicholas, "Idei i zhizn'. Khomyakov i svyashch. P. A. Florenskii" (Ideas and life. Khomyakov and the priest P. A. Florensky), *Russkaya mysl'* (Russian thought), 32, no. 2 (1917): 72-81.

———————, "Stilizovannoe pravoslavie" (Stylized Orthodoxy), *Russkaya mysl'* 29, no. 1 (1914): 109-25.

Bulgakov, Sergius, "Svyashchennik o. Pavel Florenskii" (The priest Fr. Pavel Florensky), *Vestnik,* 101-102 (1971): 126-37.

Costante, Altissimo, *Gli elementi tradizionali della contemplazione nell' interpretazione filosofico-teologica di Pavel Florenskij* (The traditional elements of contemplation in the philosophical-theological interpretation of Pavel Florensky). Vicenza, Italy, 1979.

Feodor, Bishop (Pozdeevsky), review article of *O dukhovnoi istine,* TM, 2, no. 5 (1914): 141-81.

Filipoff, Boris, "O. Pavel Florenskii" (Fr. Pavel Florensky), in N. P. Poltoratzky, ed., *Russkaya religiozno-filosofskaya mysl' XX veka* (Russian religious-philosophical thought of the 20th century). Pittsburgh: University of Pittsburgh, 1975. Pp. 356-71.

"Florenskii, Pavel Aleksandrovich," *Entsiklopedicheskii slovar' Russkogo Bibliograficheskogo Instituta Granat* (Encyclopedic dictionary of the Russian Bibliographical Institute Granat), 7th ed. (n.d.), 44:144.

———————, *Filosofskaya entsiklopediya,* 5:377-79. Moscow: Izdatel'stvo "Sovetskaya entsklopediya," 1970.

Florovsky, Georges, "Tomlenie dukha" (The pining of the spirit), *Put'* (The way), no. 20 (1930): 102-7.

Ganchikov, L., "Florenskii, Pavel (Paolo) Aleksandrovich," *Enciclopedia filosofica,* 3:698f. Roma, 1979.

Glagolev, Sergii, review of student Pavel Florensky's composition, "O religioznoi istine" (Of religious truth), TM, 1, no. 2 (1909): 129-35.

Il'in, V. N., review of *Stolp i utverzhdenie istiny, Put',* no. 20 (1930): 116-19.

Innokentii (Prosvirnin), Archimandrite, "O tvorcheskom puti svyashchennika Pavla Florenskogo" (On the creative path of the priest Pavel Florensky), JMP, no. 4 (1982): 65-76. Eng. ed., 56-68.

Ivanov, V. V., "Estetika svyashchennika Pavla Florenskogo" (The aesthetics of the priest Pavel Florensky), JMP, no. 5 (1982): 75-77. Eng. ed., no. 9 (1982): 75-78.

Jakovenko, B., "Filosofiya otchayaniya" (Philosophy of despair), *Severnyya zapiski* (Northern notes), no. 3 (1915): 166-77.

Levitzky, Sergei, "K 100-letiyu o. Pavla Florenskogo" (To the centenary of Fr. Pavel Florensky), *Posev* (Sowing), 38, no. 4

242 PAVEL FLORENSKY: A METAPHYSICS OF LOVE

(April 1982): 49-51. This article is a reprint of a chapter from the author's *Ocherki po istorii russkoi filosofskoi i obshchestvennoi mysli*, vol. II. (See below, sec. II.2, p. 244.)

Marxer, François, "Le problème de la vérité et de la tradition chez Pavel Florensky" (The problem of truth and tradition in Pavel Florensky), *Istina*, 25 (1980): 212-36.

Mashkin, Serapion, Archimandrite, "Pis'mo k P. A. Florenskomy" (A letter to P. A. Florensky), *Voprosy religii*, 1 (1906): 174-83.

Meyendorff, John, untitled commemorative article on Pavel Florensky in *L'Osservatore Romano*, CXXII (N. 28 [36.913]) (February 4, 1982), p. 3.

Modestov, Evgenii, "P. A. Florenskii i ego sovetskie gody" (P. A. Florensky and his Soviet years), *Mosty* (Bridges), 2 (1959): 419-34.

Morra, Licia, "Conoscenza, amore, mistero e simbolo in Pavel Florenskij" (Knowledge, love, mystery, and symbol in Pavel Florensky), *Russia Cristiana*, 181 (1982): 48-66.

Nikitin, V., "Pamyati svyashchennika Pavla Florenskogo" (To the memory of the priest Pavel Florensky), JMP, no. 4 (1982): 10-12 (Eng. ed., 9-12).

——————, "Vecher pamyati svyashchennika Pavla Florenskogo v LDA" (An evening to the memory of the priest Pavel Florensky at the L[eningrad] T[heological] A[cademy]), JMP, no. 7 (1982): 24-26. A shorter notice under the title of "Meeting Devoted to Father Pavel Florensky's Memory at LTA" is found in JMP (Eng. ed.), no. 7 (1982): 37.

Novikov, M. P., "Antinomizm kak apologeticheskii printsip" (Antinomism as an apologetical principle) in *Krizis sovremennoi khristianskoi apologetiki* (The crisis of contemporary Christian apologetics). Series: *Nauchnyi ateizm* (Scientific atheism), no. 12 (1981). Moscow: Izdatel'stvo "Znanie," 1981. Pp. 50-54.

Obolensky, Serge, "La sophiologie et la mariologie de Paul Florensky," *Unitas*, It. ed., 1, no. 3 (1946): 63-70; 1, no. 4 (1946): 31-49.

Papin, J., "Florenskii, Pavel Aleksandrovich," New Catholic Encyclopedia, 5:974. New York: McGraw-Hill Book Co., 1967.

Sabaneeff, Leonid, "Pavel Florensky—Priest, Scientist, and Mystic," The Russian Review 20 (1961): 312-25.

Scanlan, James P., "Florensky, Paul Alexandrovich," *The Encyclopedia of Philosophy*, 3:205f. New York: Macmillan Co. and the Free Press, 1967.

Slesinski, Robert, "Filosofiya kul'ta po ucheniyu o. Pavla Florenskogo" (The philosophy of cult according to the teaching of Fr. Pavel Florensky), *Vestnik*, 135 (1981): 39-53.

——————, "Fr. Paul Florensky: A Profile," *St. Vladimir's Theological Quarterly*, 26 (1982): 3-27, 67-88.

——————, "Pavel Florenskij: nuovi orizzonti per il pensiero ortodosso" (Pavel Florensky: new horizons for Orthodox thought), *L'Osservatore Romano*, CXXII (N. 28 [36.913]) (February 4, 1982), p. 3.

—————, "La sofiologia di Pavel Florenskij e la sua attualità oggi" (The sophiology of Pavel Florensky and its relevance today), *Unitas*, It. ed., 37, no. 4 (1982): 250-66.

Struve, Nikita, "K stoletiyu svyashchennika Pavla Florenskogo" (For the centenary of the priest Pavel Florensky), *Vestnik*, 135 (1981): 3f.

Sviridov, I. A., "Bogoslovskaya kontseptsiya svyashchennika Pavla Florenskogo" (The theological conception of the priest Pavel Florensky), JMP, no. 5 (1982): 73-75. Eng. trans., "Father Pavel Florensky's Theology," JMP, no. 10 (1982): 73-76.

Troitsky, German, "In Memory of the Reverend Pavel Florensky," JMP, Eng. ed., no. 11 (1972): 74-80.

Trubetskoy, E. P., "Svet favorskii i preobrazhenie uma" (The Taboric light and the transfiguration of the intellect), *Russkaya mysl'*, 29, no. 5 (1914): 25-54.

Tyszkiewicz, S., S.J., "Réflexions du théologien russe moderniste Paul Florensky sur l'Eglise" (Reflections of the modernist Russian theologian, Paul Florensky, on the Church), *Gregorianum*, 15 (1934): 255-61.

Udelov, F. I. (pseudonym for S. I. Fudel'), *Ob o. Pavle Florenskom* (Of Fr. Paul Florensky). Paris: YMCA Press, 1972.

Velikov, G. and A. Elchaninov, review of Florensky's *Antonii romana i Antonii predaniya, Voprosy religii*, 2 (1908): 386.

Vetukhov, A. V., *Osnovy very i znaniya (religii i nauki) po dannym yazyka (Zametki o feoditsei svyashch. P. Florenskogo)* (Foundations of faith and knowledge [religion and science] according to the givens of language [Notes on the theodicy of the priest P. Florensky]). Khar'kov, 1915.

"V kakom godu umer o. Pavel Florenskii?" (In what year did Fr. Pavel Florensky die?), *Vestnik* 115 (1975): 151-54. Correspondence on the year of Florensky's death.

Zhegin, Lev, "Vospominaniya o P. A. Florenskogo" (Reminiscences about P. A. Florensky), *Vestnik*, 135 (1981): 60-70.

Zolla, Elémire "Introduzione" in It. ed. of *Stolp i utverzhdenie istiny*, 5-77.

—————, "Prefazione" in It. ed. of *Ikonostas*, 11-16.

2. *Books and Articles Partially on Florensky or with a Brief Discussion of Him*

Andronik, Hierodeacon, "Episkop Antonii (Florensov)—dukhovnik svyashchennika Pavla Florenskogo" (Bishop Antony [Florensov] —spiritual father of the priest Pavel Florensky), JMP, no. 9

(1981): 71-77; no. 10 (1981): 67-73. Eng. ed., no. 4 (1982): 69-78.

Berdyaev, Nicholas, *Russkaya ideya* (The Russian idea). Paris: YMCA Press, 1946.

_____, "Tipy religioznoi mysli v Rossii" (Types of religious thought in Russia), *Russkaya mysl'*, 31, nos. 6-7 (1916): 1-31; 52-72.

Bori, Pier Cesare and Paolo Bettiolo, *Movimenti religiosi in Russia prima della rivoluzione (1900-1917)* (Religious movements in Russia before the revolution [1900-1917]). Brescia, Italy: Queriniana, 1978.

Bulgakov, Sergius, *Avtobiograficheskie zametki* (Autobiographical notes). Paris: YMCA Press, 1946.

_____, *Svet nevechernii* (The light which does not fade). Westmead, Farnborough, Hants, England: Gregg Internation Publishers, Ltd., 1971.

Clément, Olivier, "Antropologia trinitaria," *Servitium*, VII/Series II, 3 (1974): 345-51.

Dell'Asta, Adriano, "La bellezza splendore del vero" (Beauty, splendor of the true), *Russia Cristiana*, 174 (1980): 32-53.

Elchaninov, A., "Episkop-starets" (Bishop-staretz), *Put'*, no. 4 (1926): 157-65.

Evdokimov, Paul, *Cristo nel pensiero russo* (Christ in Russian thought). Rome: Città nuova editrice, 1972.

Florovsky, Georges, *Puti russkogo bogosloviya* (The ways of Russian theology). Paris, 1937.

Gippius-Merezhkovskaya, Zinaida, *Dmitrii Merezhkovskii*. Paris: YMCA Press, 1951.

_____, *Zhivye litsa* (Living portraits). Munich: Wilhelm Fink Verlag, 1971.

Graves, Charles, *The Holy Spirit in the Theology of Sergius Bulgakov*. Geneva, 1972.

Jakovenko, B., *Ocherki russkoi filosofii* (Outlines of Russian philosophy). Berlin: Russkoe Universal'noe Izdatel'stvo, 1922.

Kol'man, E., "Protiv noveishikh otkrovenii burzhuaznogo mrakobesiya" (Against the latest revelations of bourgeois befuddlement), *Bol'shevik*, no. 12 (1933): 88-96.

Kosharnyj, B. P., *U istokov sovetskoi filosofii* (At the sources of Soviet philosophy). Moscow: Izdatel'stvo Moskovskogo Universiteta, 1981.

Levitzky, S. A., *Ocherki po istorii russkoi filosofskoi i obshchestvennoi mysli* (Outlines for the history of Russian philosophical and social thought). Vol. II. Frankfort am Main: Posev, 1981.

Lossky, Nicholas O., *History of Russian Philosophy*. New York: International Universities Press, Inc., 1951.

_____, "Preemniki Vl. Solov'eva" (Successors of Vl. Soloviev), *Put'*, no. 3 (1926): 14-28.

_____, *Vospominaniya* (Reminiscences). Munich: Wilhelm Fink Verlag, 1968.

Maloney, George A., S.J., *A History of Orthodox Theology Since 1453*. Belmont, Mass.: Nordland Publishing Co., 1976.

Men', Aleksandr, "L'eredità di Vladimir Solov'ëv" (The heritage of Vladimir Soloviev), *Russia Cristiana*, 169 (1980): 13-28.

Meyendorff, John, "Creation in the History of Orthodox Theology," *St. Vladimir's Theological Quarterly*, 27 (1983): 27-37.

Novikov, M. P., *Krizis sovremennogo pravoslavnogo bogosloviya* (The crisis of contemporary Orthodox theology). Series: *Nauchnyi ateizm*, n. 1 (1979). Moscow: Izdatel'stvo "Znanie," 1979.

Pitirim, Archbishop (Nechaev), "Osnovnye problemy sovremennogo bogoslovskogo issledovaniya v ikh razvitii s kontsa XIX veka" (Fundamental problems of contemporary theological investigation in their development from the end of the 19th century), TS, 5 (1970): 215-26.

Poltoratsky, N. P., ed. *Russkaya religiozno-filosofskaya mysl' XX veka* (Russian religious-philosophical thought of the 20th century). Pittsburgh: University of Pittsburgh, 1975.

Radlov, E., *Ocherk istorii russkoi filosofii* (An outline of the history of Russian philosophy). Petersburg: Nauka i Shkola, 1920, 2nd ed.

Regel'son, Lev, "L'ideale della sobornost' e la personalità umana" (The ideal of *sobornost'* and the human personality), *Russia Cristiana*, 172 (1980): 27-53.

Shaginyan, Marietta, "Chelovek i vremya—Vospominaniya—Chast' III" (Man and time—Memoirs—Part III), *Novyi mir* (The new world), no. 4 (1973): 113-31; no. 5 (1973): 160-86; no. 6 (1973): 128-53.

Schmemann, Alexander, ed., *Ultimate Questions: An Anthology of Modern Russian Religious Thought*. New York: Holt, Rinehart & Winston, 1965. This work contains a translation of Florensky's fifth letter from *The Pillar and Foundation of Truth*, entitled "The Comforter." See pp. 135-72.

Schultze, Bernard, S.J., "La mariologie sophianique russe," in Humbert du Manoir, S.J., ed., *Maria. Etudes sur la Sainte Vierge*, Paris: Beauchesne, 1961. 6:213-39.

_____, "L'unicità di Maria Madre di Dio" (The unicity of Mary, Mother of God), *Scripta de Maria*, 1979, 449-59.

Sobolev, Archbishop Seraphim, *Novoe uchenie o Sofii Premudrosti Bozhiei* (The new teaching about Sophia, the Wisdom of God). Sophia, 1935.

Solzhenitsyn, Aleksander, *Arkhipelag GULag, III-IV*. Paris: YMCA Press, 1974. Eng. trans., *The GULAG Archipelago Two*. New York: Harper & Row, 1975.

Spidlík, Tomás, S.J., "L'icône, manifestation du monde spirituel," *Gregorianum*, 61 (1980): 539-54.

246 PAVEL FLORENSKY: A METAPHYSICS OF LOVE

246 PAVEL FLORENSKY: A METAPHYSICS OF LOVE

246 PAVEL FLORENSKY: A METAPHYSICS OF LOVE

246   PAVEL FLORENSKY: A METAPHYSICS OF LOVE

—————, *La spiritualité de l'Orient chrétien*. Rome: Pontificium Institutum Orientalium Studiorum, 1978.

Staniloae, Dumitru, *Theology and the Church*. Crestwood, N.Y.: St. Vladimir's Seminary Press, 1980.

Tareev, M., "Novoe bogoslovie" (The new theology), TM, 2 (1917): 3-53; 168-224.

Van Der Mensbrugghe, Alexis, *From Dyad to Triad*. London: Faith Press, Ltd., 1935.

Zenkovsky, V. V., *Istoriya russkoi filosofii* (History of Russian philosophy) (2 vol.). Paris: YMCA Press, 1950. Eng. ed., George Kline, trans. New York: Columbia University Press, 1953.

—————, *Osnovy khristianskoi filosofii* (Foundations of Christian philosophy) (2 vol.). Paris: YMCA Press, 1964.

Zernov, Nicolas, *The Russian Religious Renaissance of the Twentieth Century*. London: Darton, Longman & Todd, 1963.

3. Background and Cognate Readings

Allers, Rudolph, "Intuition and Abstraction," *Franciscan Studies*, 8 (1948): 47-68.

Arsen'ev, Nikolai, *Mudrovanie v bogoslovii? Po povodu "sofianskoi" polemiki* (Musing in theology? Concerning the "sophianic" polemic). Warsaw: Drukarnia Synodalna, 1936.

Askol'dov, S. A., *et al., Iz glubiny* (Out of the depths), 2nd ed. (enlarged). Paris: YMCA Press, 1967.

Berdyaev, N. A., *et al., Vekhi* (Landmarks). Moscow, 1909.

Bergson, Henri, *An Introduction to Metaphysics*. Indianapolis: Bobbs-Merrill Company, 1955.

Bilaniuk, Petro B. T., "The Mystery of *Theosis* or Divinization," in David Neiman and Margaret Schatkin, eds., *The Heritage of the Early Church* (Essays in honor of the Very Rev. Georges Vasilievich Florovsky), *Orientalia Christiana Analecta*, 195. Rome, 1973. Pages 338-59.

Bloom, Antoine, "Il cristiano e la trinità," *Servitium*, VIII/Series II, 3 (1974): 303-34.

Brunner, Emil, *Truth as Encounter*. Philadelphia: Westminster Press, 1964.

Buber, Martin, *I and Thou*. New York: Charles Scribner's Sons, 1958. 2nd ed.

Bulgakov, Sergius, *Dokladnaya zapiska Mitropolitu Evlogiyu po povodu opredeleniya arkhiereiskogo sobora v Karlovtsakh otnositel'no ucheniya o Sofii Premudrosti Bozhiei* (Memorandum to Metropolitan Evlogy in regard to the determination of the Synod of Bishops in Karlovci concerning the teaching about Sophia, the Wisdom of God). Paris: YMCA Press, 1936.

_____, *Kupina neopalimaya* (The burning bush). Paris: YMCA Press, 1927.

_____, *The Orthodox Church*. New York and Milwaukee: Morehouse Publishing, 1935.

_____, "Sofiologiya smerti" (Sophiology of death), *Vestnik*, 127 (1978): 18-41; 128 (1979): 13-32.

_____, *The Wisdom of God*. London: Williams & Norgate, 1937.

Cavarnos, Constantine, *Byzantine Thought and Art*. Belmont, Mass.: Institute for Byzantine and Modern Greek Studies, 1968.

Clark, F., "Pantheism and Analogy," *Irish Theological Quarterly*, 20 (1953): 24-38.

Coreth, Emerich, *Metaphysics*. New York: Herder & Herder, 1968.

Cuttat, Jacques-Albert, *The Encounter of Religions*. New York: Desclée Co., 1960.

Day, Sebastian J., O.F.M., *Intuitive Cognition: A Key to the Significance of the Later Scholastics*. St. Bonaventure, NY: Franciscan Institute, 1947.

De Finance, Joseph, "Etre et subjectivité" (Being and subjectivity), *Doctor Communis*, I (1948): 240-58.

Dell'Asta, Adriano, "L'uomo nella tradizione bizantina" (Man in Byzantine tradition), *Russia Cristiana*, 169 (1980): 58-69; 170 (1980): 56-71.

Denzinger, Henricus, and Adolphus Schönmetzer, S.J. eds., *Enchiridion Symbolorum Definitionum et Declarationum de Rebus Fidei et Morum*, 34th ed. Freiburg im Breisgau: Herder, 1965.

Dhavamony, Mariasusai, *Phenomenology of Religion*. Rome: Università Gregoriana Editrice, 1973.

Diggs, Bernard James, *Love and Being*. New York: S. F. Vanni, 1947.

Edie, James E., J. P. Scanlan, *et al.*, eds. *Russian Philosophy*, vol. 1-3. Chicago: Quadrangle Books, 1965.

Elchaninov, Aleksander, *Zapisi* (Jottings). 3rd ed. Paris: YMCA Press, 1962. Eng. trans., *The Diary of a Russian Priest*. London: Faber & Faber, 1967.

Ern, Vladimir, "Priroda mysli" (The nature of thought), TM, 1, nos. 3-4 (1913): 500-31, 803-43; 2, no. 5 (1913): 107-20.

Evdokimov, Paul, *La teologia della bellezza* (Theology of beauty). Rome: Edizioni Paoline, 1971.

Fabro, Cornelio, "The Intensive Hermeneutics of Thomistic Philosophy: The Notion of Participation," *Review of Metaphysics*, 27, no. 3 (1974): 449-91.

Faraon, Michael Joseph, O.P., *The Metaphysical and Psychological Principles of Love*. Dubuque, Iowa: Wm. C. Brown Co., 1952.

Fedotov, George P., *The Russian Religious Mind*. Cambridge, MA: Harvard University Press, 1946.

Flick, M., S.J., Z. Alszeghy, S.J., *Fondamenti di una antropologia teologica*. Libreria Editrice Fiorentina, 1970.

Florovsky, Georges, "The Idea of Creation in Christian Philosophy," *The Eastern Churches Quarterly*, 7 (1949), supplementary issue, 53-77.

Florovsky, G. V., "O pochitanii Sofii, Premudrosti Bozhiei, v Vizantii i na Rusi" (On veneration of Sophia, the Wisdom of God, in Byzantium and in Rus'), *Trudy V-go sezda russkikh akademicheskikh organizatsii za granitsei*, Chast' I (Studies of the 5th congress of Russian academic organizations abroad, part I), (1932): 485-500.

Frank, S. L., *Nepostizhimoe* (The unfathomable). Munich: Wilhelm Fink Verlag, 1971.

_____, *Predmet znaniya* (The object of knowledge). Petrograd, 1915.

_____, *Real'nost' i chelovek* (Reality and man). Paris: YMCA Press, 1956. Eng. trans., Taplinger Publishing, 1966.

_____, *Smysl zhizni* (The meaning of life). Brussels: Zhizn' s Bogom, 1976.

_____, *Svet vo t'me* (Light in the darkness). Paris: YMCA Press, 1949.

Freud, Sigmund, *The Standard Edition of the Complete Psychological Works of Sigmund Freud*, 11:57-137. London: Hogarth Press, 1957.

Gilbert, M., ed., *La Sagesse de l'Ancien Testament*. Leuven: Leuven University Press, 1979.

Grégoire, Franz, "Note sur les termes intuition et experience," *Revue Philosophique de Louvain*, 44 (1946): 401-15.

Hartshorne, Charles, *Aquinas to Whitehead: Seven Centuries of Metaphysics of Religion*. Milwaukee: Marquette University Publishing, 1976.

_____, *The Logic of Perfection*. La Salle, IL: Open Court Publishing, 1973.

_____, "Whitehead and Berdyaev: Is There Tragedy in God?" *The Journal of Religion*, 37, no. 2 (1957): 71-84.

Heidegger, Martin, *An Introduction to Metaphysics*. Garden City, NY: Anchor Books, 1961.

_____, *Being and Time*. New York: Harper & Row, 1962.

_____, *Discourse on Thinking*. New York: Harper & Row, 1962.

_____, *Identity and Difference*. New York: Harper & Row, 1969.

_____, *What Is Called Thinking?* New York: Harper & Row, 1968.

Hume, David, *An Enquiry Concerning Human Understanding*, in *The Empiricists*, pp. 307-430. Garden City, N.Y.: Doubleday & Co.

—————, *A Treatise of Human Nature.* Glasgow: Wm. Collins & Co., Bk I (1962), Bks II-III (1972).

Ignat'ev, A., "Antinomichnost' religioznogo soznaniya" (The antinomism of religious consciousness). *Vestnik,* 120 (1977): 14-26.

The Jerome Biblical Commentary. Englewood Cliffs, N.J.: Prentice Hall, 1968.

Johann, Robert, S.J., *The Meaning of Love.* Glen Rock, N.J.: Paulist Press, 1966.

Kant, Immanuel, *Critique of Pure Reason.* Garden City, N.Y.: Doubleday & Co., 1966.

Karsavin, L. P., *Noctes Petropolitanae.* Peterburg, 1922.

—————, *Poema o smerti* (Poem on death). Kaunas, 1932.

—————, *Saligia.* Paris: YMCA Press, 1978.

Khomyakov, Aleksei Stepanovich, *Polnoe sobranie sochinenii—tom I* (Complete collected works—vol. I), Moscow, 1900, 3rd ed.

—————, *Tserkov' odna* (The Church is one). Montreal: Monastery Press, 1975.

Kireevsky, Ivan Vasilevich, *Polnoe sobranie sochinenii,* I-II (Complete collected works, I-II). Moscow, 1861.

Korsakov, F., "Russkie sud'by" (Russian destines), in A. Solzhenitsyn, M. S. Agurskij, et al., *Iz-pod glyb* (From under the rubble), pp. 159-76. Paris: YMCA Press, 1974. Eng. ed., pp. 151-71. This surname is a pseudonym.

Leskovec, Paolo, S.J., *Basilio Rozanov e la sua concezione religiosa* (Basil Rozanov and his religious conception), *Orientalia Christiana Analecta,* 151. Rome: Pontificium Institutum Orientalium Studiorum, 1958.

Levitzky, Sergei, "On Some Characteristic Traits of Russian Philosophic Thought," *St. Vladimir's Theological Quarterly,* 13, no. 3 (1969): 149-61.

Lewis, C. S., *The Four Loves.* New York: Harcourt Brace Jovanovich, 1960.

Lialine, C., "Le débat sophiologique," *Irénikon,* 13 (1936): 168-205.

Litva, Aloiz, S.J., "La 'Sophia' dans la création" ("Sophia" in creation), *Orientalia Christiana Periodica,* 16 (1950): 39-74.

Lonergan, Bernard J. F., S.J., *Insight: A Study of Human Understanding.* New York: Philosophical Library, 1970, 3rd ed.

—————, "Metaphysics as Horizon," *Gregorianum,* 44 (1963): 307-18.

—————, *Method in Theology.* London: Darton, Longman & Todd, 1971.

—————, *The Way to Nicaea.* London: Darton, Longman & Todd, 1976.

Lossky, Nicholas O., "The Absolute Criterion of Truth," *Review of Metaphysics,* 2, no. 8 (1949): 47-96.

—————, *Chuvstvennaya, intellektual'naya i misticheskaya intuit-*

siya (Sensual, intellectual, and mystical intuition). Paris: YMCA Press, 1938.

—————, *Intuitivism.* Prague: Russian Free University, 1935.

—————, "Intuitivizm," *Grani* (Frontiers), 77 (1970): 144-70; 78 (1970): 212-40.

—————, *Mir kak organicheskoe tseloe* (The world as an organic whole). Moscow, 1917.

—————, *Obosnovanie intuitivizma* (Foundations of intuitivism). Berlin: Obelisk-Verlag, 1924.

—————, *Uchenie o. Sergiya Bulgakova o vseedinstve i o Bozhestvennoi Sofii* (The teaching of Fr. Sergius Bulgakov about pan-unity and about Divine Sophia). South Canaan, Pa.: St. Tikhon Press, n.d.

Lossky, Vladimir, *In the Image and Likeness of God.* Crestwood, N.Y.: St. Vladimir's Seminary Press, 1974.

—————, *The Mystical Theology of the Eastern Church.* Crestwood, NY: St. Vladimir's Seminary Press, 1976.

—————, "La notion des 'analogies' chez Denys le pseudo-Aréopagyte," *Archives d'histoire et littéraire du moyen-âge*, 5 (1930): 279-309.

—————, *Spor o Sofii* (The dispute about Sophia). Paris, 1936.

Maloney, George A., S.J., *The Cosmic Christ.* New York: Sheed & Ward, 1968.

—————, *A Theology of "Uncreated Energies."* Milwaukee: Marquette University Press, 1978.

Marcel, Gabriel, *The Mystery of Being*, 2 vols. Chicago: Regnery, 1960.

Maritain, Jacques, *Existence and the Existent.* Garden City, N.Y.: Doubleday & Co., 1956.

Mascall, E. L., *He Who Is.* London: Darton, Longmann & Todd, 1966.

Meyendorff, John, *Byzantine Theology.* New York: Fordham University Press, 1974.

—————, *Christ in Eastern Christian Thought.* Crestwood, N.Y.: St. Vladimir's Seminary Press, 1975.

Mondin, Battista, S.X., *The Principle of Analogy in Protestant and Catholic Theology.* The Hague: Martinus Nijhoff, 1968, 2nd ed.

Newman, John Henry Cardinal, *An Essay in Aid of a Grammar of Assent.* New York: Longmans, Green and Co., 1947.

Nicholas of Cusa, *Opere Filosofiche* (Philosophical works), ed. Graziella Federico-Vescovini. Turin: Unione Tipografico-Editrice Torinese, 1972.

—————, *The Vision of God.* New York: Frederick Ungar Publ. Co., 1960.

Nikol'skii, A., "Ikona sv. Sofii, Premudrosti Bozhiei" (The icon of Holy Sophia, the Wisdom of God), *Rodnaya starina* (Native land), nos. 5-6 (1928): 17f.

Noël, L., *Le réalisme immédiat*. Louvain: Editions de l'Institut Superieur de Philosophie, 1938.

Pascal, Blaise, *Pensées*. New York: Penguin Books, 1966.

Paulos Gregorios, *The Human Presence*. Geneva: World Council of Churches, 1978.

Pieper, Josef, *About Love*. Chicago: Franciscan Herald Press, 1972.

Plato, *Collected Dialogues*, ed. Edith Hamilton and Huntington Cairns. Princeton, N.J.: Princeton University Press, 1961.

Pozo, Cándido, *Teologia dell'aldilà* (Theology of the hereafter). Rome: Edizioni Paoline, 1970.

Pseudo-Dionysius (Dionysius the Areopagite), *The Divine Names and the Mystical Theology*. London: S.P.C.K., 1975.

Radlov, E., "Teoriya znaniya slavyanofilov" (The theory of knowledge of the Slavophiles), *Zhurnal Ministerstva Narodnogo Prosveshcheniya* (The journal of the Ministry of Public Education), no. 2 (1916): 153-65.

Roland-Gosselin, M.-D., "Peut-on parler d'intuition intellectuelle dans la philosophie thomiste?" (Can one speak of intellectual intuition in Thomistic philosophy?), *Philosophia perennis*, 2 (1930): 708-30.

Schultze, B., S.J., "La nuova soteriologia russa" (The new Russian soteriology), *Orientalia Christiana Periodica*, 9 (1943): 406-30; 11 (1945): 165-215; 12 (1946): 130-76.

_____, *Pensatori russi di fronte a Cristo* (Russian thinkers before Christ). Vol. I (1947); vols. II-III (1949). Florence: Mazza Editore.

_____, "Problemi di teologia presso gli ortodossi" (Problems of theology among the Orthodox), *Orientalia Christiana Periodica*, 9 (1943): 135-70.

Seifert, Josef, *Essence and Existence: A New Foundation of Classical Metaphysics on the Basis of "Phenomenological Realism," and a Critical Investigation of "Existential Thomism"* in *Aletheia*, 1 (1977): 17-157; 371-459.

Sergius, Metropolitan of Moscow (Stragorodskii), *Ukaz Moskovskoi Patriarkhii preosvyashchennomu Mitropolitu Litovskomu i Vilenskomu Elevferiyu* (Decree of the Moscow Patriarchate to the Most Reverend Metropolitan Eleutherius of Vilna and Lithuania). Two decrees bear this title. They are dated September 7, 1935, and December 27, 1935, respectively.

"Skazanie, chto est' Sofia Premudrost' Bozhiya" (Legend, what is Sophia the Wisdom of God), *Rodnaya starina*, no. 5-6 (1928): 18f.

Soloviev, V. S., *Sobranie sochinenii* (Collected works). Vols. 1, 2, 11. Brussels: Foyer Oriental Chrétien, 1966.

_____, *The Meaning of Love*. London: Geoffrey Bles, Centenary Press, 1946.

Solzhenitsyn, Alexander, M. S. Agurskij, *et al.*, *Iz-pod glyb* (From under the rubble). Paris: YMCA Press, 1974. Eng. trans., Boston-Toronto: Little, Brown and Co., 1975.

Spassky, T. G., *Russkoe liturgicheskoe tvorchestvo* (Russian liturgical works). Paris: YMCA Press, 1951.

Spidlík, Tomás, S.J., "The Heart in Russian Spirituality," in David Neiman and Margaret Schatkin, eds., *The Heritage of the Early Church* (Essays in honor of the Very Rev. Georges Vasilievich Florovsky), *Orientalia Christiana Analecta*, 195, pp. 361-74. Rome: Pontificium Institutum Orientalium Studorium, 1973.

_____, *La sophiologie de s. Basile*. *Orientalia Christiana Analecta*, 162. Rome: Pontificium Institutum Orientalium Studorium, 1961.

Spinoza, Benedict de, *The Ethics*, in *The Rationalists*. Garden City, NY: Doubleday & Co., 1960.

Stokes, Walter E., S.J., "Freedom as Perfection: Whitehead, Thomas and Augustine," *Proceedings of the American Catholic Philosophical Association*, 36 (1962): 134-42.

_____, "Is God Really Related to the World?" *Proceedings of the American Catholic Philosophical Association*, 39 (1965): 145-51.

Strémooukhoff, D., *Vladimir Soloviev et son oeuvre messianique*. Paris, 1935. Eng. trans., Belmont, MA: Nordland Publishing, 1980.

Tatakis, Basile, *La philosophie byzantine*. Paris: Presses Univeritaires de France, 1949.

Tillich, Paul, *The New Being*. New York: Charles Scribner's Sons, 1955.

Tresmontant, Claude, *Christian Metaphysics*. New York: Sheed & Ward, 1965.

Trubetskoy, Evgeny, Prince, *Smysl zhizni* (The meaning of life). Moscow, 1918.

_____, *Umozrenie v kraskakh* (Contemplation in colors). Paris: YMCA Press, 1965. Eng. trans by Gertrude Vakar, *Icons: Theology in Color*. Crestwood, NY: St. Vladimir's Seminary Press, 1973.

von Balthasar, Hans Urs, *Love Alone*. New York: Herder & Herder, 1969.

von Hildebrand, Dietrich, *The Heart: An Analysis of Human and Divine Affectivity*. Chicago: Franciscan Herald Press, 1977.

_____, *What Is Philosophy?* Chicago: Franciscan Herald Press, 1973.

Walicki, Andrzej, *A History of Russian Thought*. Stanford, CA: Stanford University Press, 1979.

Walker, Anselm, "Sophiology," *Diakonia*, 16, no. 1 (1981): 40-54.

Whitehead, Alfred North, *Adventures in Ideas*. New York: Free Press, 1967.

_____, *Process and Reality.* New York: Free Press, 1978, corrected edition.

_____, *Religion in the Making.* New York: World Publishing, 1954.

Wild, Robert, "Pathos Meets Panentheism," *Spiritual Life,* 19, no. 2 (1973): 130-36.

Wilhelmsen, Frederick D., *The Metaphysics of Love.* New York: Sheed and Ward, 1962.

Wojtyla, Cardinal Karol (Pope John Paul II), *The Acting Person.* Dordrecht, Holland: D. Reidel Publishing, 1979.

Zenkovsky, V. V., "Ideya vseedinstva v filosofii Vladimira Solov'eva" (The idea of pan-unity in the philosophy of Vladimir Soloviev), *Pravoslavnaya mysl'* (Orthodox thought), 10 (1955): 45-59. Paris: YMCA Press, 1955.

_____, "Preodolenie platonizma i problema sofiinosti mira" (The overcoming of Platonism and the problem of the sophianity of the world), *Put',* no. 24 (1930): 3-40.

Zernov, Nicolas, *Eastern Christendom.* London: Readers Union, 1963.

Zuzek, Roman, S.J., "Las ciencias eclesiásticas rusas en la Unión Soviética, según la revista 'Bogoslovskie Trudy' " (Russian ecclesiastical science in the Soviet Union, according to the journal *Bogoslovskie Trudy*), *Orientalia Christiana Periodica,* 46 (1980): 281-305.

_____, "Una mística para hoy: La visión sofiánica de la realidad" (A mysticism for today: the sophianic vision of reality), *Orientalia Christiana Periodica,* 46 (1980): 161-77.

Index

255